CUSTODY OF INVESTMENTS:
LAW AND PRACTICE

CUSTODY OF INVESTMENTS: LAW AND PRACTICE

by

A. O. AUSTEN-PETERS

OXFORD

UNIVERSITY PRESS

OXFORD
UNIVERSITY PRESS

Great Clarendon Street, Oxford OX2 6DP

Oxford University Press is a department of the University of Oxford.
It furthers the University's objective of excellence in research, scholarship,
and education by publishing worldwide in

Oxford New York

Athens Auckland Bangkok Bogotá Buenos Aires Calcutta
Cape Town Chennai Dar es Salaam Delhi Florence Hong Kong Istanbul
Karachi Kuala Lumpur Madrid Melbourne Mexico City Mumbai
Nairobi Paris São Paulo Shanghai Singapore Taipei Tokyo Toronto Warsaw
and associated companies in Berlin Ibadan

Oxford is a registered trade mark of Oxford University Press
in the UK and in certain other countries

Published in the United States
by Oxford University Press Inc., New York

© A.O. Austen-Peters 2000

The moral rights of the author have been asserted

Database right Oxford University Press (maker)

First published 2000

Crown copyright material is reproduced with the permission of the
Controller of Her Majesty's Stationery Office

British Library Cataloguing in Publication Data

Data available

Library of Congress Cataloging in Publication Data
Austen-Peters, A.O.
Custody of investments: law and practice / by A.O. Austen-Peters.
p. cm.
Revision of the author's thesis (Doctoral), 1998 under the title:
Legal aspects of the custody of assets under investment management.
Includes bibliographical references and index.
1. Securities industry—Law and legislation—Great Britain.
2. Investments—Law and legislation—Great Britain.
3. Global custody (Securities). I. Title.
KD1774.A98 2000 346.41'092—dc21 00–045293
ISBN 0–19–829858–7

1 3 5 7 9 10 8 6 4 2

Typeset by Hope Services (Abingdon) Ltd.
Printed in Great Britain
on acid-free paper by
Biddles Ltd.,
Guildford & King's Lynn

For Ayodele, Bolanle and 'Tamilayo

PREFACE

This book is a revision of my DPhil thesis, 'Legal Aspects of the Custody of Assets under Investment Management', for the Faculty of Law, University of Oxford (1998). Whilst some additional material has been included in this work up until December 1999, the principal focus of the revision has been to make the book one that is more relevant to practitioners than the academic treatise it started out in life as.

I first became interested in this topic whilst preparing legal opinions on custody whilst practising in Lagos, Nigeria. At the time, little attention had been paid by academics in England to the complex legal questions raised by the custody of investments. With few articles in journals and no single volume dedicated to this issue, there existed a serious dearth of academic or practice-oriented literature in England on an area of law which is of major importance in international banking and securities dealing. Since then, some articles on this topic have been published in legal journals, as well as Joanna Benjamin's *The Law of Global Custody* (Butterworths, 1996).

This book does not attempt to examine specific instances of custody—there are a myriad of possible custodial scenarios. Reference is only made to specific forms of custody by way of example. My aim, rather, is to provide an analysis and identify principles by which the highly technical legal problems raised by the custody of investments may be resolved.

I address the nature of legal relationships that arise when investment securities are transferred into custody. The operational practices of modern custody are considered and an assessment undertaken of the impact of these on the nature of the investor's interest, particularly on the insolvency of the custodian. The analysis in Chapters 2 to 5 suggests that, except when custodians are employed to safeguard certificates to registrable securities, where securities are transferred into custody, investors' rights against issuers are replaced by rights exercisable through their custodian. The thing to which investors' rights attach depends on the method of holding and the number of tiers of custody. With non-intermediary or single-tier intermediary custody, investors' rights may attach to the securities in custody. With tiers of intermediary custody, investors' rights may only attach to the custodian's own rights in the custodial structure. In Chapter 3, the case is made for the proposition that fungible holdings are not incompatible with the retention by investors of proprietary rights.

Chapter 6 considers how custody assets may be used for security and suggests that tiers of intermediated custody may be significant for the ordering of priorities. Chapters 7 and 8 examine the duties of custodians and investors' remedies upon breach; and Chapter 9 examines the regulatory response to custody business. In Chapter 10 the impact of foreign law on custody is considered. It is suggested that where foreign securities are held, the rights of investors against their English custodian will ordinarily be governed by English law; whilst the investor or English custodian's rights in relation to foreign intermediaries and assets may be governed by foreign law.

My debts of gratitude to all of those who have helped me in one way or another are too numerous to mention in full. However, I would wish to single out the staff at the Bodleian law library for their courtesy and efficiency in dealing with all my requests whilst writing the doctoral dissertation. My thanks also go to the staff of the Law Society of Namibia and librarians at the University of Namibia for affording me access to their facilities whilst I was visiting Namibia during part of the process of revision.

I am grateful too to Roy Goode of St John's College, Oxford and Philip Wood of Allen & Overy who examined my doctoral dissertation. They read the text with careful and critical eyes and their thoughtful and perceptive comments were much appreciated and contributed to the sharpening of my arguments. Dan Prentice was also kind enough to read and comment on early drafts of parts of the thesis. For the revision of the thesis into a practitioner-oriented book, Guy Morton of Freshfields and Richard Potok of Davis, Polk & Wardwell were kind enough to discuss with me issues of particular concern to practitioners.

Finally, my greatest debt is to Fidelis Oditah, initially my thesis supervisor and then my friend. Whilst I was writing the doctoral dissertation, he provided guidance and encouragement, and was a constant source of inspiration. His understanding of my work, and unwavering intellectual support for it, has over the years played an invaluable part in both the production of this book and the development and working out of my own ideas. My debts to him, both intellectual and personal, are enormous.

TIMI AUSTEN-PETERS
Lagos, Nigeria
April 2000

CONTENTS—SUMMARY

CONTENTS

TABLE OF CASES

TABLE OF LEGISLATION

1

INTRODUCTION

When an investor holds his investments through another party, he will be con- **1.01**
cerned by the risk that he may be denied profit and/or return of his capital for
reasons other than market forces. Since investments are increasingly held by custodians, this work addresses one of the principal concerns of investors by
analysing some of the legal aspects of custody business.

Broadly, custody business involves the holding of investment assets by parties **1.02**
other than the investor, including brokers, investment managers, specialist custodians and central depositories. Although modern custodians perform other services, the analysis here focuses on the custody of securities. The principal question
addressed is how assets are held and how the chosen method affects investors'
rights to the assets in custody.

This work identifies some of the operational features of the custody of invest- **1.03**
ments and examines these with reference to the legal concepts on which custody
is most often based. The object of this exercise is to provide a framework, using
these legal concepts, for analysing the nature of an investor's interest in relation to
assets held in custody as well as the relationship between an investor and any custodians or sub-custodians engaged in the custody of the assets.

A. Custody Business

1.04 Although the origins of the modern custody of investments may be traced to the traditional safe custody service offered by banks in relation to the physical security of things, the custody of investments has outgrown its modest origins and now encompasses ancillary services relevant to the protection of investments.

1.05 The ancient business of the safe custody of physical things[1] consists only of safe-keeping. It is directed at the custody of things as things, notwithstanding that they may also be investments,[2] and is therefore exclusively concerned with the protection of the physical integrity of the thing. This service requires little more from a custodian than secure premises. Although safe custody services may be offered by specialist companies with purpose-built structures, the service of safe-keeping of things is primarily offered by banks for the convenience of their customers,[3] as an adjunct to the primary business of banking.

1.06 The custody of investments,[4] however, is a distinct commercial activity. It is aimed at the custody of things as investments, and therefore encompasses intangible value. Where undertaken by banks it constitutes a significant proportion of their overall commercial activity, not just an incidental appendage to their operations. The service may also be offered by central securities depositories, securities brokers, non-bank investment managers and global custodians. The custody of investments requires significant expenditure on information technology and highly skilled staff to deliver the service according to the demands of customers and the dictates of regulation. The fees charged for the service are also significant, often calculated in relation to the value of the assets in custody. In addition to the safe-keeping aspect of investments, a significant element of the operations of the custody of investments often consists of administration, which will encompass record-keeping, valuation, reporting, accounting and performance measurement. Custodians may also be responsible for stock-lending, collecting and accounting for dividends and other benefits, communications from companies to shareholders, cash management, acting as intermediary on corporate actions, including the exercise of voting rights.

1.07 Whether things in traditional safe custody happen to be investments or merely of sentimental or other non-monetary value does not materially alter the safe cus-

---

[1] W Blair, A Allison, K Palmer and P Richards-Carpenter, *Banking and the Financial Services Act* (1993) 3.45; EP Ellinger and E Lomnicka, *Modern Banking Law* (2nd edn, 1994) 568–573; and M Hapgood, *Paget's Law of Banking* (11th edn, 1996) 132.
[2] This distinction is well brought out in an article by B Rudden, 'Things as Things and Things as Wealth' (1994) 14 OJLS 81.
[3] M Hapgood, *Paget's Law of Banking* (11th edn, 1996) 132.
[4] R Cranston, *Principles of Banking Law* (1997) 359–363.

tody function. The custodian in such circumstances is concerned with receipt of the thing, protecting its basic physical integrity and returning it intact. A safe custody service does not necessarily involve knowledge by the safe custodian of the thing in his custody because the thing will often be in a sealed container to which the safe custodian does not have access. Conversely, a custodian of investments knows what is in his charge and is ordinarily empowered to act in relation thereto to enhance the monetary value of the thing. This may involve the settlement of trades and the collection of dividends and bonus issues. Indeed, these other functions may constitute the very reasons a custodian of investments is appointed.

B. Practical Importance of Custody Business

Custodians are employed for the benefits they confer on the particular user and **1.08** for the increased efficiency they offer to the capital markets. The growth in participants in the capital markets and ever-increasing volume of assets traded has been reflected in the increased use of custodians for one or more of the purposes set out below.

Whether directly or indirectly, most people in any developed economy benefit **1.09** from the use of custodians. Whereas a wealthy individual may employ a direct custodian to hold his investment portfolio, moderately affluent investors may be the indirect beneficiaries of custodial services when investing in pooled investment vehicles such as unit trusts. Indeed, anybody who is the beneficiary of a pension is likely to be a beneficiary of assets held by a custodian. Definitive figures as to the volume and value of assets held in custody are not readily available but the sums are likely to be vast. In 1993, the Securities and Investments Board (SIB) estimated that there was £800 billion worth of UK equities held by custodians.[5] In 1997, one market operator estimated that there was $40,000 billion worth of assets in custody world-wide and that this figure was set to rise to $50,000 billion by the year 2000.[6]

In the retail and wholesale investment markets, a custodian may be utilised to **1.10** reduce the risk of theft or accidental destruction of investments. Custodians will have invested and developed specific strategies with this in mind that may not be cost-effective for a small retail investor or fund manager to undertake.[7] The additional advantage to a fund-manager in doing this is that it enables him to devote

---

[5] SIB, *Custody Review—Discussion Paper* (August 1993) 5.9.
[6] See the reported comments of Jurgen Marziniak, global head of custody services for Deutsche Bank, in 'Survey on Global Custody: The Big Get Bigger as the Sector Grows', *The Financial Times*, 11 July 1997, I.
[7] 'Focus on Global Custody: New Worlds to Conquer and a Game for Big Players', *The Times*, 28 April 1995, 28.

his energies to his core business, ie selection of investments.[8] Clients of custodians may also wish to benefit from the range of services on offer, including the taking of corporate action (dividend or interest collection, bonus shares, etc), payment of taxes and to exercise voting rights on the investor's behalf.

1.11 In the wholesale capital markets, custodians may be employed as settlement systems to facilitate the transfer of interests in investments. Where investment in an asset ordinarily involves the movement of the thing, such as a negotiable security, if both transferor and transferee use the same custodian the asset does not need to move; transfer of ownership is merely recorded on the books of the custodian. By effecting transfers of ownership in this way, the depository or other form of custodian offers a securities settlement service. This type of transfer, in immobilised investments, avoids the risk of loss or destruction of the thing in the process of moving it. Further, the risk of loss upon a failed transfer is reduced because the diminution in time between payment and transfer should reduce the chance that one side suffers by performing his side of a transaction prior to receiving performance from a counter-party. The settlement service offered by custodians reduces the investor's risk of loss in the event that his counter-party becomes insolvent.

C. Scope and Relevance of This Work

1.12 Although the principal focus of this work is on the custody of debt and equity securities, much of the analysis will be of direct application to the custody of other types of investments, including derivatives. Beyond that, various issues of importance to both investors and custodians are examined, including how assets under custody may be used to raise finance, the typical duties of a custodian and the options for an investor upon a misapplication of custody assets. The regulatory response to some of the issues raised is also considered. For the most part, it is assumed that the custodian is located in England, that the agreement for custodial services is subject to English law and that the assets under custody are located in England. However, given that much of modern investment is cross-border, the impact of the conflict of laws on the foregoing is assessed.

1.13 It is not the intention of this work to analyse any specific custodial arrangements. Given the infinite possible variations of custodial arrangements, it is preferable to identify some of the principal operational features underpinning modern arrangements for the custody of investments and to analyse these. Reference is made to particular custodial systems only by way of illustration.

---

[8] The withdrawal of the Prudential from custody business would seem to support this. See 'Focus on Global Custody: Wisdom of the Prudential', *The Times*, 28 April 1995, 28.

As with any process, the use of custodians entails its own risks. There are the **1.14** inevitable risks that the investment could yet be destroyed, lost or misapplied in the hands of the custodian. The custodian may also be negligent in the care exercised in guarding the integrity or record-keeping of the investments. Legal risk in the use of custodians may also arise where the relationship between investor and custodian is not recognised by law as conferring a proprietary interest on the investor in respect of custody assets, the principal consequence of such risk being that the investment is characterised as an asset of the custodian that would be available to his creditors in case of his insolvency. The investor would become a creditor of the custodian rather than an owner of the custody assets.

The legal analysis of the operational features of custody business allows investors **1.15** to identify legal risks they face, to evaluate and manage such legal risks and, above all, to enable an informed decision to be made by the investor as between the alternative methods of structuring the holding of their investments. This analysis also enables regulators of banks and non-bank financial intermediaries to determine the most appropriate method of regulating custodians.

D. Investment Assets

The principal focus of this book is the custody of securities, both debt and equity. **1.16** It is not that the safeguarding of cash is unimportant to the custodial process.[9] Cash is ordinarily not an investment asset. Cash paid to a deposit-taker is essentially a question of banking, which raises different considerations from the custody of investments. It is inevitable in the process of the custody of investments that some cash will be dealt with, if only to execute trades for clients or in transmitting dividends and other payments. Accordingly, some consideration is given to cash held by custodians. The importance of the analysis of cash in the cash management service offered by custodians is reduced by the fact that the custodian will often turn cash not needed immediately into a securitised asset,[10] enabling it to be dealt with in the same fashion as any other security.

In restricting the principal scope of this book to securities, several of the features **1.17** of the assets encompassed by this term need to be clearly identified.

---

[9] Whilst securities in custody with Barings were relatively unthreatened by the collapse of the bank (see 'Survey on Pension Fund Investment: a More Cautious View of Risk Prevails', *The Financial Times*, 27 April 1995, I), more than £600 million client cash from its custodial operations was in jeopardy until the rescue of the bank: see 'SIB Seeks Safeguards for Investors' Assets', *The Financial Times*, 1 September 1995, 6.

[10] 'Survey on Pension Fund Investment: a More Cautious View of Risk Prevails', *The Financial Times*, 27 April 1995, I; also advocated by W Filonuk, of JP Morgan, in a presentation to the Sixth Annual Conference on Global Custody Services at the Hyatt Carlton Tower, London (31 October 1995).

1.18 Securities are of various types, which, beyond their use as a vehicle for investment, perform different functions. Securities may embody debt, such as bonds or notes entitling the title-holder to future payments. Alternatively, they may reflect equity in an enterprise. These are the principal forms of securities but there are others such as convertible loan stock, which are a hybrid combining elements of debt and equity, and depository receipts, by which the holder thereof is entitled at least to the benefit of a given number of underlying securities.[11] Beyond these, an investor may hold warrants that entitle him to purchase certain securities at a future date for a pre-determined price or he may seek to acquire other derivatives of securities as part of his investment strategy.

1.19 Securities may also be classified by the manner in which they are transferred. In England, this occurs in one of two ways, either by a change in the register which records entitlement to the securities (registrable securities) or by transfer of tangible tokens of evidence of entitlement to the securities (negotiable securities).[12] Negotiable securities may be further sub-divided into those of bearer form and those transferable by indorsement.[13]

1.20 Further, securities may be either wholly dematerialised, without any tangible manifestation of the investment; essentially dematerialised, but the investment is evidenced by a tangible token;[14] or tangible,[15] perhaps better described as documentary intangibles[16] to reflect their true nature, whereby the token is treated as if it embodies the securities it represents. The distinction between the two forms of securities with tangible tokens is as follows. For essentially dematerialised securities, the fact of the tangible evidence does not alter their fundamental nature. The token is merely evidence of the intangible underlying securities. Any transfer must occur in the fashion set out by the terms of issue, most likely by amending the register. For documentary intangibles, the token is all but the security itself. Whilst there may remain a conceptual distinction between the underlying securities and

---

[11] Depository receipts are the system by which it is anticipated that members of CREST will be able to enjoy interests in relation to offshore assets via CREST. Nominee companies established by CREST for this purpose in various jurisdictions will hold foreign securities on behalf of CREST members. These nominees will then issue UK securities held via CREST entitling the title-holder to the UK securities to the underlying offshore securities. In effect, it is by enjoying title to the UK (depository receipt) securities issued by the nominee that CREST members are identified as beneficial owners of securities held by the nominee. See CRESTCo Limited, *CREST: Cross-Border Settlement* (December 1997) 16–17.

[12] The transfer of negotiable securities confers on the transferee good title notwithstanding a defect in the title of the transferor.

[13] In principle, the obligations under bearer securities are transferable by mere delivery of the relevant certificate, whilst those under securities transferable by indorsement require that the obligations are discharged in favour of the person named therein or to his order. Negotiable securities transferable by indorsement may in effect be made bearer securities by being indorsed in blank.

[14] Such as a non-negotiable share certificate.

[15] Such as a negotiable bond.

[16] RM Goode, *Commercial Law* (2nd edn, 1995) 33, 53–55.

the document which represents them, documentary intangibles are treated as if they are the securities themselves, thus enabling them to be dealt with like chattels. In this sense, the securities are reified as the document that represents them, with transfer of the securities occurring by transfer of the token.

E. Operation of Custody Business[17]

In this section, many of the principal operational features of custody business will be introduced. In so doing, some indication will be given of the practical importance to custody business of the type of operation and any legal problems that it raises. Any perceived legal problems are more fully addressed in subsequent chapters. **1.21**

Beneficial Entitlement to Assets in Custody

Does the custodian take the assets beneficially with the obligation to re-deliver equivalent assets, or does he undertake to hold them for the investors as beneficial owners? Another question is who, if at all, may use the custody assets for sale and repurchase (repo) transactions, stock-lending or otherwise as collateral to raise financing. **1.22**

If the particular type of custody assets permits this,[18] it may be that assets transferred to the custodian are taken by him beneficially, with a duty merely of equivalent re-delivery. In this way, the custodian holds custody assets in a similar fashion to the manner in which banks take money deposited with them for the account of customers. Although this type of holding may be less onerous for a custodian, in case of the insolvency of the custodian, the claim of the investor will be that of a mere creditor with no guarantee of being met. The assets transferred into custody may be claimed by any of the creditors of the insolvent custodian, with the investors responsible for the transfer into custody not enjoying any special priority in this regard. **1.23**

In order to protect their investments, investors may seek to establish custodial relations by which they are recognised at law to be beneficially entitled to the assets in custody. Recognition of such entitlement should ensure that the creditors of an insolvent custodian could not claim the assets. Regardless of such intent, there are features of the assets kept in custody, as well as a number of custodial **1.24**

---

[17] Many of the developments in the modern custody of investments are examined in: CW Mooney, Jr, 'Beyond Negotiability: A New Model for Transfer and Pledge of Interests in Securities Controlled by Intermediaries' (1990) 12 Cardozo Law Review 307; and JS Rogers, 'Negotiability, Property and Identity' (1990) 12 Cardozo Law Review 471.

[18] This may not be possible with non-negotiable certificates to registrable investments.

practices, that pose a significant challenge to this. The challenges posed are explored in Chapters 2, 3 and 4.

Custodian's Duties

1.25 Where assets are held by a custodian appointed by the investor, it is likely that the obligations of the custodian will be owed directly to the investor. Where custodial services are offered by a fund manager or broker, the obligations are also likely to be owed directly to the investors. However, in the event of the use of nominees or third party custodians by brokers or fund managers, the obligations of the nominee or third party (actual) custodian may be owed to the broker or fund manager.

1.26 One question which arises is the source of any duties, in particular whether they are exclusively as set out in the agreement for custodial services or whether general law has a significant role to play in this area. Assuming the relevance of general law, it remains to be seen to what degree it may be circumscribed by the parties to a custodial agreement. Another issue is whether the duties are owed exclusively to the appointing party or, where appointed by an intermediary, duties may be owed to the investor. Assuming the possibility of the latter, it then falls to be determined whether the duty owed to the investor is instead of or parallel to that owed to the appointing intermediary.

Dematerialisation

1.27 Paper-based systems for the transfer of securities are labour-intensive. For registrable securities the certificate must be surrendered and re-issued in the name of the new owner of the securities evidenced by the certificate. In the case of negotiable securities, the certificate must ordinarily be physically transferred into the possession of the new owner. The issue and movement of large quantities of certificates following transactions in the capital markets has severely strained settlement and clearance systems. Other demerits of paper-based systems of transfer include the fact that the paper is expensive to produce because it must be made to include features that prevent forgery. There are also great risks that the certificates may be stolen, with most significant consequences for negotiable securities, and overriding title passed to a bona fide purchaser for value. Finally, the *situs* of securities evidenced or represented by certificates may be peripatetic, with the consequence that transfer of the security whether by sale or security interest will need to accord with varying systems of law depending on where it is at the time of the transaction.

1.28 In view of these shortcomings, investments are increasingly dematerialised.[19] They are neither evidenced nor represented by a tangible token of the underlying

---

[19] Around £1 trillion of stock is held electronically in CREST, representing about 80 per cent of the value of all listed companies in the United Kingdom, and approximately 130,000 transactions are settled per day with a value of about £20 billion; see *CREST: Briefing* (November 1997) 2, 4.

security. One example of this is CREST, the paperless system for the settlement of equities, albeit with an option for those who wish to keep their paper to opt out of the system.[20] The system is said to offer greater efficiency in the settlement of equity, together with reduced costs and risks for users.[21] Another example is the Central Gilts Office ('CGO') of the Bank of England for the settlement of gilt-edged securities by electronic book entry in real time against an assured payment.[22]

There are likely to be membership and IT costs involved in effecting transactions **1.29** in a dematerialised settlement system which may not be justified by the volume of transactions which many investors undertake. This presents a powerful motive for their use of custodians. When employing a custodian that undertakes transactions in that settlement system for numerous parties, the various investors spread the cost of using the settlement system amongst themselves by the custodian spreading this cost between his clients as a part of the fees he charges them.

Dematerialisation in itself does not necessarily influence the structure of legal **1.30** relationships that existed when there were certificates.[23] With registrable securities, the difference is minimal. Instead of having to surrender the certificate and obtaining a change in the register to effect a transaction, all that is required is a change in the register—there is no longer a certificate to have to surrender. With negotiable securities, although the difference is greater,[24] dematerialisation still does not necessarily alter the kind of legal structures that would exist by virtue of negotiable certificates. The principal difference is that some kind of book or register is introduced to reflect ownership of the securities. Where transfer of possession of the certificate would ordinarily have been required for a transaction, one obtains a change in the book-entry records of ownership instead. Nothing has to move, there is merely a change of record.

Immobilisation[25]

Whilst it might have been assumed that dematerialisation would have been the **1.31** most significant development for the holding of financial assets, this has not proved to be the case. Dematerialisation still entails the (at least notional) transfer

---

[20] CREST Project Team at the Bank of England, *CREST: The Business Description* (December 1994) 4, 61–62.

[21] ibid 4, 5.

[22] *Central Gilts Office Reference Manual*, version No 1 (October 1997) 1.1.3.

[23] In relation to CREST see Uncertificated Securities Regulations 1995, SI 1995/3272, especially reg 20; and CREST Project Team at the Bank of England, *CREST: The Business Description* (December 1994) 16–17, 90. In relation to CGO, see reg 1(2) of Government Stock Regulations 1965, SI 1965/1420; and *Central Gilts Office Reference Manual*, version No 1 (October 1997) 2.5.3.

[24] JS Rogers, 'An Essay on Horseless Carriages and Paperless Negotiable Instruments: Some Lessons from the Article 8 Revision' (1995) 31 Idaho Law Review 689. See also J Benjamin, *The Law of Global Custody* (1996), ch 3.

[25] N Papaspyrou, 'Immobilisation of Securities' Part One [1996] JIBL 430 and Part Two [1996] JIBL 459.

of the relevant securities each time they are traded. With the growing volume of trades, even if this notional transfer only requires an amendment to the electronic records of the issuer, this could still prove to be unduly onerous for the issuer.

1.32 For this reason it has been thought advantageous to sever the link between investors and the investment, by issuers depositing the securities with a custodian depository as legal title-holder thereof so that it is only possible to invest in the security indirectly by opening an account with the custodian. Instead of the investor enjoying a direct relationship with the issuer, he enjoys a direct relationship with the custodian. The benefits of this structure are that whether the underlying security is dematerialised or not, any formalities relating to the transfer of the securities on the register of the issuer are avoided. Transfers or other transactions affecting the securities are reflected on the books of the custodian, hence the term 'book entry transfers'.

1.33 An example of immobilisation in England is the Central Moneymarkets Office (CMO) which acts as depository and settlement system for sterling money market securities.[26] Although CMO regards itself as bailee for account-holders in CMO in relation to the negotiable instruments held in CMO,[27] implying that the legal relationship between investor and investment is a direct one, this is doubtful. As contended in Chapters 2 and 4, it is likely that the structure of immobilisation severs the legal relationship between investor and issuer,[28] with the result that CMO may be better characterised as trustee of securities in the system.

1.34 Immobilisation may be established by an issuer giving one global certificate or note to a custodian attesting to the custodian's legal title to an entire issue of securities,[29] with the result that investors may only enjoy an interest in relation to such securities by opening an account with the custodian. These certificates or notes may be permanent, semi-permanent or temporary. Where permanent, no investor will ordinarily ever enjoy a direct relationship with the issuer, unless, for instance, the custodian ceases to offer its services or upon the insolvency of the issuer. Temporary notes or certificates are intended to be replaced by certificates of smaller denominations to be held directly in the name of the investors who take an interest in the issue. In either case the immobilisation or termination of immobilisation applies to all investors with an interest in the relevant issue. A semi-

---

[26] *Central Moneymarkets Office Reference Manual,* version No 2 (updated May 1997) A.3.1. The workings of the CMO are summarised by Jennifer Donohue and Clifford Atkins, 'Settling Trades in the UK Moneymarkets' (1993) 12(3) IFLR 35.

[27] *Central Moneymarkets Office Reference Manual,* version No 2 (updated May 1997) J.2.5.

[28] In contrast with CREST and CGO holdings which have statutory backing that the legal relationship between investor and investment is unchanged by those types of holdings (see n 23 above), the nature of relationship between investor and investment in CMO is left for general law to determine.

[29] F Christie and H Dosanjh, 'The Practical Elements of Settlement and Custody' in F Oditah (ed), *The Future for the Global Securities Market: Legal and Regulatory Aspects* (1996) 132–134. See also J Benjamin, *The Law of Global Custody* (1996), 13, 14.

permanent note or certificate is different in that the issuer deposits a global certificate or note with a custodian on terms that it is essentially permanent but that investors may at their option elect to call for the issue of a certificate representing their holdings, with corresponding reductions in the volume of securities evidenced by the global certificate or note. Where some investors elect to take their own definitive certificates, the global indirect holding is ended for those investors but not for those who wish to continue to take their interest via the global note or certificate—the immobilised portion of the issue is merely reduced correspondingly.[30]

Immobilisation may also be effected by the issue of securities into custody, with a further issue of depository receipts (DRs) by the custodian based thereon giving those entitled to the DRs an interest in relation to the underlying securities or benefits flowing therefrom.[31] The degree of separation between the investor and the underlying securities where the investor acquires DRs depends on the particular structure by which the DR is established.[32] It may be that the underlying securities are beneficially owned by investors in the DRs, with investment in the DR, in effect, being a method of identifying by whom the underlying securities are beneficially owned. This would be the case where a nominee enjoys title to the underlying securities for the benefit of those who acquire new securities (DRs) issued directly by it or any other party it recognises for this purpose. If, however, the nominee holds the underlying securities for another party who in turn issues new securities (DRs), investment in the depository receipts will not constitute beneficial ownership of the underlying securities. Beneficial ownership is for the intermediary who issues the new securities. An investor enjoys legal title to the new securities and beneficial entitlement to whatever benefits the intermediary gets from the underlying securities. In such circumstances, the investor does not have any direct link with the underlying securities. **1.35**

Immobilisation need not be established at the instance of issuers. It may be established by investors transferring their holdings to custodians. In so doing, investors exchange their direct rights against issuers for direct rights against the custodian. **1.36**

Immobilisation obviates the need for every issuer to invest in the costly computer systems that are required for dematerialisation, a wasteful duplication of computer capacity with every issuer. Even if dematerialisation is effected with a **1.37**

---

[30] Due to operational difficulties which may arise from an issue of securities being definitively represented by a global certificate or note, as well as by certificates withdrawn by an individual investor, there is now a trend away from semi-permanent immobilisation; see F Christie and H Dosanjh, 'The Practical Elements of Settlement and Custody' in F Oditah (ed), *The Future for the Global Securities Market: Legal and Regulatory Aspects* (1996) 133.

[31] For a detailed discussion of these see J Benjamin, *The Law of Global Custody* (1996), ch 9.

[32] The implications of tiered holdings on the interests of investors in relation to assets deposited into custody are examined in Chapter 4.

centralised settlement system, such as CREST, to avoid each issuer having to maintain such computer capacity, traders in various securities may still need to invest in and become conversant with the different types of software operated by the different settlement systems. With immobilisation, only depositories and intermediaries who wish to offer settlement services would have to undertake significant investment in information technology.

1.38 It was suggested above that dematerialisation need not impact on the legal structures by which investment is carried out and that the investor may still enjoy direct relations with the issuer. Immobilisation is very different. It is this operational practice which, perhaps more than any other feature of modern custody, affects the legal analysis of the custody of investments. By definition, immobilisation is a system by which investors can only enjoy indirect holdings. The investor enjoys direct relations only with the custodian, leaving the investor, at best, with an indirect interest in the investment. The principal evidence of the investment of the investor is no longer a certificate, or even the register of the issuer of the relevant security. It is the book entries reflected in the books of the custodian that indicate the investor's entitlements. Consequently, the transfer of the investor's rights in relation to the investment need not be reflected by any change in the register of the issuer. If the transferee of the investor uses the same custodian, as would obtain in the case of transfers within a depository, the legal title to the underlying investment remains the same, the custodian remains legal title-holder, and the transfer is only reflected in the change of book entries in the books of the custodian/depository. The principal consequences of this in various contexts, including for the use of custody assets as collateral and the conflict of laws analysis of the custody of assets, are explored in later chapters.

Settlement Netting

1.39 If immobilisation (whether accompanied by dematerialisation or not) was the ultimate evolution and all investors dealt with this depository, the significant saving would only be that issuers would not have to invest in substantial information management systems. However, the type of system necessary to cope with real time trading by every buyer and seller of securities on the books of the depository would still be vast.

1.40 In pursuit of ever-greater efficiencies, some securities markets have introduced the settlement of trades by netting. Trades are not reflected on a real time basis. When a trade is agreed upon, settlement takes place at predetermined settlement times, at which point reciprocal obligations for the same class of security are calculated and settled, with only net transfers being made.

1.41 This process of netting may take place at various levels. Assuming the use of sub-custodians, a concept that is considered below, netting may occur variously in the books of the custodian and in the books of the sub-custodian. Only net move-ments in the positions of the account-holders with the custodian are reflected post-netting. Similarly, the only movements on the sub-custodian's books are those necessary to reflect changes (if any) to the net position of the account-holder with the sub-custodian post-netting.

The implications of netting where there are tiered holdings is to reduce drastically **1.42** the reflections, and necessary verification, of changes of entitlements. Assuming 1,000 transactions between 100 customers of 10 custodians in relation to a single type of asset in one settlement period, these may as a result of netting be reduced to 100 changes[33] on the books of the custodians (a saving of 900 changes over transfers being reflected on a real time basis). This may in turn be reduced post-netting to 10 changes in the books of the sub-custodian/depository, assuming that the positions of all 10 custodians in relation to the type of asset had changed (a sav-ing of 990 changes over transfers being reflected on a real time basis). Assuming immobilisation with a depository, or that the net position of the sub-custodian has not changed, there would be no change in the underlying legal title (a saving of 1,000 changes over transfers being reflected on a real time basis). On a two-tier structure with 1,000 transactions at the top tier in relation to one type of invest-ment asset, there is a saving of 2,890 changes: see Figure 1.1. Given that in prac-tice there may be millions of transactions in relation to many different financial assets, where the holdings structures involve numerous tiers, the savings of time and energy afforded by netting are enormous.

Figure 1.1: Benefits of netting

No of transactions	Level of transaction	Amendments
1000	customer's records	1000
1000	custodian's records post-netting	100
1000	sub-custodian's records post-netting	10
1000	issuer's register	0
4000	Total transactions	1110

Beyond the benefits set out above, netting affords participants in capital markets **1.43** a significant reduction in the risk of loss upon the failure of a counter-party to per-form his side of the transaction after one side has already performed. Ordinarily, it is all but impossible, given the different mechanisms that may be involved in the transfer of funds required to pay for the transfer of securities for instance, to ensure that the two sides of a transaction occur absolutely simultaneously. As such, there arises the risk that the party who has completed his side of the bargain

---

[33] This assumes that the account balance of each client has changed. In fact, it may be the case that it is the balance of only a few clients who trade heavily that alters, leading to a smaller number of post-netting adjustments.

may lose out if the counter-party fails before he has completed the other side of the bargain.

1.44 Whatever the benefits of netting, however, there arises one significant problem. By the process of netting, it becomes difficult to establish how the securities of any one party are applied. The problem is not simply derived from the possible similarity of assets netted. Even with similar assets, if transactions were effected on a real time basis one could reasonably clearly establish that the securities of XYZ were transferred in favour of ABC. Netting poses a significant challenge to the process of identification which may be necessary for the acquisition of proprietary rights generally, as well as for remedies for breach of duty which are dependent on tracing.

Fungibility[34]

1.45 Securities holdings may or may not be fungible,[35] a state where one unit of assets is considered replaceable by another unit. This is critical to some of the operational practices of custody business. It enables client assets to be pooled, it is also critical to the process of netting where there is no in specie transfer for the settlement of trades. Fungibility is partly a function of the features of the assets. It is unlikely that dissimilar assets will be considered fungible, although at the election of all concerned they may be. Conversely, even if assets are identical they will not be considered fungible if the holder is obliged to return them in specie to their respective owners. Ultimately, therefore, it appears that it is the re-delivery obligation in relation to assets held by a custodian that determines whether assets are fungible.

1.46 Securities represented or evidenced by a tangible token may be fungible or non-fungible. Although the underlying obligations of any issuer in respect of the various securities that make up an issue are indistinguishable in principle, they may be separated in practice by segregating the tokens evidencing or representing the securities. If the securities are numbered, this serves as another means of separating the securities in practice. Notwithstanding the foregoing, where securities are deliberately transferred into fungible holdings of securities with identical features, so that the investor is satisfied by the re-delivery of similar securities to the ones transferred into the pool, the securities transferred will be fungible whether numbered or not.

---

[34] This issue is treated more fully in Chapter 3. See also J Benjamin, *The Law of Global Custody* (1996), 38, 39.

[35] An example of a fungible holding is holding via CREST, to which securities are only admitted on condition that the units are not numbered or otherwise individually identifiable, CREST Rules (1996), r 19(13). Conversely, an example of non-fungible holdings is in CMO, where specifically identifiable securities are credited to a member's account; see *Central Moneymarkets Office Reference Manual*, version No 2 (updated May 1997) F.1.4–5.

Wholly dematerialised securities raise peculiar problems. By definition, there can **1.47**
be nothing to distinguish one unit out of a set of identical securities, nor is there
any tangible token by which this might be notionally achieved in practice. Thus,
where wholly dematerialised securities are unnumbered they can only be fungible.
Even if numbered, they would, like with numbered certificates evidencing or
representing securities, also be fungible if deliberately transferred into fungible
holdings.

However, the treatment of wholly dematerialised but numbered securities may be **1.48**
different when kept out of fungible holdings. Can they be considered non-
fungible? They cannot be physically identified because they do not have any
physical features by which they may be distinguished. Further, in the absence of a
physical existence they cannot be identified by reference to a geographical location. Yet, just as with otherwise identical securities represented by numbered certificates, the numbering may be taken as a form of notional identification so that
the different securities that make up a wholly dematerialised issue may be distinguishable in practice. The very essence of the numbering is to counteract in practice the actual indistinguishability of the securities.[36] The numbering enables the
securities to be distinguished according to the manner in which they are applied.[37]
Even if this position does not accord fully with logic, it is defensible based on the
intention of all concerned. The fundamental question at issue relates to the allocation of transactions. With non-fungibility it is certain how each investor's assets
are applied; conversely, fungibility leaves this to be resolved by the records of the
custodian. If the facts suggest that specific transactions are allocated to specific
investors, this is clearly incompatible with fungible holdings.

Pooling

Pooling is the practice of keeping like assets in indistinguishable omnibus hold- **1.49**
ings. This may occur at the various tiers of custodial holdings, for instance in the
books of a depository and in the books of an ordinary custodian.

A custodian may pool both client and its own assets in its name without anything **1.50**
on the face of the investment to distinguish that any of the assets belong to its
clients.[38] This would most likely occur where the investment does not permit any
type of designation in the title to the securities. This does not mean that the
investors necessarily lose all means of identifying that assets are held for them, it

---

[36] LD Smith, *The Law of Tracing* (1997) 222–227.
[37] RM Goode, 'The Nature and Transfer of Rights in Dematerialised and Immobilised
Securities' [1996] BJIBFL 176, 170; J Benjamin, 'Custody: An English Law Analysis—Part 2'
[1994] BJIBFL 187, 189. In relation to international central depositories, see F Christie and
H Dosanjh, 'The Practical Elements of Settlement and Custody' in F Oditah (ed), *The Future for
the Global Securities Market: Legal and Regulatory Aspects* (1996) 132.
[38] The title to such securities may read ABC Bank.

just means that this can only occur in the books of the custodian and not in the title to the securities.

1.51 Where some degree of designation on the title to the investments held by the custodian is possible, whether on the books of the issuer[39] or on the books of a sub-custodian, the custodian may pool only client assets and hold its own assets separately by adding something in the title to some securities to indicate that they belong to clients as a whole.[40] Whether designation is allowed or not, custodian and client assets may be effectively separated, albeit pooling client assets, by putting client assets together in the name of a special nominee constituted for this purpose.

1.52 The opposite of pooling is segregation, of which there are degrees. Segregation may only involve separation of the custodian's assets from those of the investors, or it may involve segregation of each investor's holdings from those of another. Full segregation is best achieved where title to the investment permits some degree of designation;[41] it would be impractical to set up a nominee for each client. Whilst segregation facilitates the allocation of transactions in relation to custody assets to particular investors, as well as the process of reconciling client assets, it is a more labour intensive, and therefore costly, method of holding assets.

1.53 The benefits of pooling include savings on the expense and efforts that would be necessary to administer and reconcile separate holdings for every contributor or interested party in the pool. It also reduces the risk of administrative errors in the process of administering different holdings for every interested party. However, pooling raises a number of difficulties. In the first place, there are questions as to the possibility of acquisition or retention of proprietary rights in relation to pooled assets. Assuming that these difficulties can be overcome, pooling also reduces the ease with which entitlement to assets in the pool may be identified. Consequences of this include the fact that misapplication of pooled assets may be more difficult to detect and, where detected, it may be more difficult to ascribe the loss to a particular party. Thus, upon the insolvency of the custodian where client assets are pooled with the custodian's own assets, there is an increased risk that client assets may be mistaken for the custodian's assets. The pooling of client assets separately from the custodian's own assets does not jeopardise client assets in case of the custodian's insolvency. Although difficulties may arise as to who owns which unit in the pool, it is clear that none of the units in the pool belongs to the custodian and so may not be claimed by his creditors.

---

[39] CREST Project Team at the Bank of England, *CREST: The Business Description* (December 1994) 16; CREST, *CREST Reference Manual* (May 1996) 22.

[40] The title to such securities may read ABC Bank for its own securities and ABC Bank-Clients for client securities.

[41] The title to such securities may read ABC Bank for its own securities and ABC Bank-XYZ or 123, the suffix may be the initials or code by which particular clients are identified.

Sub-Custodians

Modern custody is now most often constituted by tiers of holdings. A number of **1.54**
factors encourage and sometimes necessitate this.

Where securities are immobilised in a depository, which constitutes one tier of **1.55**
custody, it may be impractical for an individual investor to deal directly with the
depository custodian. As with dematerialised settlement systems, there may be
membership and IT costs involved which the volume of transactions that many
investors undertake cannot justify. However, as already indicated in the section on
dematerialisation, investors can effectively spread this cost by using a custodian.
The implication of the investors using a custodian to interface with the custo-
dian/depository will be that there will be a two-tier structure to the holding of that
type of investment.

The use of nominees by the custodian may also introduce tiered holdings to a cus- **1.56**
todial structure. This will be the case if client assets are vested in a nominee who
holds on behalf of the custodian, and the custodian takes any benefit to be passed
on to the clients. The result of this is a two-tier holding of assets held by a nominee to the order of the custodian, who takes for the benefit of his clients.

As indicated earlier, the particular structure by which depository receipts are **1.57**
issued may also constitute the direct owner of the underlying securities a sub-
custodian where the securities are held for the benefit of an intermediary. Where
the intermediary issues the depository receipts that the investor acquires, such
intermediary will be constituted the lead or first-tier custodian.

The practice of 'white-labelling' of custodial services also results in a tiered custodial **1.58**
structure. White-labelling is the practice whereby the operations of custody are carried out by one party but it is another party that offers the custodial services in its
own name. The parties involved in white-label custody services may do this for a
number of reasons. The party carrying out the actual custodial operations clearly
does so for remuneration. The party who offers the service to be performed by
another may do so for any number of strategic reasons. For example, a fund-manager
may do so in order to offer a fuller range of financial services than he would otherwise be capable of offering or in order to prevent the actual custodian, who may also
offer fund-management services, from coming into contact with the investor.

One of the most important reasons for using sub-custodians is for investment in **1.59**
foreign assets. The local laws of the assets may not recognise foreign ownership of
the type of investment and so it may be necessary to constitute or employ a local
nominee to hold the investments. This will create a two-tier holding structure
where the investor uses a (global)[42] custodian himself and the local nominee holds

---

[42] See generally J Benjamin, *The Law of Global Custody* (1996).

for the custodian. The result will be the same where the foreign assets are immobilised in a central custodian/depository and an investor employs his own custodian as well.[43] Even if there are no local impediments to direct foreign ownership of investments, it may be more practical and efficient to use one of the international central securities depositories (ICSD) as a means of effecting foreign investments.[44] The typical ICSD will have constituted or employed nominees in all of the jurisdictions to which its service extends to hold assets to its order. If the investor interfaces with the ICSD directly, this will constitute a two-tier structure. However, if, as is more likely to be the case, the investor uses a (global) custodian to interface with the ICSD, a three-tier custodial structure will have been constituted. The assets are held by a local nominee to the order of the ICSD, who in turn holds for the (global) custodian, who in turn holds for the benefit of the investor.

1.60   It is not inconceivable, assuming the particular type of investment permits this or the local laws of the situs of the investment permit this, that the sub-custodian is instructed by the (global) custodian to hold directly for the investors. In such a scenario, there is only one tier of holding, in spite of the existence of two levels of custodian. The sub-custodian holds directly for the investor.

1.61   Whilst the foregoing has focused on one, two or three-tier holding structures, in practice there may be many more tiers than that. There is no limit to the number of tiers of any structure. As many tiers will be created as are necessary to achieve the desired investment objective. Depending on the structure of each tier of a custodial structure, the investor may or may not be increasingly removed from the underlying assets. A full analysis of the effects of tiered holdings is undertaken in Chapter 4.

Use of Custody Assets

1.62   It is not uncommon for custodians to make use of custody assets or for the assets to be made use of by other parties. This may arise upon the stock-lending of custody assets by the custodian, a practice which is essential to the liquidity of capital markets as it allows market-makers to cover short positions for the purposes of settlement. Custodians benefit by being able to borrow the assets or by charging fees for arranging stock-lending to other parties. Investors benefit by being able to generate additional income from their assets. Investors may also seek to make more active use of idle custody assets by undertaking repo transactions or otherwise using the assets as collateral for the raising of finance. The credit sought may be from the custodian itself or a third party.

---

[43]   An example of this is the Depository Trust Corporation of New York, USA, which uses a nominee, Cede & Co, to hold securities participating in the depository scheme.

[44]   Euroclear and Cedel are prominent examples: see F Christie and H Dosanjh, 'The Practical Elements of Settlement and Custody' in F Oditah (ed), *The Future for the Global Securities Market: Legal and Regulatory Aspects* (1996).

In the above scenarios the assets may need to be transferred from the beneficial **1.63** ownership of the investor to that of the other person who seeks to make use of them or, for certain types of collateral arrangements, the person from whom credit is sought. Where the party who seeks to use the assets is the custodian as stock borrower, or the custodian is the party from whom the investor seeks secured credit, the practice of stock-lending or pledging may impact on the rights of the investors in relation to the custody assets. It may affect the characterisation of the investor as beneficial owner of the custody assets, and on occasion may leave him with mere creditor rights if it appears that the custodian can use the assets as if they are his own. These issues are more fully addressed in Chapter 3.

Nominees

In the foregoing sections, nominees are said to be used for various purposes. They **1.64** may be used to segregate client holdings from those of a fund manager who provides custodial services or a custodian who engages in proprietary trading. Nominees may also be used to hold foreign assets where the client or custodian is not permitted to enjoy title in relation to the particular thing, or where it is simply more convenient for custody to be structured in this way.[45]

A nominee serves only as repository for title to assets. Although the nominee does **1.65** not enjoy such title beneficially, the structure of the nominee may be critical to the question of who enjoys beneficial entitlement to the assets held in its name. This question may be resolved exclusively with regard to the books of the nominee itself or, as will often be the case, a combination of the books of the nominee and the books of another party, such as the custodian or fund-manager who set up the nominee arrangements.

The party or parties recognised by the nominee to be beneficially entitled to the **1.66** assets it holds will impact on the number of tiers of custody. If the nominee recognises the investors to be beneficially entitled, even if the investors may only be identified from the records of another party, such as the settlement system, custodian or fund-manager who constituted or employed the nominee, then there is only one tier of holding. The nominee holds for the investors directly.[46] However, where the nominee holds for the custodian who holds in turn for its client investors, there will have been constituted two tiers of holding.

Nominee holdings, as with any other type of custodial holding, may involve **1.67** pooled or segregated holdings. If the nominee holds for clients directly, the

---

[45] These are the reasons why it is currently being contemplated that CREST establishes a network of nominees especially around Europe, so that CREST members may via CREST enjoy interests in relation to offshore securities. See CRESTCo Limited, *CREST: Cross-Border Settlement* (December 1997) 14–15.

[46] An example of this is how foreign assets are held by CREST offshore nominees for CREST members; see CRESTCo Limited, *CREST: Cross-Border Settlement* (December 1997) ch 2.

holdings are pooled if the records of the nominee do not indicate who the individual clients are. Even if the individual clients are identified, the assets will be pooled if the records of the nominee do not indicate which client is beneficially entitled to what assets.

Custody of Offshore Assets

1.68   As suggested above, notwithstanding that the investor may be English, that his custodian is also English, and that the agreement for custodial services may be subject to English law, it may yet be impossible to avoid the impact of foreign law on the custodial structure. This will arise in the event that the custodian provides custodial services for offshore investments and the investor makes use of that facility. Such custodians are known as global custodians in view of the geographical reach of the services they offer.

1.69   The offshore assets may be such that the investor enjoys direct legal title to registrable securities held for him. Where custodians are employed, title to registrable securities may be vested in a global custodian or one of a tier of custodians, with negotiable securities held for the benefit of one of the tier of custodians. As already suggested, the introduction of tiers may affect the investor's rights in relation to the assets transferred into custody.

1.70   Where cross-border holdings are concerned, it is imperative that investors, custodians and their counter-parties are able to predict with some degree of certainty the governing law or laws relating to the custody assets. This issue must be addressed for every tier of holding in order to determine how the stream of benefits is passed to the investor from the ultimate (sub-) custodian. Certainty of governing law is also important for transactions in relation to offshore custody assets as this leads to the avoidance of disputes and promotes the finality of transactions, thereby facilitating the manner in which investors may alienate the assets.

2

SINGLE-TIER CUSTODY

Typically, custody business involves a number of parties, which may include: the **2.01** investor who transfers assets into custody or acquires assets via a custodian; a fund manager who may be entitled to issue investment orders directly to the custodian in relation to the asset; the custodian or its nominees, into whose name or to whose order the assets are transferred; sub-custodians; and central depositories in whose name the assets may be registered.

This chapter is concerned with the most basic form of custodial relationships. At **2.02** its most elemental, a custodial arrangement would consist of the investor, issuer of the relevant security and the custodian only. The custodian may be an external party to the relationship between the investor and the issuer or, where the custodian is the legal owner of the asset, an intermediary between the investor and the issuer of the securities.

When an investor transfers assets into custody or acquires assets via a custodian, **2.03** the investor may be described by the custodian as having become entitled to a certain number of securities or may be described as having had a securities account with the custodian opened or credited with a number of securities. In sum, the investor becomes the beneficiary of a number of securities. Regardless of labels, an analysis of the form of beneficial entitlement that identifies the nature of the investor's interest in relation to assets transferred into or acquired via custody is important for a number of reasons.

A. Importance of the Nature of the Investor's Interest

2.04 Although investors would ordinarily enjoy contractual rights of a personal nature against their custodian for re-delivery of custody assets, it may be their common intention that the investor retains a proprietary, beneficial interest in assets in custody in order to insulate the assets from the insolvency of the custodian. However, the label attached to the investor's entitlement or declared intent of custodian and investor does not of itself determine the legal relationship between investor and custody assets. The relationship must be of such a nature that it produces the results desired according to legal principle.

2.05 As a rule, the issuer of securities is concerned only with the legal owner of the securities, to whom all benefits are passed. This raises the question of the treatment of such benefits as between the custodian legally entitled to the benefits and investors. The investor may be a creditor of the custodian or beneficial owner of the securities and their fruits. If the investor is a creditor of the custodian, he is limited to purely personal rights against the custodian. On the other hand, if the investor is beneficially interested in the custody assets, he may be in a position to determine how the fruits of the custody assets are applied.

2.06 As already indicated, the typical custodian will be under a personal obligation to return assets transferred into custody to the investor upon the conclusion of the term of custody. The re-delivery obligation may be specific or non-specific and the implications of this for the characterisation of the relationship between custodian and investor will be explored in the next chapter. It has already been asserted that many investors would, in addition, wish to establish a relationship with their custodian that confers on them, the investors, proprietary rights in relation to the custody assets. The principal reason for this relates to the risk to an investor of transferring his assets into the custody of another that turns on the distinction that English law draws between property rights and personal rights.[1] In the event of the custodian's insolvency, those investors able to assert proprietary rights in relation to assets in custody will enjoy priority *vis-à-vis* the custodian's general creditors in the recovery of the assets or their traceable substitutes,[2] whilst those enjoying personal rights will have to compete with the custodian's general creditors for a dividend. In case of insolvency, it is unlikely that those enjoying personal rights against the insolvent will have their claims fully satisfied.

2.07 The nature of the investor's interest is also of importance to potential creditors of the investor who might want to take security over the assets in custody. The cred-

---

[1] RM Goode, 'Ownership and Obligations in Commercial Transactions' (1987) 103 LQR 433, 434–453.

[2] *Re Nakashidze (No 2)* [1948] 2 DLR, 522, 529–534 per Urquhart J, Ontario SC; *Re Ord, Wallington, etc.* (1971) 15 CBR (NS) 66, 70 per Poultney, Registrar, Ontario SC.

itor will want to know the precise nature of the asset he is getting as security, as this would in part determine the quality of his security and the ease with which it could be realised.[3]

In the event of fraudulent or negligent misapplication of custody assets, the char- **2.08** acterisation of the relationship of the various parties with the custody assets may be critical in determining who bears any losses, as well as the form of remedy which may be obtained by the aggrieved party.

The nature of the investor's rights may also raise regulatory issues as to the capital **2.09** regime to be demanded of institutions offering custodial services. If the custodian is regarded as the debtor of the investor, as are banks in relation to depositors of funds, there may be a case to be made for significant capital adequacy standards being imposed on custodians in order to increase the likelihood that an investor who has deposited assets in custody will be able to have his claims satisfied.

The nature of the interest and the legal characterisation of the relationship **2.10** between the parties may affect the custodian's duties. Beyond any agreement between custodian and investor, fiduciary and other obligations may be imposed by general law because of the investor's interest in the assets in custody.

B. Proprietary Rights

Whilst the term 'proprietary rights' has been employed, no indication of the **2.11** meaning of the term has so far been given. It is necessary to have an understanding of what is meant by the term in order to be in a position to assess whether the interests enjoyed by an investor in relation to custody assets are proprietary or not.

'Property can be defined as that which is capable of being the subject-matter of **2.12** property rights.'[4] This definition relates to the use of the word 'property' in the sense of things that can be the subject of ownership. However, it should be recognised that the word may be applied to the state of ownership itself. Concentrating for the moment on the former use of the word, the way in which it is there defined indicates that the concept of property as the subject-matter of ownership is flexible, capable of application to both tangible and intangible assets.[5] The concept of property as subject-matter is limited only by the type of rights that society is willing to recognise in relation to the particular asset. That willingness may be influenced, but not necessarily determined, by a number of factors, such as the

---

[3] R Ryan, 'Taking Security over Investment Portfolios Held in Global Custody' (1990) 10 JIBL 404.

[4] AP Bell, *Modern Law of Personal Property in England and Ireland* (1989) 3.

[5] WN Hohfeld, *Fundamental Legal Conceptions As Applied in Judicial Reasoning* (WW Cook (ed), 3rd printing, 1964), 85–91.

prevailing religion or morality of a society, economic considerations, as well as the practical feasibility of the recognition of proprietary rights in relation to the particular type of asset. If this definition is accepted, an examination of the nature of the asset claimed in a custodial arrangement will not be of particular significance in establishing whether the interests enjoyed in relation thereto are proprietary or not.

2.13   It is recognised that ownership is the '*greatest possible interest in a thing which a mature system of law recognizes*'[6] and that ownership of any asset is comprised of a number of different interests in relation thereto. Depending on the asset, and general circumstances, ownership may entitle one, *inter alia*, to possess, use, manage, enjoy and alienate the asset.[7] Further, the incidents of ownership in relation to any asset may be separated between different parties. Yet, even if the typical incidents of ownership are termed proprietary, this does not lead to a clearer understanding of why they are proprietary. Since some personal rights enable one, for example, to manage or use an asset, what makes an interest proprietary as opposed to personal?

2.14   Proprietary rights have been described as rights in or over things[8] or against other persons in relation to a particular thing (*res*),[9] the implication of the latter view being that rights or interests which arise out of contractual or fiduciary relations between individuals may be considered proprietary.[10] Without entering into the debate as to whether the rights are in, against or simply in relation to a thing, the emphasis of proprietary rights would seem to be that they bind the generality of mankind. In the words of one commentator, a proprietary right is '*one* of a large *class* of *fundamentally similar* yet separate rights, actual and potential, residing in a *single* person (or single group of persons) but availing *respectively* against persons constituting a very large and indefinite class of people'.[11]

2.15   One point needs to be made in relation to the question of rights being good against the generality of mankind. Proprietary rights are perceived as binding the generality of mankind, not necessarily every man. In this sense, they are not absolute rights. They do permit exceptions, and are therefore limited thereby. For instance, it is recognised that existing proprietary rights would be invalid in the face of the new interest of a bona fide purchaser for value without notice, regardless of whether the owner of the prior right knew of or consented to the sale. Thus,

---

[6] AM Honoré, 'Ownership' in AG Guest (ed), *Oxford Essays in Jurisprudence* (1st Series, 1961) 107, 108.

[7] For a fuller discussion, see Honoré (n 6 above) 113; and Hohfeld, *Fundamental Legal Conceptions* (n 5 above) 28–29.

[8] *National Provincial Bank Ltd v Ainsworth* [1965] AC 1175, 1243 per Lord Wilberforce.

[9] Hohfeld, *Fundamental Legal Conceptions* (n 5 above) 75–76.

[10] *Federal Commissioner of Taxation v United Aircraft Corporation* (1943) 68 CLR 525, 548 per Williams J, HC of Australia.

[11] Hohfeld, *Fundamental Legal Conceptions* (n 5 above) 72.

the fact that an interest may be defeated or is invalid against an exceptional class of persons does not necessarily deprive an interest of its proprietary status.[12]

Whilst the general nature of rights is significant in the case of tangible assets such **2.16** as land, the importance of interests in relation to intangibles is not best explained by the fact of their availing against the whole world. For instance, whilst it may be important that the owner of a plot of land is recognised to have proprietary rights in relation to the land which may preclude others from enjoying the land, where a share entitles an investor to rights against X company, the recognition or not of this right by third parties is largely irrelevant. Entitlement to exercise the rights that make up shares is essentially between issuer and shareholder only. Nevertheless, it is established that the investor's interest in the share is proprietary.[13] This would suggest that there are other factors that may determine the classification of an interest as proprietary.

The nature of proprietary rights has been considered by the House of Lords,[14] **2.17** where it was declared that as regards the distinction between property rights and personal rights, 'Before a right or an interest can be admitted into the category of property, or of a right affecting property, it must be definable, identifiable by third parties, capable in its nature of assumption by third parties, and have some degree of permanence or stability'.[15] Examination of these criteria provides a further clue as to the constituent elements of proprietary rights. To the extent that a right must be definable, identifiable by third parties and possess some degree of permanence, it is not fundamentally different from any personal right. The real distinction turns on the need for it to be 'capable in its nature of assumption by third parties'; in short, it should be capable of alienation.

In view of the foregoing, it is submitted that proprietary rights are rights in rela- **2.18** tion to determinate or identifiable assets that may be exercised against the generality of mankind and/or are assignable.[16] Depending on the nature of the *res*, it may be sufficient that they are either good against the generality of mankind or assignable.

C. Relationship between Investor and Custodian

The typical custodial scenario could bring about a whole range of legal relation- **2.19** ships between investor and custodian, including contracting counter-parties, debtor-creditor, agency, bailment, fiduciary and trust. In order for investors to

---

[12] ibid 73, 104–106.
[13] *The Colonial Bank v Frederick Whinney* (1886) 11 AC 426.
[14] *National Provincial Bank Ltd v Ainsworth* [1965] AC 1175.
[15] ibid 1247–1248, per Lord Wilberforce.
[16] For a similar view, see Bell, *Modern Law of Personal Property* (n 4 above) 12–13.

enjoy beneficial proprietary rights in the assets transferred into custody, the relationship established between investor and custodian will need to amount to a bailment, whereby the investor is not deprived of legal title to the assets bailed, or a trust, whereby the investor enjoys beneficial title to the trust assets. The question is whether the structure of custodial operations permits recognition of these.

(1) Non-Intermediary Custody

Figure 2.1: Non-intermediary custody

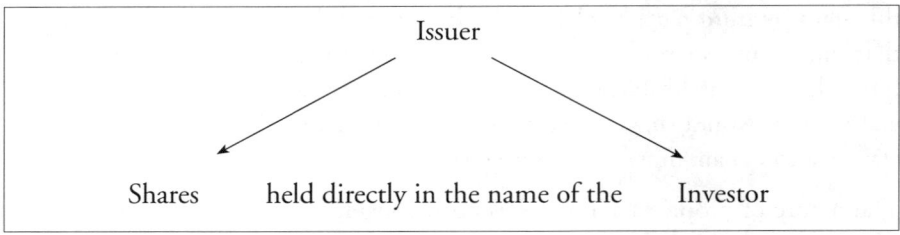

2.20   With non-intermediary custody, the link between the issuer of the relevant securities and the investor is maintained. Investors enjoy continuing legal ownership of the securities represented by the certificate or other token of the securities transferred into custody. Custody here takes the form of depositing with a custodian the share certificate or certificate of negotiable securities indorsed to the investor.

2.21   This type of arrangement is of little import for the question of the investor's ownership of the securities. The investor is recognised by the issuer, as well as the custodian,[17] as the owner of the securities. The certificate attesting to the investor's ownership is issued in the investor's name, and the investor remains entitled to, and continues to enjoy the features of ownership of, the securities. The certificate of negotiable securities will have been indorsed in favour of the investor or to his order. In order for the custodian to be able to act in relation to those securities for the investor, the investor may execute a power of attorney in favour of the custodian.

Bailment

2.22   With non-intermediary custody, the form of relationship which may be established to enable an investor to preserve proprietary rights is one of bailment. Fundamental to any bailment are various elements. There must be a transfer of possession to the bailee of a tangible thing belonging to someone other than the bailee on condition of the bailee's undertaking to do something with the thing, such as to return it to the bailor or deliver it according to the order of the bailor.[18]

---

[17] A clause to this effect may be included in a custodial agreement.
[18] *The Queen v McDonald* (1885) 15 QBD 323; *Sutcliffe v Chief Constable of West Yorkshire* [1996] RTR 86, 90 per Otton LJ. See also F Pollock and RS Wright, *An Essay on Possession in the Common Law* (1888) 163.

Further, for the receipt of possession to lead to the establishment of bailment, such receipt needs to have been voluntary.[19] As such, bailment is simply the voluntary assumption of possession of a tangible thing,[20] it does not arise by the actions or wishes of the bailor but by the actions and intentions of the bailee.

The issue of bailment relates only to the safe-keeping of the token evidencing the investor's interests in relation to the securities. Since the securities represented by the token transferred into custody remain the property of the investor, so do the tokens. Therefore when the tangible tokens are transferred into custody, as typically obtains in non-intermediary custody, this would appear to conform to one of the basic requirements of bailment. Given that the typical custodial agreement will have expressed that the taking of possession by the custodian is voluntary, such possession will have occurred with the requisite intent, ie voluntariness, necessary to conform to the establishment of a bailment. The requisite intent need not be express; all that is required is that the custodian actually takes possession voluntarily. Thus, even in the absence of a custodial agreement expressing in terms the intent of the parties to form a bailment, or even that the custodian takes possession of the assets voluntarily, if the possession was taken voluntarily a bailment could nonetheless arise. **2.23**

Assuming that the establishment of a bailment is accepted, the distinction between the certificate and the underlying security must be underlined. The bailment under discussion is established only with respect to the certificate.[21] Nevertheless, since the underlying rights continue to belong to the investor, the omission of these rights from the bailment relationship does not adversely affect the investor. **2.24**

(2) Intermediary Custody

The combination of the trends toward dematerialisation and immobilisation of securities, as well as the desire of investors to reap the efficiencies to be gained by the use of custodians, has increasingly led to a break in the link between investors and issuers. Custodians become legally entitled to the custody assets on the undertaking to hold the benefit of such for the investors who transferred the assets into custody. This may arise where registrable securities are registered in the name of the custodian or bearer securities are held by a custodian. Notwithstanding the fact that the benefits to be transmitted may be intangible rights, such as rights to a dividend, etc, it is proper to use the term 'custody' to describe the activity of holding these intangible assets for investors.[22] **2.25**

---

[19] *The Pioneer Container* [1994] 2 AC 324, 339–340.

[20] ibid 342.

[21] 'There can be no bailment of the rights of action represented by such documents': NE Palmer, *Bailment* (2nd edn, 1991) 8.

[22] Support for this view may be derived from cases where it is stated that there may be custody, as distinguished from acquisition, of information, *North & South Trust Co v Berkely* [1971] 1 All ER

Figure 2.2: Intermediary custody

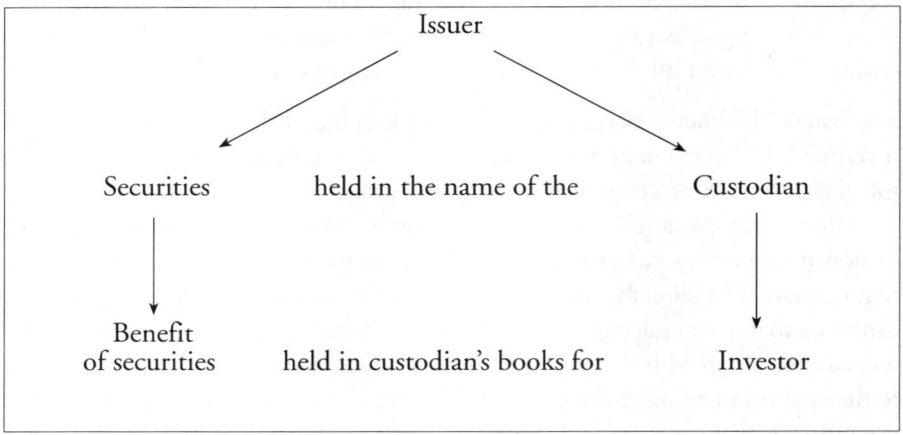

2.26 Which form of legal relationship would permit a beneficiary of custody assets proprietary rights in relation to the assets where the investor has exchanged full legal entitlement for beneficial entitlement in this way? Putting aside the issue of intent, which in these circumstances should not pose any real difficulties, the question is whether the assets held by the custodian in intermediary custody may form the basis of bailment. The custodian is invested with, and may thus be notionally described as holding: a legal title to securities, a certificate to evidence entitlement to securities, as well as rights against the issuer for the benefits of the securities which he may be obliged to pass on to the investor. Can any of these form the basis for a bailment?

Bailment?

2.27 Title by its very nature is intangible and cannot be possessed in order to form a bailment, nor can the intangible benefits of securities that the custodian may hold for an investor. Although the argument has been made that it may be possible to establish bailment in the absence of physical possession of a thing,[23] and analogies drawn between custody of an intangible and bailment,[24] the orthodox view

---

980, 993 per Donaldson J; and custody of goodwill, *Hospital Products Ltd v United States Surgical Corporation* (1984) 156 CLR 41, 101 per Mason J, HC of Australia.

[23] *Federal Commissioner of Taxation v United Aircraft Corporation* (1943) 68 CLR 525, 534 per Latham CJ, HC of Australia; *Roufos v Brewster* (1971) 2 SASR 218, 233 in a dissenting judgment per Zelling J, SC of South Australia. See also AW Beaves, 'Global Custody: A Tentative Analysis of Property and Contract' in NE Palmer and E McKendrick (eds), *Interests in Goods* (1993) 267, 274, 275–277.

[24] *Hospital Products Ltd v United States Surgical Corporation* (1984) 156 CLR 41, 101 per Mason J, HC of Australia.

remains that it is necessary for a bailment that there be physical possession of a chattel.[25]

Even if there is a certificate to evidence legal entitlement to the securities, custodi- **2.28** ans cannot be constituted bailees of the certificates because in intermediary custody the certificates are legally owned by the custodian. The fact that the custodian may be obliged to hold the benefit of securities legally owned by him for an investor does not detract from the proposition that it is only the custodian that is recognised as legal owner of the securities.[26] As such, the certificate would be held by the custodian for himself, *qua* legal owner.[27] Such a scenario cannot ordinarily constitute a bailment because the custodian would have to constitute the bailment based on his own things. Although it has been held on one peculiar set of circumstances that a bailor may become (joint-) bailee of his own assets,[28] the general proposition is that a bailor cannot become bailee of his own assets.[29]

The foregoing suggests that the structure of intermediary custody is not compat- **2.29** ible with the establishment of a bailment.[30] The impediments to bailment in this case are that the things which might conceivably form the basis for bailment either belong at law to the custodian, with the result that he cannot become bailee thereof, or the things are intangible, incapable of possession, and therefore equally incapable of forming the basis for a bailment.[31]

Trust

If the relationship between investor and intermediary custodian is incompatible **2.30** with bailment, the fact that there is a division between legal title and the entitlement to enjoy the benefit of the securities suggests that it could be a trust.[32]

---

[25] *Coggs v Bernard* (1703) 2 Ld Raym 909, 912–914 per Holt CJ, 92 ER 107. See also PV Baker and PStJ Langan (eds), *Snell's Equity* (29th edn, 1990) 91; NE Palmer, *Bailment* (2nd edn, 1991) 8, 99.

[26] Companies Act 1985, s 360: 'No notice of any trust, express, implied or constructive, shall be entered on the register, or be receivable by the registrar, in the case of companies registered in England and Wales'. In relation to bearer securities, the obligation of the issuer is to the holder or bearer.

[27] *MCC Proceeds Inc v Lehman Brothers International (Europe)*, *The Times*, 14 January 1998, per Hobhouse LJ.

[28] *Harding v CIR* [1977] 1 NZLR 337, 341–342 per Coates J, SC of NZ.

[29] *Dows v Nat Exch Bank of Milwaukee* 91 US 618, 23 L Ed 214, 219 per Strong J (1875). See also Palmer, *Bailment* (n 25 above) 2, 86.

[30] See J Benjamin, *The Law of Global Custody* (1996), 37–40.

[31] This issue is addressed in J Benjamin, *The Law of Global Custody* (1996), ch 5.

[32] A custodial relationship where legal title of the investment assets is vested in the custodian, whilst the benefit of the assets is for the investor, would appear to fit most modern definitions of a trust.

See *Underhill and Hayton, Law Relating to Trusts and Trustees* (15th edn, 1995) 1. 'A trust is an equitable obligation, binding a person (who is called a trustee) to deal with property over which he has control (which is called the trust property), for the benefit of persons (who are called the beneficiaries or cestuis que trust), of whom he may himself be one, and any one of whom may enforce the obligation.' This definition, as expressed in earlier editions of the work, was approved in *Re*

Indeed, some form of ownership by the custodian is a condition *sine qua non* for the recognition of a trust in relation to the assets in his custody. The establishment of a trust does not need a precise formulation of words; the necessary intent for the establishment of a trust may be inferred from any words that carry such intent, as well as the context of the relevant parties.[33] It is therefore likely that the typical intermediary custody scenario would suffice to form the basis for a trust. The necessary intent should be evident from the custodial agreement by which the assets were taken into custody or the general words and actions of the parties at the time, assuming that the words and actions led to the conclusion that the transfer of assets into custody was not a gift or loan to the custodian, but that the assets were to be held by the custodian for the benefit of others.

2.31   If the concept of intermediary custody seems to accord in general with the establishment of a trust, one question remains outstanding. The trust is a transitive concept and the question arises whether certain operational methods of custodians allow for sufficient identification of the relevant assets to permit the recognition of a trust. Since this question is likely to prove to be the most fundamental obstacle to the recognition of proprietary interests by investors, this question is dealt with separately in Chapter 3 on the identification of custody assets.

2.32   If a trust may be recognised in these circumstances, does it achieve the intention of the parties? It would seem so. Although the beneficiary of a trust does not enjoy legal title to trust assets, he enjoys equitable rights directly in relation to the assets. There used to be doubts as to whether the beneficiary of a trust enjoyed proprietary rights directly in relation to trust assets,[34] personal rights against the trustee[35] or an amalgamation of the two.[36] The argument may be made that because the beneficiary is recognised to enjoy more than personal rights against the trustee, the beneficiary must enjoy a direct interest in relation to the asset. Thus, the recog-

---

Marshall's Will Trusts [1945] Ch 217, 219 per Cohen J and in *Green v Russell* [1959] 2 QB 226, 241 per Romer LJ.

　　See also *Lewin on Trusts* (16th edn, 1964) 1; *Keeton and Sheridan's The Law of Trusts* (12th edn, 1993) 3; and Recognition of Trusts Act 1987, Schedule, para 2, which incorporates into English law the Hague Convention on the Law Applicable to Trusts and on Their Recognition.

　　[33] *Re Endacott* [1960] Ch 232, 241 per Lord Evershed MR; *Paul v Constance* [1977] 1 WLR 527, 530, 532 per Scarman LJ.

　　[34] See WG Hart, 'What is a Trust?' (1899) 15 LQR 294, 301; AW Scott, 'The Nature of the Rights of the Cestui Que Trust' (1917) 17 Columbia Law Review 269; Hohfeld, *Fundamental Legal Conceptions* (n 5 above) 96–114; PH Winfield, *The Province of the Law of Tort* (1931) 112; EJ Mockler, in an untitled note (1962) 40 Canadian Bar Review 265, 272; *Snell's Equity* (n 25 above) 23; and DJ Hayton, *Underhill and Hayton, The Law Relating to Trusts and Trustees* (15th edn, 1995) 40.

　　[35] See HF Stone, 'The Nature of the Rights of the Cestui Que Trust' (1917) 17 Columbia Law Review 467; and FW Maitland, *Equity: A Course of Lectures* (AH Chaytor and WJ Whittaker (eds), revised by J Brunyate 1936) 117.

　　[36] See HG Hanbury, 'The Field of Modern Equity' (1929) 45 LQR 196, 199; *Snell's Equity* (n 25 above) 24; and *Parker and Mellows, The Modern Law of Trusts* (6th edn, by AJ Oakley, 1994) 12.

nition of a trust where there is custody by intermediation allows investors to retain a direct proprietary link to the assets in custody.

D. Direct Proprietary Link?

The above suggests that most investors in single-tier custody would enjoy some **2.33** sort of direct proprietary link with the assets in custody.

With non-intermediary custody, the direct link is the same as with any direct secu- **2.34** rities holding, with the exception that the tangible token is in the custody of a party other than the owner.

Where the link is via intermediary custody, the link differs radically from the typ- **2.35** ical direct ownership of securities. It is unlikely that the issuer would be aware of the investor's interest and, even if it was, the issuer is not likely to recognise the subsidiary interest.[37] Enjoyment of the benefits of the right is indirect, via the custodian through whom the investor claims. Instead of rights against the issuer of the underlying securities, the investor will enjoy a number of rights against the custodian in order to ensure that he, the investor, takes the economic benefit of the relevant securities holding. This does not deny the existence of the direct equitable right enjoyed by the investor. However, this direct right is largely only of utility upon the insolvency of the custodian, so that the securities can be claimed by the investors before they are appropriated by the custodian's creditors. These rights would also be of utility in the event of a misapplication of custody assets in circumstances where the custodian could not otherwise make good the loss and the misapplied assets remain identifiable. Other than that, they do not serve him in any meaningful way for the enjoyment of the benefit of the securities. For the enjoyment of the benefit of the securities, the investor will have to claim through his custodian and take from him.

Thus, whilst investors in non-intermediary custody retain the same direct owner- **2.36** ship rights as any owner of securities would enjoy, an investor with assets in intermediary custody would effectively have exchanged his rights in the relevant securities against the issuer for a new set of rights against the custodian through whom he claims. Beyond the rights against the custodian, however, the investor would also be recognised as enjoying direct equitable rights with respect to the securities so that the securities are not appropriated by the custodian's creditors in the event of his insolvency.

---

[37] Companies Act 1985, s 360.

E. Delegated Power of Disposition

2.37 Although we have indicated that investors may retain a proprietary interest in the securities kept in custody, in an active custodial arrangement the investor may at the outset have conferred a power on the custodian to alienate the entirety of the interests linked to the security, including the investor's beneficial interest. The delegation of this power would appear to be inconsistent with the earlier asserted importance to the investor of his retention of a proprietary interest in the custody assets.

2.38 The efficiencies which active investors seek in using custodians can only be achieved if the custodian is free to deal with the securities, including to alienate the entirety of the ownership interests of the security to buyers, borrowers, for sale and repurchase (repo) transactions and the like. If custodians need to take the time and undertake the costs of contacting the investor for express mandate each time it is needed to take action in relation to custody assets, there would be much delay in capital market activity, as well as increased costs to the investors. Such impediments would defeat one of the principal *raisons d'être* of using custodians, that of carrying out transactions on behalf of the investor in a timely and cost-effective manner. The provision of a delegated power of disposition neatly marries the twin needs of the investor retaining proprietary interests in relation to custody assets and leaving custodians with a free hand to deal with the custody assets.

2.39 Whether delegation of a power of disposition constitutes a disposition of the equitable interest in the custody assets by the investor may be important because of section 53(1)(c) of the Law of Property Act 1925,[38] which requires the disposition of equitable interests to be effected in writing. *Grey v Inland Revenue Commissioners*[39] indicates that disposal is to be construed from the perspective of the purported disposer and that a disposal of an equitable interest will only have been effected when the disposer loses an equitable interest that he previously enjoyed. The mere delegation of the power to dispose of the equitable interest does not of itself dispose of the equitable interest. The delegation is in the nature of a power of appointment. The interest that is the subject of the power remains where it was, ie with the investor, until further action is taken. This would suggest that the delegation of a power of disposition does not fall within section 53(1)(c) of the Law of Property Act 1925.

2.40 Furthermore, *Vandervell v Inland Revenue Commissioners*[40] indicates that section 53(1)(c) is directed to dealings with equitable interests divorced from the legal

---

[38] This provision is more fully discussed in Chapter 4, in the section on formalities for dealing with equitable interests.
[39] At the Court of Appeal, [1958] 1 Ch 690, 723 per Ormerod LJ, and at the House of Lords, [1960] AC 1.
[40] [1967] 2 AC 291.

title. Hence, the provision is of no application where the holder of the equitable interest also controls the legal interest and intends that both be transferred to a third party beneficially. Thus, where an investor instructs his custodian to transfer assets in which he enjoys an equitable interest to a third party, there will be no need for the disposal to be in writing where the third party takes the entirety of the interests related to the assets or takes the assets via his own separate intermediary custodian. However, where the transferee is using the same custodian as the investor, and it is only the equitable interest that is affected by the transfer, it is submitted that such a disposition may be caught by section 53(1)(c). In this scenario the legal interest remains in the custodian, it is only the equitable interest which is transferred.

In view of the speed, volume and back-to-back nature of transactions, the upset of **2.41** just one transaction could cause great loss in terms of the cost and time of having to unravel the many subsequent and consequent transactions. It is therefore essential to the smooth workings of capital markets that this power be exercised without dispute. If investors can effectively challenge the right of custodians to dispose of the interests in relation to custody assets, this would bring about unwelcome uncertainty in the finality of transactions from the risk that investors may seek to overturn transactions entered into by custodians. In view of this, it may be wise for custodians to benefit from a power expressly conferred on them in the agreement for custodial services, possibly with a provision expressly excluding the investor from interfering in such transactions.[41] The exclusion of investors in this way is not without precedent. In the case of shares, for instance, section 360 of the Companies Act 1985 has this effect by not permitting the legal recognition of subsidiary interests in the legal title of a shareholder. A shareholder who delegates his legal title to another is excluded from direct contact with the issuer of the shares. There is also authority for the view that one who delegates his interest in certain situations may be excluded from dealings by the delegate in relation to that interest. This is seen in relation to undisclosed principals[42] and disclosed but unnamed principals.[43] The exclusion may be rationalised on the basis that the investor takes a calculated business risk in entrusting his assets to the custodian so that the investor may be able to benefit from the efficiency gains to be derived thereby.

The idea that a custodian exercising a delegated power of disposition may alienate **2.42** the investor's interest would seem to run counter to the general rule of *nemo dat quod non habet*. By this rule, it is generally not possible under English law for one

---

[41] Of course, a necessary corollary of this delegation of power is a duty on the custodian to exercise the power only in execution of instructions issued by a person with a right to demand assets out of the pool. It is this duty that should ensure there will always be sufficient assets to meet the entitlements of all contributors.

[42] *Siu Yin Kwan v Eastern Insurance Co Ltd* [1994] 2 AC 199, 207.

[43] *Tudor Marine Ltd v Tradax Export SA, The Virgo* [1976] 2 Lloyd's Rep 135; *N & J Vlassopulos Ltd v Ney Shipping Ltd, The Santa Carina* [1977] 1 Lloyd's Rep 478.

to alienate something that does not belong to him. However, there are exceptions to the rule. One obvious example of this is the ability of one who does not enjoy an interest to confer such interest on a bona fide purchaser for value without notice.[44] Another example that used to exist is that of sales in market overt.[45] Although this latter exception has now been abolished, the fears that led to its abolition may not be applicable to the trade of securities.[46]

---

[44] *Burgis v Constantine* [1908] 2 KB 484, 501 per Farwell LJ.

[45] Goode, *Commercial Law* (2nd edn, 1995) 461; and B Davenport and R Ross, 'Market Overt' in NE Palmer and E McKendrick (eds), *Interests in Goods* (1993) 469, in which this exception to the rule *nemo dat quod non habet* was criticised. The market overt exception to the *nemo dat* rule was abolished by the Sale of Goods (Amendment Act) 1994, s 1.

[46] Law Reform Committee Twelfth Report, *Transfer of Title to Chattels* (Cmnd 2958, 1966) 13–14, and the reservation by Lord Donovan to the recommendations of the Committee, 18–19; Davenport and Ross (n 45 above) 471, 474; and D Miller, 'Transfer of Title: A New Legal Regime in only Three Paragraphs' [1994] LMCLQ 322, 325.

The principal fear that led to the abolition of market overt was that it facilitated the sale of stolen goods, thus leaving the lawful owner to proceed against, in all likelihood, an impecunious thief. It was felt that even if recovery of value against the thief/seller was successful, this would be scant compensation for the loss of a treasured heirloom of sentimental, as well as material, value. These fears are not significant to the custody of securities. Custodians are often banks with deep pockets, so there should be something to recover, and investments generally do not have any other value than that which is measurable in financial terms.

3

IDENTIFICATION OF CUSTODY ASSETS

The analysis in Chapter 2 suggests that the practice of custody is often generally **3.01** compatible with the establishment of a bailment or trust. In this way, investors may retain a direct legal or equitable interest in relation to custody assets so that in the event of the insolvency of the custodian the assets would not be available to his general creditors and could be retrieved by investors as their own. However, the transitive nature of such legal structures requires that they relate to something. This chapter seeks to determine whether the types of investments under consideration and modern custodial practices permit sufficient identification to accommodate a bailment or trust.[1]

In the discussion of proprietary rights in Chapter 2, it was suggested that propri- **3.02** etary rights may only exist in relation to determinate or identifiable assets. However, there are varying degrees of identification. In the present context, there are at least three possible approaches: specific identification of assets; identification by reference to a particular pool of identical units without the need for specificity; or identification by generic description of assets which may come from any source. The position taken in this work is that although specific identification will always suffice, this requirement may impose an unduly costly or onerous administrative obligation on the custodian. Generic description, on the other hand, is insufficient because the proprietary rights relate to units that may not exist or cannot be reached by the person claiming the right, so rendering the purported identification and rights meaningless. It is suggested that identification by reference to a particular pool of unallocated identical units should be adequate because the rights relate to assets that are known to exist and can be claimed. Since the pooled units are identical, it should not matter to the person asserting the right to which

---

[1] This issue is addressed in J Benjamin, *The Law of Global Custody* (1996), ch 5.

units of the pool his rights attach.[2] If the particular assets claimed become important, such as in the event of misapplication or a shortfall in the pool, the records of the custodian or common law rules on mixtures can resolve this.

A. Identification of Securities

3.03 The first issue is whether securities are capable of discrete identification. It may be recalled that securities may be negotiable; registrable certificated securities; or registrable intangible securities. With all of these types of securities the units of any issue may or may not be numbered according to the wishes of the issuer.

3.04 Regardless of the form in which they are established, securities are essentially choses in action and may be equated with rights under a contract constituted by the terms of issue. In the case of equity securities the interest of a shareholder 'is the interest of a person in the Company, that interest being composed of rights and obligations which are defined by the Companies Act and by the memorandum and articles of association of the company'.[3] With debt securities the investor may be entitled under a trust deed, or other document of issue, to the payment of interest, repayment of a lump sum and other rights to enforce repayment from the issuer of the debt securities. However, securities constitute more than a series of personal rights. The bundles of interests that constitute securities are themselves the object of proprietary rights,[4] constituting intangible assets.

3.05 The rights of any person subscribing to units of an issue against an issuer are indistinguishable from those of any other person enjoying rights against the issuer under the same issue.[5] There is authority for this view, both domestic[6] and foreign.[7] This is also a premise of company law legislation.[8]

3.06 Where securities are issued with a certificate of evidence as to legal entitlement, the argument may be made that securities represented by one certificate are different from those represented by another certificate, notwithstanding that they belong to the same issue. The argument is unsound. A certificate of entitlement to

---

[2] It is a separate question whether the terms on which the custodial service was agreed permit the holding of custody assets in this way.

[3] *Commissioners of Inland Revenue v Crossman* [1937] AC 26, 66 per Lord Russell of Killowen; see also *Borland's Trustee v Steel Brothers & Co* [1901] 1 Ch 279, 288 per Farwell J.

[4] *Commissioners of Inland Revenue v Crossman* [1937] AC 26, 66 per Lord Russell of Killowen.

[5] This is certainly true at the moment of issue. However, securities may yet be distinguishable on the basis of whether the owner has complied with terms which form a condition of ownership, such as whether shares in a company are paid up or not.

[5] *Ind's case, Re the International Contract Company* (1872) LR 7 Ch App 485, 487 per Mellish LJ: 'one share, an incorporeal right to a certain portion of the profits of the company, is the same as another'.

[7] *Skiff v Stoddard* 26 A 874, 880 per Prentice J (SC of Errors of Connecticut, 1893).

[3] Companies Act 1985, s 182(2).

securities does not constitute the securities themselves; the securities are made up of the bundle of intangible rights against the issuer.[9] For registrable securities, a certificate is merely prima facie evidence of entitlement to a certain number of securities with no impact on entitlement itself.[10] Even in relation to bearer securities, where possession of the document of title entitles the bearer to securities represented thereby, a conceptual distinction may be drawn between the certificate and the underlying securities. A certificate of entitlement to bearer securities no more constitutes the securities it represents than do the register and any certificate of entitlement for registrable securities. Therefore, the existence or otherwise of certificates of evidence of entitlement to securities does not render one unit out of an issue inherently distinguishable from any other unit of the same issue.

Where units of an issue of securities are numbered, the argument may be made **3.07** that by virtue of numbering, each unit is inherently distinguishable from another in one issue. Swinfen Eady J in *Platt v Rowe*[11] has expressed such a view. This is doubtful. The rights represented by unit number one are in no way distinguishable from those represented by unit number two, and so on. So, even though units of an issue of securities may be numbered, this does not of itself affect the inherent indistinguishability of the units.[12]

Although intrinsically indistinguishable, it is thought desirable to be able to iden- **3.08** tify securities so that title thereto may be traceable.[13] There is authority for the view that securities are capable of discrete identification.[14] This view has been expressed notwithstanding recognition of the indistinguishable nature of securities.[15]

Indistinguishability of units does not ineluctably mean that they may not be **3.09** separately identified. For instance, with identical tangible objects they may be identified by their physical location. However, securities are choses in action which do not possess a physical presence that would allow this. Nevertheless, the existence of certificates of evidence to title or numbering is useful in appropriating inherently indistinguishable securities to particular investors or transactions.

Securities may be identified by reference to the particular certificate that repre- **3.10** sents them. For instance, 10 certificates may be taken to identify 10 securities each out of an issue of 100. If a party who owned four such certificates, ie 40 securities, sought to transfer 20 securities, he would need to transfer two of his certificates.

---

[9] *Skiff v Stoddard* 26 A 874, 880 per Prentice J (SC of Errors of Connecticut, 1893).
[10] Companies Act 1985, s 186.
[11] (1909) 26 TLR 49, 51 per Swinfen Eady J.
[12] See J Benjamin, *The Law of Global Custody* (1996), 32.
[13] On this point *Ind's case, Re the International Contract Company* (1872) LR 7 Ch App 485, 487 per Mellish LJ and *Platt v Rowe* (1909) 26 TLR 49, 51 per Swinfen Eady J are in accord.
[14] *Platt v Rowe* (1909) 26 TLR 49, 51 per Swinfen Eady J.
[15] *Brady v Stapleton* (1952) 88 CLR 322, 345 per McTiernan J, HC of Australia.

The particular 20 securities transferred could then be identified, if only for administrative purposes, by reference to the two certificates transferred.

3.11 Similarly, if each unit of an issue is allocated a number, whether on the register of the issuer or the certificates that represent them, action taken in relation to any securities may be by reference to particular numbers. Therefore, the man with 40 bearer securities represented by four certificates numbered 1 to 10, 11 to 20 and so on would be able to identify which of the 40 securities he wished to alienate by reference to their number. He could determine that it is the securities numbered 21 to 30 and 31 to 40 that he wished to alienate. If the 40 securities were registrable, the transferor was the registered owner of securities 31 to 70, and he sought to alienate 20 of them, he could identify which 20 by number. Thus, he could determine to alienate securities numbered 41 to 60.

B. Non-Intermediary Custody

3.12 By definition, where there is non-intermediary custody the investor remains the legal title-holder of the relevant securities. Title to the securities is in his name, any certificate of entitlement belongs to him and the underlying securities are his.

3.13 As discussed in Chapter 2, the only likely relevance of custodians in these circumstances is in relation to the physical custody of a certificate. Since the certificate remains in the name of the investor, this readily satisfies the need for identification for a bailment relationship.

C. Intermediary Custody

3.14 There are at least three forms of intermediary custody, including: where a custodian physically holds certificates of bearer securities for the investor; where registrable securities with a tangible token are registered in the name of the custodian for the benefit of the investor; and where dematerialised securities are registered in the name of the custodian. As observed in Chapter 2, since there is no question of a bailment arising, because the custodian cannot be bailee of things which technically belong to him and/or which cannot be taken into physical possession, the issue that arises is whether there may be sufficient certainty of subject-matter for the establishment of a trust.

(1) Non-Fungible Holdings

3.15 A custodian may hold client assets in segregated holdings, ie in a manner that identifies assets as belonging to particular investors. In the case of negotiable certificates, this may be done by holding them in a segregated pile for a particular person. In the case of registrable securities, this may be effected in at least two ways. Where the securities are numbered, particular numbers may be allocated to particular clients. In the absence of numbering, segregation may be achieved by adding a suffix to the name of the custodian in the title to the securities representing the name, initials or code by which the relevant investor may be identified. This is expressly provided for by CREST with the facility for a member to operate several accounts with different designations under his one general membership.[16]

By these methods of segregation, there would be sufficient identification of the **3.16** assets in relation to which a trust may arise in favour of the investor.

(2) Fungible Holdings

In order to reduce costs and increase the efficiency of administering custody assets, **3.17** investments may be held by custodians in fungible holdings. Fungibility is the quality accorded to assets that are accepted to be freely interchangeable upon the substitution of an equivalent weight, number or measure of assets from the class.[17]

In view of the indistinguishability of units of securities from a single issue, these **3.18** investment assets readily lend themselves to fungible holding. Unnumbered securities, whether represented by negotiable certificates or registrable, automatically conform to fungibility. Even if numbered, especially in view of the intrinsic indistinguishability of the securities, an investor can surrender the right/ability to identify his securities by number. In this way, even numbered securities may be made the subject of fungible holdings.

As the essence of fungibility is that there should not be specific identification of **3.19** the fungible units, this quality poses difficulties for the identification of assets necessary for the establishment of a trust. Nevertheless, it is accepted in principle that it is possible for one to constitute himself trustee over fungible assets in his care.[18] In accepting this, however, a distinction must be drawn between absolute fungibility and limited fungibility, for example as practised in custody business.

Absolute fungibility in the context of custody would mean that a custodian's **3.20** obligations to an investor in relation to securities deposited are intended to be capable of being satisfied by the custodian's delivery of any other similar unit, regardless of its allocation or provenance. In such a scenario, a custodian holding 10 ABC shares for an investor would not be obliged to effect re-delivery upon termination of the custodial period from his holdings; he would be within his rights to seek out 10 ABC shares in the marketplace and have those transferred to the

---

[16] CREST, *CREST Reference Manual* (May 1996) 22.
[17] *Res quae pondere, numero, et mensura constant.* See Gaius, *Institutes* 3.90; Justinian, *Institutes* 3.14. The term 'fungible' is said to have been first used by the German jurist Zase in the sixteenth century, see *Roman Law: Lord Mackenzie* (7th edn, J Kirkpatrick (ed), 1898) 276, n 1.
[18] *Re Goldcorp Exchange Ltd* [1995] 1 AC 74, 91.

investor instead. The investor's claim in such a scenario would not relate to any assets identifiable other than by generic description. However, the result of this type of holding is to constitute the custodian-investor relationship a debtor-creditor relationship, denying the investor a proprietary interest in the assets held by the custodian.[19] It may be this sort of analysis that led to early suggestions that the deposit of securities into fungible custody constituted a loan.[20]

3.21 The characterisation of the transfer of securities into fungible holdings as a loan is incompatible with the intention of investors to retain proprietary interests in custody assets. Because fungible holdings as practised in the custodial industry are not necessarily absolutely fungible, it may be possible to escape this characterisation. The quality of fungibility in custodial holdings may be limited, restricted to similar units that are actually held by the custodian, so that the interest claimed by investors refers to assets from a precise source, and not an open-ended generic description. With limited fungibility, the custodian satisfies his obligation to the investor by reference to assets held by him (the custodian) even if such assets had not previously been specifically allocated to the particular investor.

Pooled Holdings

3.22 The question that arises is whether it is possible for a custodian to properly constitute himself trustee over pooled holdings, so that claimants of the benefits of the assets in the pool may be recognised as beneficiaries under a trust or several trusts, retaining equitable proprietary interests in the pooled assets which would afford them a degree of protection in case of the custodian's insolvency. The view may be taken that there is no reason in principle why this should not be possible, because the 'difficulty which arises in such a case is a difficulty of fact and not of law'.[21]

3.23 There is abundant authority in support of the proposition that the mere fact of mixture does not deny participants in the mixture proprietary interests in the units that constitute the pool. This proposition stands whether the mixing is consensual[22] or non-consensual, both accidental[23] and wrongful.[24] Therefore, the

---

[19] *Re London Wine Co Ltd* (1975) [1986] PCC 121, 137 per Oliver J; *Re Goldcorp Exchange Ltd* [1995] 1 AC 74, 90–91, 99–100.

[20] RM Goode, 'Ownership and Obligations' (1987) 103 LQR 433, 452; R Ryan, 'Taking Security over Investment Portfolios held in Global Custody' [1990] 10 JIBL 404.

One may be influenced by the reference to fungible assets in Roman law in relation to loans: Gaius, *Institutes* 3.90; Justinian, *Institutes* 3.14. However, this was merely by way of example of the type of asset that readily conforms to the typical requirements of a loan. It is a non sequitur to suggest that simply because fungibles are often the subject of loans, transactions in relation to fungibles are therefore loans.

[21] *Taylor v Plummer* (1815) 3 M & S 562, 575 per Lord Ellenborough, 105 ER 721.

[22] *South Australian Insurance Company v Randell* (1869) 3 LRPC 104, 113; *Coleman v Harvey* [1989] 1 NZLR 723, 727 per Cooke P, CA of NZ.

[23] *Spence v Union Marine Insurance Co* (1868) 3 LRCP 427, 437 per Bovill CJ.

[24] *Indian Oil Corpn v Greenstone Shipping SA* [1988] QBD 345, 370–371 per Staughton J.

mere fact of pooling is not necessarily inimical to the enjoyment of proprietary interests therein by investors who had contributed thereto.

However, a number of difficulties persist. Chief amongst these, given the fact of **3.24** fungible holdings whereby units are not allocated to particular claimants, is the evidential difficulty of demonstrating that the investor contributed to the pool. Logically, and at law,[25] it cannot be proper for a claimant to enjoy any kind of interest in a pool unless he can prove, or it is admitted by other claimants to the pool, that he has contributed thereto. Even if some contribution is established, the extent of the contribution must also be ascertained. Beyond that, the precise nature of interest that contributors to pooled assets enjoy is unclear.

(a) Initial Contribution to Pool

Where an investor enjoys an interest in units that are proved to be added to a pool, **3.25** the mere fact of their transfer into the pool is proof of contribution to the pool.[26] This is the case when an investor first transfers assets into custody.

Where there is a pool of assets and it is possible, but there is no proof, that one has **3.26** contributed thereto, a number of possibilities arise. The consideration of this scenario is relevant if the custodian's records were for some reason irretrievably destroyed and the pool was insufficient to satisfy all those who can be demonstrated to have transferred assets of a particular type to the custodian and it is uncertain how the assets of all such claimants have been applied. The difficulty that arises for investors is in proving participation in the remaining pool; proof of participation in the original pool is not conclusive because the assets of the investor may have been applied out of the pool.

The various claimants who may have contributed to the pool could, in the **3.27** absence of proof, agree as to whose units constitute the remaining pool.[27]

It may be the case that there is no proof and the claimants cannot agree as to whose **3.28** units make up the remaining pool. In *Sandeman & Sons v Tyzack and Branfoot Steamship Company, Limited,*[28] Lord Moulton stated that 'there cannot possibly be a presumption of law' of contribution to the remaining pool.[29] The implication of this is that any claimant who cannot prove contribution, where other claimants do not agree, is excluded from participating in the pool. This view may be criticised because it is capable of working great iniquity. Any resolution of this type of dispute will, in effect, involve some kind of presumption, that the disputed units

---

[25] *Sandeman & Sons v Tyzack and Branfoot Steamship Company Limited* [1913] AC 680, 696 per Lord Moulton.

[26] *Buckley v Gross* (1863) 3 B & S 566, 574–575 per Blackburn J, 122 ER 213.

[27] *Jones v Moore* (1841) 4 Y & C Ex 351, 160 ER 1041.

[28] [1913] AC 680, 696 per Lord Moulton.

[29] For the view that presumptions should not be permitted, see P Birks, 'Mixtures' in NE Palmer and E McKendrick (eds), *Interests in Goods* (1993) 466.

form part of the pool or that they do not.[30] An automatic presumption of exclusion is harsh.

3.29 Decisions such as these are made 'not upon the notion, that strict justice was done, but upon this; that it was the only justice, that could be done'.[31] Therefore, rather than adopting a position whereby a court in effect presumes that the disputed units do or do not contribute to the pool, an all or nothing approach, it may be better for a court to presume that the units of all possible contributors to the pool contributed to the remainder in proportion to the amount of units transferred to the custodian in the first place. Where claimants may have been affected by a common loss, and it is not known who precisely suffered the loss, it is fairer for all claimants to share in the results of the misfortune, rather than heaping the effects of the misfortune onto a few. *Spence v Union Marine Insurance Co*[32] suggests that on appropriate facts contribution may be inferred. In the absence of evidence or agreement between the parties, the court adopted the principle of proportion, by which it was determined that contribution to the remaining pool occurred in proportion to the amount of units that the various parties had started out with in the original pool.

(b) Acquisition of Interest in Pool

3.30 The more difficult case is where the claimant did not enjoy a prior interest, but claims to have acquired an interest in a pool of fungible units, none of which has been specifically allocated to him. This may arise, for instance, where an investor seeks to acquire an interest in relation to assets pooled in the name of a depository. The general rule is that one cannot acquire a proprietary interest in a definite number of pooled units in the absence of specific allocation or appropriation of the relevant units to which such interest attaches.[33] By this principle, a person who claims to have acquired an interest in a fungible pool will not be able to satisfy the need for proof that he enjoys a proprietary interest in the pool so that a trust is established in his favour unless there is specific allocation of units in his favour.

3.31 The general rule is demonstrated by the divergent results of two similar scenarios that differ in one respect. In *Aldridge v Johnson*[34] P agreed to buy 100 units of barley ex-bulk. Some of the units were removed from the bulk to be sent to P but were eventually put back in the bulk. It was held that property in the units that had been removed from the bulk had passed to P, notwithstanding the fact that the

---

[30] *Spence v Union Marine Insurance Co* (1868) 3 LRCP 427, 439 per Bovill CJ.

[31] *Lupton v White* (1808) 15 Ves Jun 432, 441 per Eldon LC, 33 ER 817.

[32] (1868) 3 LRCP 427, 439 per Bovill CJ.

[33] *Re London Wine Company (Shippers) Limited* (1975) [1986] PCC 121, 137 per Oliver J; *Re Goldcorp Exchange Ltd* [1995] 1 AC 74, 90.

[34] (1857) 7 El & Bl 885, 119 ER 1476, KB.

units had been returned to the bulk. This contrasts with *Re Wait*[35] where W bought 1,000 tons of wheat to be imported from the USA and resold 500 thereof to H who paid the purchase price. However, W was declared bankrupt before the wheat arrived and before any physical appropriation had been made to H. It was held that property in relation to the wheat had not passed to H, therefore he had to prove in the bankruptcy of W for the recovery of the purchase price paid like any ordinary creditor.

The difference between the two cases is that in the former, assets were for a period **3.32** allocated to the contract. However, at the time the claims were made the plaintiffs were not in materially different positions. The brief allocation in the former case had by the time of claim become irrelevant. Neither of them would have been in a position to point to the specific assets in the bulk in relation to which his contract related. They might as well both have been claiming purely ex-bulk. To insist on specific identification in the circumstances is capable of working great iniquity to claimants. The rights of a claimant to assets ex-bulk would on this analysis appear to be based not on their own actions, but on the possibly arbitrary actions of the bulk-holder, of which they may have no knowledge and over which they may have no control.

It must be noted, however, that the view that specific allocation is required for **3.33** acquisition of a proprietary interest in a pool has most often been expressed in relation to the sale of goods ex-bulk where specific allocation was a statutory requirement. It is not clear that this requirement is essential in other contexts where proprietary interests in a pool are to be acquired. This doubt is supported by a number of cases that permit the acquisition of proprietary rights in a pool by way of tenancy in common or without any need for allocation of assets.

It is recognised that instead of specific allocation a proprietary interest may be **3.34** acquired in relation to constituent units of a pool if the interest is expressed to be a proportion of the pool, with the relevant contributors taking as tenants in common.[36] Although a claim to a specific number of units in a pool will not readily be translated into a proportion of the pool in order for the claimant to be able to enjoy an interest via a tenancy in common,[37] where it is clear that this is intended the claimant's proprietary interest will be recognised by these means.[38] In this way, the claimant will be able to prove his interest in the pool for the establishment of a trust in his favour. In *Re Stapylton Fletcher Ltd*,[39] Judge Paul Baker QC suggested that ascertainment for the passing of property should be determined in the light

---

[35] [1927] 1 Ch 606.
[36] *Re London Wine Company (Shippers) Limited* (1975) [1986] PCC 121, 137 per Oliver J.
[37] ibid.
[38] ibid; *Re Stapylton Fletcher Ltd* [1994] 1 WLR 1181, 1198–1199 per Judge Paul Baker QC.
[39] [1994] 1 WLR 1181.

of the governing circumstances,[40] and that where assets are sold but retained by the vendor or his agent for the purchaser, and the vendor or his agent holds the assets 'not mingled with the trading stock, in store for a group of customers, . . . even though they are not immediately appropriated to each individual customer. Property will pass by common intention . . . They will take as tenants in common'.[41]

3.35 Yet, there will be circumstances in which acquisition of rights to pooled fungibles is not envisaged to take place by a fraction of the pool or by a tenancy in common but by a definitive number of units in the pool. Is it an unavoidable conclusion that such a claimant would not be recognised as enjoying proprietary rights in the pool? Is there any reason why the purchaser in this type of scenario cannot simply succeed by common intention to the same interest as was previously enjoyed by the vendor?

3.36 In *Hunter v Moss*[42] the requirement of specific identification was not required. The court recognised the establishment of a trust over a definite number of unallocated equity securities in a bulk, without reference to a tenancy in common.[43] At first instance, Colin Rimer QC, sitting as a Deputy High Court Judge, drew a distinction between a pool of fungible tangible assets, the constituent units of which may be different in fact, and a pool of fungible intangibles, which by definition must be indistinguishable; and concluded that the certainties requisite for the establishment of a trust over tangibles were not necessarily applicable to a trust over intangibles.[44] He stated that specific identification of fungible assets was 'unnecessary and irrelevant. . . . Any suggested uncertainty as to subject matter appears to me to be theoretical and conceptual rather than real and practical'.[45] On appeal, Dillon LJ, with whom the rest of the court concurred, also drew a distinction between trusts over tangible and intangible assets[46] and made the point that if one could alienate a certain sum of shares out of a larger shareholding by making a bequest, there is no reason in principle why one could not declare a trust over the same.[47]

3.37 These judgments support the proposition that a claimant may acquire an interest in relation to a definite number of unallocated units in a pool,[48] depending on its

---

[40] ibid 1199.

[41] ibid 1200.

[42] [1993] 1 WLR 934 at first instance; and [1994] 1 WLR 452, CA.

[43] At first instance at 946, on appeal at 459.

[44] At 940, distinguishing *Re London Wine Company (Shippers) Limited* (n 35 above). This distinction is described as specious by D Hayton, 'Uncertainty of Subject-Matter of Trusts' (1994) 110 LQR 335, 337.

[45] First instance at 946.

[46] On appeal at 458.

[47] ibid 459.

[48] W Norris, 'Uncertainty and Informality: Hunter v Moss' [1995] Private Client Business 43, 45; B Sharp, 'Insolvent Banks as Custodians' in F Oditah (ed), *Insolvency of Banks: Managing the Risks* (1996) 93, 97.

subject-matter, a view that is welcomed by some practitioners.[49] *Hunter v Moss* has been explicitly followed, albeit seemingly reluctantly, in at least one subsequent case.[50] Nevertheless, *Hunter v Moss* has been the subject of strong criticism.[51] It is suggested that one could not ascertain the precise shares to which the interest attaches and so it is unclear whose assets are affected by action taken in connection with the pooled shares; that because a bequest only requires certainty at the time the administrator grants the assets to the intended beneficiary it is fundamentally distinct from a trust which grants an immediate equitable interest in favour of the beneficiary; that the distinction between tangible and intangible assets is specious; and that it would be wrong to burden a donor-settlor with legal rather than purely moral obligations.

These criticisms may be met by the following three points. First, with fungible **3.38** assets, it should not matter to which out of a given number of pooled assets the interest of the investor attaches.[52] If it does become important, such as because of a sale of a portion of the pool, the trustee can be made to declare for whose account the sale was effected or this will ordinarily be capable of being established from his records. In case of loss, wrongful alienation or other misapplication of the pooled assets, the law of trusts has numerous rules by which evidential difficulties are resolved.[53] Furthermore, in a consensual matter where one party has recognised an unequivocal state of affairs over which he has exclusive control there is no reason why the person so declaring should not be kept to his word,[54] more so where the declarant has received consideration for recognising the state of affairs as such.[55] Finally, the tenancy in common is merely an artificial way of quantifying units in a pool where other means of quantification are impossible or impracticable. Quantification by number, where this is possible, should not impede the

---

[49] See, for example, case notes by Simmons & Simmons, 'Security over unascertained shares: In re Harvard Securities' (1997) 12(8) BJIBFL 399 and (1997) 11(9) *Corporate Briefing* 3–4.

[50] *Re Harvard Securities Ltd* [1997] 2 BCLC 369, 381 per Neuberger J, where he acknowledged the force of criticism that has been levelled against *Hunter v Moss*.

[51] D Hayton, 'Uncertainty of Subject-Matter of Trusts' (1994) 110 LQR 335; M Ockelton, 'Share and Share Alike?' (1994) 53 CLJ 448; *Parker and Mellows, The Modern Law of Trusts* (6th edn, 1994) 96; and A Shipwright, 'Shares, Claret, Grain and Bricks: Certain Uncertainty?' (1994) *The Tax Journal* (19 May, Issue No 260), 9.

[52] RM Goode, 'Ownership and Obligations' (1987) 103 LQR 433, 459–460.

[53] For example, *Parker and Mellows, The Modern Law of Trusts* (n 51 above) ch 23; and *Underhill and Hayton, Law Relating to Trusts and Trustees*, ch 20. Many of the relevant rules are examined in the chapter of this work on the misapplication of custody assets.

[54] As may be established by a deed, estoppel, etc. If such a transaction should be enforced where expressed as a proportion of a whole, there is no reason why it should not be enforced where expressed as a definite number.

[55] *Re Stapylton Fletcher Ltd* [1994] 1 WLR 1181, 1200 per Judge Paul Baker QC: 'where the price has been paid in full, there would appear to be nothing to embarrass the ordinary operations of buying and selling goods'.

acquisition of proprietary rights in pooled assets.[56] Any uncertainty as to whose amongst the pooled assets are affected by the actions of the trustee/custodian would be more as a result of poor administration of the trust assets than as a result of the concept of carving a trust out of a larger existing holding.[57]

(e) Extent of Contribution to Pool

3.39 The second principal evidential problem with claiming an interest in pooled unallocated units is the quantification of one's contribution. Where it is clear exactly how much one's contribution is, or how much the maximum could have been, the evidential difficulty does not arise or its scope is limited.[58] However, there may be circumstances where it is wholly unclear how much of a contribution one has made to a mixture, such as if the records of allocation of the original pool are lost or destroyed and the remaining pool is insufficient to satisfy fully all claimants.

3.40 In such circumstances, where the mixing is consensual Blackstone suggests that English law allows the parties an interest in the resulting pool in proportion to the number of units they started out with.[59]

3.41 With inadvertent mixing, as would arise where a custodian pooled the units of investors without their knowledge, there is authority that the mixture be split equally amongst those who can be demonstrated to have contributed thereto.[60] However, the author of this judgment was tentative in his opinion. The reason for this is obvious. Where two parties can be demonstrated to have started out with 100 and 10,000 units of fungible assets respectively, if there is subsequently found to be a pool of only 50 units and it is unclear what happened to all of the rest of the units it is inequitable for the parties to take the 50 units in equal shares. The better approach, as adopted in *Spence v Union Marine Insurance Co*,[61] is for the parties to share the pool in proportion to the number of units they started out with.

3.42 If the mixture was brought about wrongfully in the hands of one of the parties claiming to have contributed thereto, such as would obtain if the custodian mixed client units with his own against their wishes, the general rule is that the resultant

---

[56] Law Commission, *Sale of Goods Forming Part of a Bulk* (Law Com No 215, 1993); Sale of Goods (Amendment) Act 1995; and Law Society's Standing Committee on Company Law, *Custody Review: Comments on the Discussion Paper Issued by the Securities and Investments Board* (No 291, October 1993) 10.

[57] *Hunter v Moss* [1993] 1 WLR 934, 946 per Colin Rimer QC, 'if any such uncertainty were to arise, that would not be because the trust fund was uncertain as to subject matter, but rather because the trustee had failed to keep proper accounts showing how he had subsequently dealt with it'.

[58] *Spence v Union Marine Insurance Co* (1868) 3 LRCP 427, 439 per Bovill CJ; *Indian Oil Corpn v Greenstone Shipping SA* [1988] QBD 345, 369 per Staughton J.

[59] W Blackstone, *Commentaries on the Laws of England, Volume II: Of the Rights of Things* (1766), with an Introduction by AWB Simpson (1979) 405.

[60] *Buckley v Gross* (1863) 3 B & S 566, 575 per Blackburn J, 122 ER 213.

[61] (1868) 3 LRCP 427, 439 per Bovill CJ.

pool is forfeited as a penalty to the innocent party.[62] The forfeiture is, however, not absolute. It merely shifts the onus of proof on to the wrongdoing party who has created the evidential difficulty. If the wrongdoer cannot prove what is his own in the pool, the whole is forfeited to the innocent party[63] to the maximum number of units which the innocent party started out with.[64]

(d) Nature of Interest in Pool

If individual investors may enjoy proprietary rights in relation to unallocated pooled assets, what do they own? The preponderance of judicial[65] and academic[66] opinion indicates that ownership in a mixture is by common ownership with each person owning a fraction of every unit of the mixture. Sir James Mansfield CJ stated that they will become 'tenants in common who have a right to a part of every'[67] unit therein. Birks states in relation to the co-ownership of personalty that 'each co-owner has his undivided beneficial ownership in every quantum of the whole mass, in the given proportions'.[68]   **3.43**

However, investors are unlikely to be satisfied with owning fractions of pooled units that they could not at any moment quantify. What they claim is a precise number of unascertained pooled units. If one observes the characterisation of investors' ownership rights as a tenancy in common of beneficial interests, for any withdrawal to take place it would be necessary for the tenancy in common to be ended.[69] The 'unity of possession' and ability of co-tenants in common to 'occupy promiscuously' which are the essential characteristics of a tenancy in common would be terminated. Each investor would get his share, thereby allowing the person wishing to depart with his share to do so. Of course, all of those who seek to retain their assets in pooled holdings could do so by constituting a new tenancy in common. Further, a co-owner may need to seek the agreement of all other co-owners in order to be able to deal with his portion of undivided property or seek   **3.44**

---

[62] *Warde v Aeyre* (1614) 2 Bulstrode 323, 80 ER 1157.

[63] *Lupton v White* (1808) 15 Ves Jun 432, 436, 439–441 per Eldon LC, 33 ER 817.

[64] *Indian Oil Corpn v Greenstone Shipping SA* [1988] QBD 345, 369 per Staughton J.

[65] *Buckley v Gross* (1863) 3 B & S 566, 575, 122 ER 213 per Blackburn J; *Spence v Union Marine Insurance Co* (1868) 3 LRCP 427, 437 per Bovill CJ; and *Indian Oil Corpn v Greenstone Shipping SA* [1988] QBD 345, 370 per Staughton J.

[66] For example I Brown, 'Admixture of Goods in English Law' [1988] LMCLQ 286; G McCormack, 'Mixture of Goods' (1990) 10 Legal Studies 293; R Bradgate and F White, 'Sale of Goods Forming Part of a Bulk: Proposals for Reform' [1994] LMCLQ 315, 320, n 28; and Law Commission, *Sale of Goods Forming Part of a Bulk* (Law Com No 215, 1993) 4.15–4.16.

[67] *Jackson v Anderson* (1811) 4 Taunt 24, 30, 128 ER 235.

[68] P Birks (n 29 above) 457.

[69] Blackstone, *Commentaries on the Laws of England, Volume II* (n 59 above) 194, where it is stated that 'estates in common can only be *dissolved* two ways: 1. By uniting all the titles and interests in one tenant, by purchase or otherwise; which brings the whole to one severalty: 2. By making partition between the several tenants in common, which gives them all respective severalties. For indeed tenancies in common differ in nothing from sole estates, but merely in the blending and unity of possession'.

a court order to be able to divide the pool in order to be able to alienate his share.[70] These would be highly inconvenient consequences of the tenancy in common analysis.

3.45 The analysis that co-owners together own each unit of the pool may have implications for a co-owner's ability to take assets withdrawn from the pool free of claims from other co-owners. If one co-owner is faced with a shortfall in his entitlement he may seek to assert rights in relation to units previously withdrawn from the pool on the basis that he enjoys an interest in each unit that constituted the pool. Finally, purchasers of units ex-pool may, if they do not have the benefit of contractual provisions whereby each contributor of the pool has agreed to allow the pool-holder to give valid discharge, and in an effort to avoid possible disputes with other co-owners of the pool from which the assets were withdrawn, be faced with the inconvenience of having to investigate all of the titles to the pool and to ascertain that all other co-owners consented to the partition and alienation.

3.46 If owners of pooled fungible units must be viewed as co-owners, in a commercial context this should be 'a special type of co-ownership, in relation to which the normal rules of co-ownership would be too restrictive',[71] a view advocated by OW Holmes as early as 1872.[72] Co-owners of pooled fungible units in a commercial context should be able to acquire their assets free of claims by other co-owners. More recent support for this view may be derived from the Law Commission[73] and the Sale of Goods (Amendment) Act 1995.[74] The undesired implications of the full rigours of the traditional co-ownership concept may be avoided by all participants in the bulk being deemed to approve delivery ex-bulk to other co-owners of the bulk of quantities equivalent to that which each one had contributed. The effect of this deemed approval is that it bars a contributor who faces

---

[70] *Lord Coke's Institutes of the Laws of England, the First Part, Volume I*, Lib 3, Cap 4, s 318, where it is suggested that tenants in common cannot be compelled by law to make partition. Partition is only effected 'if they will'. Contrast with s 188 of the Law of Property Act 1925, which permits co-owners to apply to court for the division of shares. Although this provision applies explicitly to chattels, this analysis could be applied by analogy to intangibles.
See also R Bradgate and F White, 'Sale of Goods Forming Part of a Bulk: Proposals for Reform' [1994] LMCLQ 315, 320, n 28; P Birks (n 29 above) 457; and Law Commission, *Sale of Goods Forming Part of a Bulk* (Law Com No 215, 1993) 4.15–4.16.

[71] ibid 4.15.

[72] 'Grain Elevators', an unsigned article in (1872) 6 American Law Review 450, 457–459, attributed to OW Holmes by S Williston, *The Law Governing Sales of Goods* (rev edn, 1948) vol 1, 412, n 16.

[73] Law Commission, *Sale of Goods Forming Part of a Bulk* (n 70 above) 4.16.

[74] Sale of Goods (Amendment) Act 1995, s 1(3), which inserts a new s 20B in the Sale of Goods Act 1979. See also R Bradgate and F White, 'Sale of Goods Forming Part of a Bulk: Proposals for Reform' [1994] LMCLQ 315; Tom Burns, 'Better Late than Never: The Reform of the Law on the Sale of Goods Forming Part of a Bulk' (1996) 59 MLR 260.

a shortfall in assets from seeking to recover from other co-owners who had earlier withdrawn their assets.[75]

Yet, one may question whether tenants in common necessarily own a fraction of **3.47** each unit in the pool. Historically, the definition of a tenancy in common was taken to be where owners 'hold by several and distinct titles, but by unity of possession; because none knoweth his own severalty, and therefore they all occupy promiscuously'.[76] The unity of possession, which in the case of custody would only be notional, does not necessarily lead to the conclusion that the co-ownership must be by fractions of each unit. That would only necessarily be the case where the tenancy in common related to a single item. Indeed, the suggestion that possession is enjoyed 'promiscuously' because no one person can identify precisely what is his simply indicates that the owners of pooled units should be able to enjoy any of the units without distinction,[77] rather than fractions of all of them at the same time.

There is authority that notwithstanding the characterisation of the contributors **3.48** to a pool as co-owners, their entitlement from the pool may be measured exclusively by reference to the whole number of units they contributed to the pool.[78] *Hunter v Moss* also serves as authority for this proposition. There is North American authority to similar effect, both from the USA[79] and from Canada,[80] in relation to both the retention of title to assets transferred into a pool and the acquisition of title ex-bulk. Support for the proposition that an investor enjoys a proprietary interest in relation to definite unallocated pooled units may also be derived from the Uncertificated Securities Regulations 1995.[81] This approach accords more with what obtains in practice than the tenancy in common analysis.

---

[75] The implication of this is that the last person to withdraw from the pool may be left with a shortfall. Such a shortfall will only arise in the event of the dishonesty of the person controlling the pool or an accident. The shared unit approach of co-ownership does not prevent either of these eventualities, merely seeking to share the consequences more evenly. The point remains that even with the shared unit approach a claimant to a pool may not get out of it what he was properly entitled to. Of course, investors facing a shortfall will be able to rely, for whatever they may be worth, on their contractual rights against the custodian.

[76] *Blackstone, Commentaries on the Laws of England, Volume II* (n 59 above) 191; see also *Lord Coke's Institutes of the Laws of England, the First Part, Volume I*, Lib 3, Cap 4, s 292 for a similar definition.

[77] *The Oxford English Dictionary, Vol XII* (2nd edn, 1989) 613.

[78] *Indian Oil Corpn v Greenstone Shipping SA* [1988] QB 345, 370 per Staughton J.

[79] *Kimberly v Patchin* 19 NY 330, 333 per Comstock J (CA of NY, 1859) on title ex-bulk; *Morgan v Gregg* 46 Barb 183, 186–187 per Parker PJ (SC of NY, 1865) on retention of separate title to pooled fungibles; *Young v Miles* 20 Wis 646, 654 per Dixon CJ (SC of Wisconsin, 1869); *Wilkinson v Stewart* 85 Penn 255, 260 per Paxson J (SC of Pennsylvania, 1877).

[80] *McDonald v Lane* (1881) 7 SCR 462, 466–467 per Strong J, SC of Canada.

[81] SI 1995/3272. In relation to the period between the issuing of instructions to change the register upon the execution of a trade, and the registration of the appropriate number of securities in the name of a transferee, reg 25(1) refers to the transferee as enjoying 'an equitable interest in the requisite number of uncertificated units of the security' out of the holding of the transferor.

In practice, to withdraw assets, investors with pooled assets do not necessarily act in concert in order to fulfil the wishes of one amongst their number. As a rule, only the investor seeking to remove his units and the custodian will be aware of the transaction. There is no question of all of the co-owners of the pool determining a tenancy in common. The investor merely indicates to the custodian his desire to obtain the equivalent of the assets he contributed to the pool and the custodian transfers this to him. The custodian does this without reference to fractional ownership of individual assets, and does not consider the consent, implied or otherwise, of other contributors to the pool but purely on the basis of the specific quantity contributed by the particular investor to the pool.

3.49   Based on the foregoing analysis, it may be argued that each investor's right is to a certain but unallocated number of assets in an identifiable pool of fungible assets. Even if this analysis is not accepted, the position of the Sale of Goods (Amendment) Act 1995 could be adopted whereby there is the deemed consent of all co-owners of assets in the pool to forego their claims to assets lawfully removed from the pool. The first approach is preferable because, whilst both approaches should allow investors who withdraw their assets from the pool to take free of competing claims by other contributors to the pool, it is the first approach that better explains the fact that co-owners are able to act autonomously. The shared ownership concept is nothing more than an evidential tool whose real strength lies in its ability to allow the contributors to a pool to divide the pool equitably in the event of a shortfall of the assets pooled. It does not avoid the possibility of a shortfall in the bulk. Indeed, such a possibility is explicitly acknowledged under the Sale of Goods (Amendment) Act 1995.[82] The fear that certain investors could be left short could just as well be addressed by other means, eg a deposit insurance scheme.

Substitution

3.50   The fact of mixture makes it likely that an investor will not receive in specie re-delivery of whatever he transferred into the pool of assets.[83] Indeed, the substitution of custody assets is a necessary feature of some operations of custody. The practices of stock-lending and repos by which investors derive additional income from their assets necessitate the transfer of assets out of the pool to which they are entitled, with a subsequent re-transfer of equivalent units back into the pool upon the conclusion of the transaction. Furthermore, in the context of custody, a transfer of intangible things may take the form of the extinction of one set of rights belonging to the transferor and the establishment of a new set of rights in favour

---

[82]   See new s 20B(3).
[83]   Such as negotiable certificates transferred into fungible pooled custody.

of the transferee.[84] By the very nature of these transactions, therefore, there may be no question of in specie transfers. Does the fact that the investor will receive substitute assets impede his enjoyment of a proprietary interest in relation to the custody assets?[85]

In *South Australian Insurance Company v Randell* Sir Joseph Napier stated that **3.51** '[w]herever there is a delivery of property on a contract for an equivalent in money or some other valuable commodity, and not for the return of his identical subject matter in its original or altered form, this is a transfer of property for value—it is a sale'.[86] This suggests that the agreement to transfer assets into custody where in specie re-delivery will not occur results in the shift of legal and equitable ownership of custody assets transferred to the custodian. However, more recent authority from the House of Lords has established that the absence of in specie re-delivery is not fatal to the enjoyment of proprietary interests in relation to pooled assets.[87]

Nevertheless, there are certain features which, when allied with the substitution of **3.52** assets, will suggest that property in pooled assets passes to the custodian. A principal determining factor of whether property in stored assets passes is the location of an option to substitute the assets for cash or equivalent assets. The reason for this is that the power to determine how the assets are applied is a major indicator of the party in whom property resides. If the option is with the custodian, he is in effect at liberty to deal with the assets as his own. In such circumstances it is likely that the terms of custody will be characterised as a loan or sale, with property in the assets passing to the custodian.[88] Where the option remains with the depositor as to whether he demands equivalent re-delivery or he retains the right to have the deposited assets alienated or returned, the transaction is likely to be characterised in terms that the property in the deposited assets remains with the depositor until the option is exercised.[89]

Other factors may illustrate the nature of the transaction. It is likely that property **3.53** in assets transferred will be held to be in the person who is declared to bear the risk of loss or destruction of the assets.[90] There are suggestions that the fact of payment

---

[84] Some support for this view may be derived from *R v Preddy* [1996] AC 815, 834 per Lord Goff, affirmed by Lords Mackay, Jauncey, Slynn and Hoffmann at 826, 841, 842 and 842 respectively.

[85] See J Benjamin, *The Law of Global Custody* (1996), 39.

[86] (1869) 3 LRPC 101, 108. See also *Chapman Bros v Verco Bros & Co Ltd* (1933) 49 CLR 306, HC of Australia.

[87] *Mercer v Craven Grain Storage Ltd* [1994] CLC 328, 329 per Lord Templeman.

[88] *Chase v Washburn* 1 Ohio St. 244, 249, 252 per Bartley J (SC of Ohio, 1853); *Kansas Flour Mills Co v Board of Com'rs* 259 P 795, 796 per Marshall J (SC of Kansas, 1927); *Latta v Transit Grain Co* 222 SW 2d 467, 470 per Stokes J (Court of Civil Appeals of Texas, 1949); and 78 Am Jur 2d, 'Warehouses' para 36 and the cases cited therein.

[89] *Burke v Boulder Milling & Elevator Co* 235 P 574, 575 per Burke J (SC of Colorado, 1925); and 78 Am Jur 2d, 'Warehouses' para 35 and the cases cited therein.

[90] *Clark v McClellan* (1893) 23 OR 465, HC of Justice for Ontario.

for storage may be indicative of the nature of the transaction as one in which property does not pass from the depositor.[91] It is also likely that a transaction whereby the depository is obliged to keep sufficient of the relevant assets to meet the demands of depositors at any time will be characterised as one in which property in the assets remains with the depositors;[92] although the absence of such an obligation will not necessarily constitute the transaction one in which property passes to the depository.[93] Such a provision may be deliberately omitted where it is known that there may be transactions in relation to the pooled assets, such as stock-lending or repos, which would at times bring the volume of assets available below that which all of the contributors to the pool could lawfully demand.

3.54 Where the depository undertakes transactions that reduce the number of fungible units in the pool below that necessary to meet the claims of depositors, there are at least two considerations to be addressed. There are questions as to whether the depositors have agreed to such transactions. There may be express or implied agreement for this, such as for stock-lending and repo transactions.[94] If there is no such agreement, this would constitute a breach of the terms of custody, possibly making the depository liable for damages. More important, however, is the fact that the depositors may lose their proprietary interest in relation to assets alienated. Repos and stock-lending transactions involve outright transfers with no question of vestigial proprietary interests being retained by custodian or investor. It is also likely that wrongful alienation by the depository would be to a bona fide purchaser who takes free. In such circumstances the depositors are left, in relation to the assets transferred out of the pool, with personal rights against the depository for return of the assets. The depository is no longer characterised as trustee of such assets; he becomes debtor of such assets in favour of the depositors.

3.55 The question of whose rights amongst the contributors to the pool of unallocated assets are reduced from proprietary to personal rights in this way becomes critical upon the insolvency of the custodian. Of course, there may have been allocations of the alienation to a particular depositor, in which case he would be the only depositor whose rights are so affected. However, with fungible accounts there would be no such allocation and the question of how individual depositors are

---

[91] *Bucher v Commonwealth* 103 Penn 528, 534 per Gordon J (SC of Pennsylvania, 1883); *Barnes v McCrea* 39 NW 392, 394 per Robinson J (SC of Iowa, 1888); see also 'Grain Elevators', an unsigned article in (1872) 6 Am LR 450, 465, attributed to OW Holmes by S Williston, *The Law Governing Sales of Goods* (rev edn, 1948) vol 1, 412, n 16.

[92] *Rice v Nixon* 97 Ind 97, 99 per Elliott CJ (SC of Judicature of Indiana, 1884).

[93] *Burke v Boulder Milling & Elevator Co* 235 P 574, 575 per Burke J (SC of Colorado, 1925).

[94] Such consent would be inconsistent with a requirement that the depository maintains sufficient assets to meet the claims of depositors at any time, because it contemplates that the depository may lawfully, if only temporarily, alienate assets with the result that the pool of assets falls below the volume necessary to meet all depositors' claims.

affected by the shortfall is addressed by the rules on mixtures: contributors are affected rateably according to their contribution to the pool.

3.56 If the depository re-delivers substitute assets into the pool to replace those that were alienated, reconstituting the pool to the same size as it formerly was, then he can turn the personal rights based on what had been alienated back into proprietary rights on the basis of the substitute assets. However, by virtue of the lowest intermediate balance rule,[95] investors do not automatically enjoy an interest in relation to assets subsequently added to the pool. For this to occur, a clear intention on the part of the party making the later addition to make good the depletion must be established. In the USA, 'in the absence of countervailing proof'[96] such intention is presumed from the mere addition of new stock to a pool from which it was withdrawn,[97] even though this presumption is 'productive of cynic smiles even in counsel advancing the same'.[98] Nevertheless, this is a perfectly reasonable inference to draw where the pool consists exclusively of depositor holdings,[99] as is accepted in England.[100]

3.57 However, for the duration that the assets are alienated the depositors do not enjoy priority in the event of the insolvency of the depository in relation to the alienated assets, nor do they bear the risk of their loss or destruction.[101] Given the rules on pooled fungibles, and the implication that depositors with assets in pools may all have to bear part of the loss of the type of asset which did not end up being substituted, depositors may wish to insist that the particular pool to which their assets are added is not utilised for transactions such as repos.[102] However, even in the event of a failed transaction where similar assets were not added to the pool, the depositors should not be prejudiced in monetary terms. In general, depositories routinely require/receive on behalf of depositors as much collateral/financing as the value of the assets transferred out of the pool. If such collateral/financing is properly allocated to the depositors, so that it is in their collective name or the custodian's as trustee thereof for them, their ultimate balance sheet position will not have been prejudiced. It is only if the depository is both insolvent and dishonest that the depositors risk financial loss.

---

[95] *Roscoe v Winder* [1915] 1 Ch 62.

[96] *James E Gorman v Charles E Littlefield* 229 US 19, 25; 33 SC 690, 692 per Day J (1913).

[97] ibid 691; *Arthur B Duel v Harry B Hollins* 241 US 523; 36 SC 615 (1916).

[98] *Re HB Hollins & Co* 212 F 317, 320 per Hough DJ (1914).

[99] 'Grain Elevators', an unsigned article in (1872) 6 Am LR 450, 467, attributed to OW Holmes by S Williston, *The Law Governing Sales of Goods* (rev edn, 1948) vol 1, 412, n 16.

[100] *Re Stapylton Fletcher Ltd* [1994] 1 WLR 1181, 1199, 1200 per Judge Paul Baker QC; *Goldcorp Exchange Ltd* [1995] 1 AC 74, 98–99.

[101] *Sering v Shafroth* 27 NE 702, 705 per Shope J (SC of Illinois, 1891).

[102] To satisfy such requests a custodian would need to maintain two separate pools of identical client assets, one where the balance always reflected the claims of the contributors thereto and another which permitted repos, stock-lending and the like.

3.58 If the foregoing analysis is accepted, depositors of assets in a fungible pool may receive substitute assets for at least one of two reasons. They may receive substitute assets because of the evidential difficulty of returning in specie assets that are by definition or agreement indistinguishable. In this case, it is not certain that substitute assets will be received but it is likely. Depositors may also receive substitute assets where the depository is permitted to alienate assets, or wrongfully does so, and replaces them with substitutes. This occurs by a trust being converted into a debt and back into a trust again.[103] There are important distinctions between this type of transaction and the characterisation of the transfer of assets as constituting a loan. With a loan, property in the custody assets is immediately transferred to the depository, where it would remain until the return to the depositor of the same or other assets upon termination of the period of deposit. The risks that this would entail for an investor upon the insolvency of the custodian have already been highlighted.[104] However, with the type of transaction under contemplation the depositor enjoys a proprietary interest in relation to the assets deposited for the duration of the transaction except whilst the assets are being properly on-lent or otherwise transferred to a third party. The depositor enjoys a proprietary interest before the substitution and once substitution has been effected although the assets remain with the depository. The risks to investors of not enjoying proprietary rights in the custody assets are limited to the period whilst they are out on loan or used for repo. These risks are ameliorated by the investors enjoying proprietary interests in relation to assets of equivalent value transferred to the custodian in exchange for the transfer of some of the pooled custody assets for loan or repo.

---

[103] 'Grain Elevators', an unsigned article in (1872) 6 Am LR 450, 465, attributed to OW Holmes by S Williston, *The Law Governing Sales of Goods* (rev edn, 1948) vol 1, 412, n 16.

[104] See the section on importance of the proprietary analysis in Chapter 2.

4

MULTI-TIER CUSTODY

This chapter examines the impact of the introduction of a chain of sub- **4.01**
custodians between the investor and 'his' securities on the interest enjoyed by an
investor with assets held in custody. Perhaps the most important reasons for the
establishment of such a chain are the fact that much investment is now cross-
border or immobilised, which may necessitate the employment of sub-custodians
if the investor uses a global custodian. In view of this, it is likely that it is the analysis in this chapter that will best illustrate the nature of a typical investor's claim.

A. Non-Intermediated Sub-Custody

If the investor uses the custodial structure purely for safe-keeping certificates to his **4.02**
securities and a sub-custodian is employed, it is likely that it is the sub-custodian
who will be in actual possession of the certificate.

The transfer into custody of registrable securities or securities indorsed in favour **4.03**
of the investor does not impact on legal title thereto.[1] Legal title to the securities
and certificate remains in the investor. The extended bailment relationship, as
with other forms of bailment, does not affect the title of the head bailor in relation
to the certificate or the underlying securities.

---

[1] The analysis of bearer certificates where legal ownership is transferred by delivery comes under
intermediary sub-custody.

4.04   The certificate may have been delivered to the sub-custodian by the investor himself, the investor's lead custodian or the sub-custodian may have collected the certificate from the issuer or previous owner (or his intermediary) of the security. Regardless of who actually delivers the certificate to the sub-custodian, the parties may establish a relationship of bailment with the investor as bailor of the certificate and the sub-custodian as bailee independent of any contractual relationship between them, though it is likely that this would also exist. Such a bailment would be valid notwithstanding the fact that the investor had not previously enjoyed possession of the certificate.[2] As indicated in Chapter 2, a bailment relationship based on the certificate to registrable securities or securities specifically endorsed in favour of the investor will not affect ownership of the underlying securities.

4.05   Where the investor himself delivers the certificate to the sub-custodian, the analysis does not differ from that of a bailment where there is single-tier custody. The investor and sub-custodian, notwithstanding the recognition of another party as the investor's lead custodian, are brought into a direct relationship of bailment.

4.06   Where the certificate is delivered by the investor to the lead custodian, who in turn hands it to the sub-custodian, the relationship between the lead custodian and the sub-custodian is technically one of sub-bailment if the lead custodian remains a part of the custodial structure,[3] and a substituted bailment if the lead custodian is thereby removed. Ordinarily, permission for the lead custodian to delegate in this way will have been expressly provided for in the contract for custodial services between the investor and the lead custodian. If no such provision has been made, there are suggestions that a sub-bailment should not be recognised.[4] However, there is support for the view that since the sub-bailee's responsibilities 'are substantially similar whether or not the sub-bailment is authorised', the question of authorisation should not determine the establishment of the sub-bailment.[5]

---

[2] *Transcontainer Express Ltd v Custodian Security Ltd* [1988] 1 Lloyd's Rep 128, 135 where Slade LJ assumed the correctness of a submission by counsel which relied on 'authorities such as *Edwards v Newland,* [1950] 1 All ER 1072 and *Johnson Matthey & Co Ltd v Constantine Terminals Ltd and Another,* [1972] 2 Lloyd's Rep 215, that it is in law quite possible for a person to create a relationship of bailor and bailee . . . between himself and another party, such as to confer on bailee . . . the possession of the goods and on himself the immediate right to possession of them, even though he himself has at no time had physical control of the goods', although Slade LJ stated that his assumption related to the purposes of the case in hand, without deciding on the point.

See also *The Pioneer Container* [1994] 2 AC 324, 337; *Re Goldcorp Exchange Ltd* [1995] 1 AC 74, 108; *Re Stapylton Fletcher Ltd* [1995] 1 All ER 192, 210; and *Spectra Internat v Hayesoak* [1997] 1 Lloyd's Rep 153.

[3] *China Pacific SA v Food Corporation of India* [1982] AC 939, 959 per Lord Diplock.

[4] See the Canadian case of *Chapman v Robinson and Ferguson* (1969) 71 WWR 515, 523–526 per Belzil DCJ and the Australian case of *Roufos v Brewster and Brewster* (1971) 2 SASR 218, 234 per Zelling J.

[5] Palmer, *Bailment* (2nd edn, 1991) 1282–1283, citing *Chellaram & Sons (London) Ltd v Butlers Warehousing & Distribution Ltd* [1978] 2 Lloyd's Rep 412 and the dictum of Yeldham J, in *RM*

There is authority for the view that the facts of sub-bailment may also constitute **4.07** the sub-bailee the direct collateral bailee of the head bailor.[6] On the present analysis, therefore, a sub-custodian could be constituted the collateral bailee of the investor even though the sub-custodian received the investor's assets from a lead custodian. The rationale for this characterisation of the relationship between the bailor and sub-bailee is based upon the view that the voluntary taking by the sub-bailee of the bailor's assets into his custody of itself results in his owing to the owner the duties of a bailee.[7] This reasoning entails two consequences. It is not necessary for the establishment of the collateral bailment that the bailor consents to the sub-bailee's possession of the assets.[8] Further, a sub-bailee should not be characterised as a collateral bailee of the (head) bailor unless 'he has sufficient notice that a person other than the bailee is interested in the goods so that it can properly be said that (in addition to his duties to the bailee) he has, by taking the goods into his custody, assumed towards that other person the responsibility for the goods which is characteristic of a bailee'.[9]

The above scenario whereby the sub-custodian comes into possession of the **4.08** investor's assets from the investor or via the lead custodian may conveniently be achieved within the context of a wholly domestic sub-custodial arrangement. However, it is sometimes the case with domestic investments, and often the case with cross-border investments, that the sub-custodian takes possession of the certificate directly from the issuer, previous owner or other party. This fact would preclude the establishment of the relationship between sub-custodian and lead custodian as a sub-bailment. Instead, it is suggested by Palmer that where 'a person, other than by direct delivery from an antecedent bailee, takes possession of goods upon the instructions or at the request of an intermediary', the recipient may be termed a quasi-bailee, with the issuer of instructions a quasi-bailor.[10] The establishment of a quasi-bailment does not require the authority of the owner of the asset. It may arise 'irrespective of any breach of contract in sub-contracting'.[11]

Campbell (Vehicle Sales) Pty Ltd v Machnig (an unreported case of SC, New South Wales, Australia, 22 May 1981).

This does not detract from the fact that the unauthorised establishment of a sub-bailment may constitute an unlawful deviation from the terms of the principal bailment, with the implications this may have for the lead custodian (bailee/sub-bailor's) liability for any loss or injury to the chattel caused thereby or that the lead custodian (bailee/sub-bailor) may be guilty of conversion.

[6] *Morris v CW Martin & Sons Ltd* [1966] 1 QB 716; *Gilchrist Watt and Sanderson Pty Ltd v York Products Pty Ltd* [1970] 1 WLR 1262; and *The Pioneer Container* [1994] 2 AC 324.

[7] *The Pioneer Container* [1994] 2 AC 324, 337 and 341.

[8] ibid 342.

[9] ibid.

[10] Palmer, *Bailment* (n 5 above) 1291; see generally 1291–1295; NE Palmer, 'Quasi-Bailment' [1988] 1 LMCLQ 34.

[11] *Metalhandel JA Magnus BV v Ardfields Transport Ltd* [1988] 1 Lloyd's Rep 197, 203 per Gatehouse J.

Palmer suggests,[12] supported by dictum,[13] that the structure of the relationships between quasi-bailor, quasi-bailee and the owner of the asset is analogous to that of a sub-bailment and as such that the quasi-bailee/sub-custodian will owe duties directly to the owner of the asset in his, the sub-custodian's, possession. There is recent authority for this view of quasi-bailment.[14]

4.09 The distinction between sub-bailment and quasi-bailment nevertheless remains important. Since the quasi-bailor never enjoyed possession of the assets bailed, and was therefore never a bailee or (subsidiary) bailor of the assets in question, it may be the case that the quasi-bailee would not owe him duties under the principles of bailment concurrent with those owed to the owner/true bailor of the assets.[15] The quasi-bailor has not enjoyed legal title, possessory or otherwise, to the assets as a basis for which such duties may be owed. It is, however, likely that the quasi-bailee would owe contractual duties to the quasi-bailor. In a sub-bailment, on the other hand, it is likely that the sub-bailee would owe concurrent duties to the intermediary bailee/sub-bailor and to the bailor under the principles of bailment, in addition to any contractual duties owed to the bailee/sub-bailor. The sub-bailor is the sub-bailee's actual bailor in their direct relationship of bailment.

4.10 Two further points may be emphasised. Since the essence of a bailment is the voluntary assumption of obligations owed to the owner of the assets, the basic terms on which the bailment exists are the terms on which possession of the assets was taken by the quasi/sub-bailee. However, any attempt by the quasi/sub-bailee to invoke terms agreed with a quasi/sub-bailor against the owner which restrict or otherwise affect the quasi/sub-bailee's responsibilities to the owner can only be made if the consent of the owner for the quasi/sub-bailor to enter into such an agreement was obtained.[16] In addition, it is important for the quasi/sub-bailee to establish clearly the terms on which assets were accepted. It is not sufficient for a quasi/sub-bailee to believe that assets were taken into possession by him on certain terms if he cannot prove this, especially if there are contractual provisions that suggest otherwise. In *The Mahkutai*[17] it was held that a sub-bailee could not rely

---

[12] Palmer, *Bailment* (n 5 above) 1292.

[13] *Metalhandel JA Magnus BV v Ardfields Transport Ltd* [1988] 1 Lloyd's Rep 197, 202–203 per Gatehouse J. Note, however, that there seems to be some confusion between the roles of quasi-bailee and quasi-bailor in the report.

[14] *The Pioneer Container* [1994] 2 AC 324, 345; *Spectra Internat v Hayesoak* [1997] 1 Lloyd's Rep 153 where although Judge Hallgarten QC spoke exclusively in terms of sub-bailments at 155–157, the case actually involved a combination of quasi-bailment and further sub-bailment. Nevertheless, the result was to bring the owner of the goods and actual bailee, notwithstanding two intermediaries, into direct relations.

[15] Palmer, *Bailment* (n 5 above) 1292.

[16] *The Pioneer Container* [1994] 2 AC 324, 342.

[17] [1996] AC 650.

on terms which were judged not to constitute one of the express terms of acceptance of the assets regardless of the fact that the sub-bailee was under the misapprehension that the assets had been accepted including those terms.

B. Intermediated Sub-Custody

Figure 4.1: Intermediated sub-custody

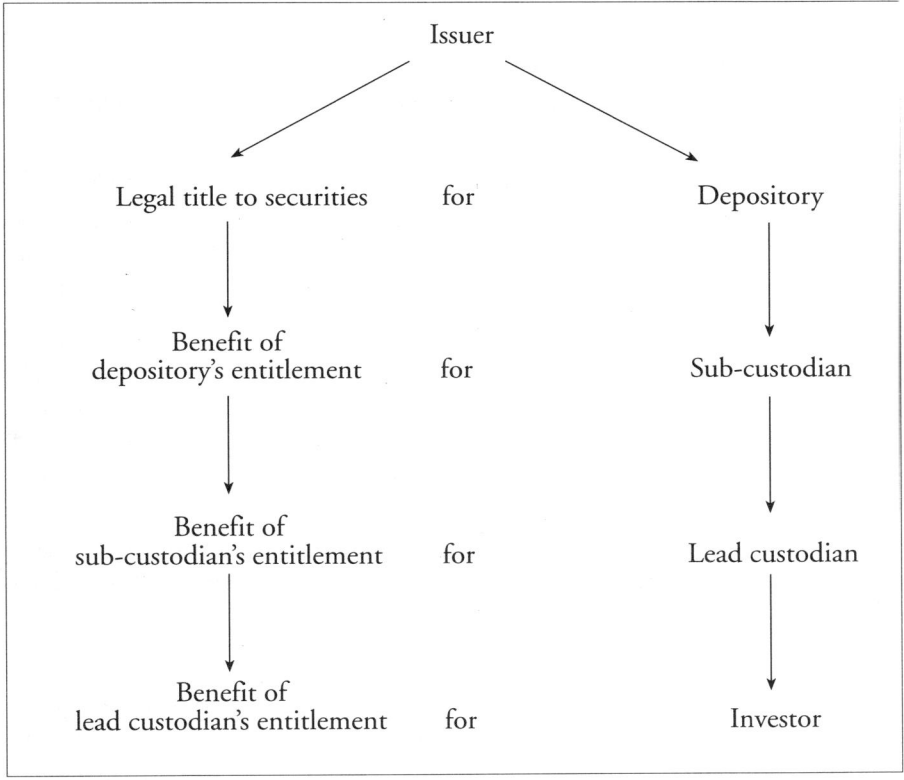

Figure 4.1 gives an indication of the levels of intermediaries that may come **4.11** between an investor and 'his' securities. The diagram is merely representative of some of the tiers of sub-custody that may exist; it is possible to extend this by adding yet more tiers of sub-custody to the top of Figure 4.1. A multiplicity of tiers of intermediaries is not unusual. Indeed, with the growth of immobilisation and cross-border investments, such tiers are increasingly the norm.

If the hierarchy of tiers is respected in a sub-custodial structure, which would be **4.12** the case if all of the tiers were true intermediaries, the structure represented by Figure 4.1 may be analysed as follows:

(1) The first tier is the depository, who is nominally entitled to the securities whilst holding the benefit thereof for the sub-custodian. The depository in this scenario may be termed the investor's sub-sub-custodian.

(2) The sub-custodian's entitlement is also not beneficial. He must in turn pass the benefit of whatever he receives by his entitlement from the assets held by the depository on to the lead custodian.

(3) Again, the lead custodian's entitlement is non-beneficial. Whatever benefit is derived by this entitlement from the sub-custodian (in relation to the sub-custodian's own entitlement to the assets held by the depository) must be passed on to the investor.

(4) The investor is entitled to benefits that accrue to the lead custodian from the sub-custodian.

4.13 If the above represents the logical structure of tiered intermediary custody, the investor appears increasingly removed from a direct link with the custody assets. The question that this leads to is whether the legal structure which is established by such tiers is to similar effect and the implications of this for the nature of the subject-matter of whatever interest is enjoyed by the investor.

4.14 As observed in Chapter 2, it is the trust concept that allows the investor to maintain proprietary rights in relation to assets held by the custodian in intermediary custody. In the case of single-tier custody, the investor enjoys a direct equitable interest in securities legally vested in the custodian as trustee. In the case of multiple tiers, assuming that a trust is established at the top tier, it is the ultimate sub-custodian who enjoys legal title and the next tier beneficiary who enjoys a direct equitable interest in relation to the securities in custody. In Figure 4.1, the depository would enjoy legal title and the sub-custodian enjoys a direct equitable title to the securities in custody.

4.15 It must at this point be emphasised that the logical or hierarchical structure of tiers of sub-custody need not be respected. The legal relationship between investor and any sub-custodian could, by appropriate action, be constituted in the same way as the direct relationship enjoyed between investor and custodian discussed in Chapter 2, possibly with the lead custodian doing nothing more than facilitating the establishment of such a relationship. Thus, the investor in Figure 4.1 could be constituted the depository's direct beneficiary, as opposed to the investor having to receive benefits via the sub-custodian and lead custodian. In such a case, the analysis of the investor's interest in the custody assets and relationship with the sub-custodian (*qua* direct trustee) remains the same as that in any other case of single-tier intermediary custody.

4.16 Where legal title is vested in a tier other than the investor's direct custodian, and the structure of the tiers is respected, so that the investor does not have access to other tiers, the question arises of the type of interest the investor enjoys and in relation to what asset. The answer to this question may lie in the manner in which the benefits of the securities held are transferred down the tiers and it is from this perspective that the issue will be analysed.

(1) Passing Benefits from Tier to Tier

Any person with an equitable interest in an asset, such as the sub-custodian in relation to the custody assets in Figure 4.1, may dispose of the substance of the equitable interest by any one of at least three principal ways.[18] The disponor may assign the totality of the interest to a third party; he may direct the trustees who are holding the asset in his favour to hold for a third party instead of him; or he may declare a trust with himself as trustee based on his equitable interest in favour of a third party.   **4.17**

The practical effect of all of these methods is for the third party to enjoy the benefit of the asset held by the trustee instead of the direct beneficiary of the trustee. There are suggestions that all three methods are of similar legal effect, amounting to 'the voluntary transfer of an equitable interest'.[19] However, there would appear to be fundamental differences between the first two and the third of these methods. By assignment or orders to his trustee, the sub-custodian, as beneficiary of the principal trust, appears to remove himself from the chain of intermediaries. He effects the substitution of another party for himself in the chain. However, where such a beneficiary, the sub-custodian in Figure 4.1, declares a (sub-) trust, he does not remove himself from the chain of events. Rather, he simply declares that although he is entitled to the benefit of the securities vested in the depository, he will give the benefit of such entitlement to another party. In Figure 4.1 this further beneficiary would be the lead custodian.   **4.18**

These three methods of transferring the benefit of assets to which one is beneficially entitled are analysed below. Much of the analysis will be related to the three-tier structure represented in Figure 4.1 where the depository holds for sub-custodian, who holds for lead custodian, who holds for investor.   **4.19**

Assignment

A direct relationship could be brought about between the investor or any intermediary and the ultimate sub-custodian. With reference to Figure 4.2, the beneficiary of the depository could effect an assignment of his entitlement under the trust established by the depository to another party. The investor or other intermediary would then become entitled to everything which the former beneficiary   **4.20**

---

[18] *Timpson's Executors v Yerbury (HM Inspector of Taxes)* [1936] 1 KB 645, 664 per Romer LJ; *Grey v Inland Revenue Commissioners* [1958] 1 Ch 375, 380–381 per Upjohn J.
[19] ibid 1 Ch 375, 380 per Upjohn J.

Figure 4.2: Assignment

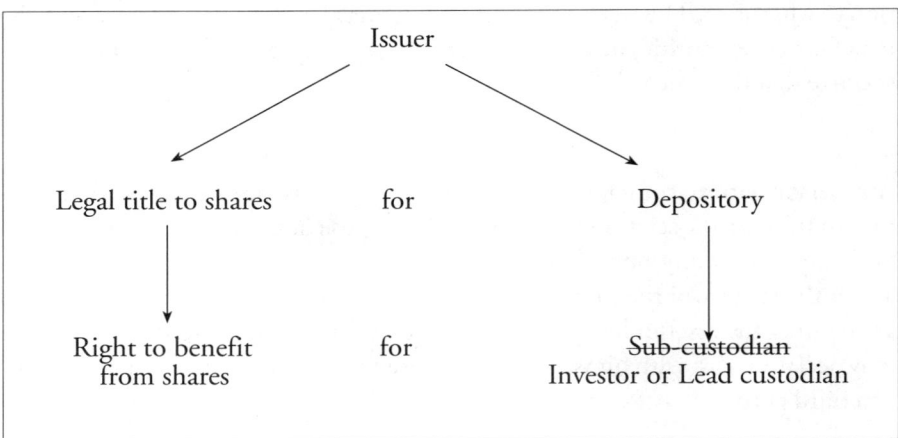

of the depository, the sub-custodian in Figure 4.2, would have been entitled to. The entire equitable interest formerly enjoyed by the sub-custodian in Figure 4.2 is transferred to the investor or other intermediary directly.[20]

4.21　However, the intention of the depository to pass the benefit of his entitlements in this way could be hampered by the existence of a non-assignability clause in the terms on which the depository holds for the sub-custodian,[21] in order perhaps for depositories to not have to deal with retail investors. It has been suggested that such a prohibition 'could no more operate to invalidate the assignment than it could to interfere with the laws of gravitation',[22] and that 'a chose-in-action which is in its own nature assignable cannot be made inalienable by a contractual undertaking not to assign it'.[23] Conversely, the view may be taken that 'there is no reason why the parties to an agreement may not contract to give its subject-matter the quality of unassignability'.[24] Such assertions conceal a number of issues. One must distinguish between the ability of an assignee to claim directly from the obligor of an assignor and an 'assignor' merely passing on the substance of his entitlement to a further beneficiary. One should also bear in mind the fact that such a prohibition may have different effect between the obligor of the benefits sought to be assigned and the assignor, and between the purported assignor and assignee. In

---

[20] *Norman v Federal Commissioner of Taxation* (1963) 109 CLR 9, 26 per Windeyer J, HC of Australia.

[21] *Linden Gardens Trust Ltd v Lenesta Sludge Disposals Ltd* [1994] 1 AC 85, 103 per Lord Browne-Wilkinson, 'every lawyer knows that the burden of a contract cannot be assigned: see for example, *Nokes v Doncaster Amalgamated Collieries Ltd* [1940] AC 1014, 1019–1020'.

[22] *Tom Shaw & Co v Moss Empires (Limited) and Bastow* (1908) 25 TLR 190, 191 per Darling J.

[23] *Hodder & Tolley Ltd v Cornes* [1923] NZLR 876, 878 per Salmond J.

[24] *Helstan Securities Ltd v Hertfordshire County Council* [1978] 3 All ER 262, 266 per Croom-Johnson J; *Re Turcan* (1888) 40 ChD 5.

relation to Figure 4.2, one must distinguish between the right of the assignee of the sub-custodian to claim directly from the depository and the sub-custodian passing on the benefit of his entitlement to the purported assignee; and distinguish between the effect of the prohibition as between the depository and sub-custodian, as opposed to between the sub-custodian and his purported assignee.

The effect of any non-assignability clause is in the first place a question of construction.[25] At least four constructions of a non-assignability clause are possible, that:[26] (i) an assignment in breach of the provision is merely a breach of a personal undertaking which would not render the assignment ineffective, but would leave the party in breach thereof (the sub-custodian) open to a claim for damages by the other party (depository) to the agreement in which the prohibition is contained; (ii) the assignment would be ineffective as against a party to an agreement which contained the prohibition, such that the aggrieved party (depository) remained at liberty to hand over the benefits to the assignor (sub-custodian), but that this would not affect the obligation of the assignor (sub-custodian), once he had actually received the benefit from the other party (depository), to deliver whatever benefit he does receive to the assignee (lead custodian or investor); (iii) the assignment would not only be ineffective against the parties to the agreement in which the prohibition is contained, the parties would also be barred from transferring the benefit to any other party, even after the benefit had become the assignor's (sub-custodian's); or (iv) an assignment would be ineffective against the parties to the agreement in which the prohibition is contained and would constitute a breach of contract between assignor (sub-custodian) and his counter-party (depository) entitling the counter-party (depository) to terminate his obligations to the assignor (sub-custodian). **4.22**

As with any other consensual relationship the parties to the custodial agreement at the top tier, the depository and sub-custodian, should in general be free to choose with whom and on what terms they form relations. With this in mind, Goode has expressed views on the legal effect of these types of clauses, which views have been accepted by the House of Lords in *Linden Gardens Ltd v Lenesta Ltd.*[27] He stated that a provision bearing construction (i) needs no comment,[28] the implication being that such a clause would be valid having the effects stated and that a clause bearing construction (ii) would also be valid, giving effect to the intentions of the parties to the contract to choose with whom they enjoy direct relations.[29] He, however, suggested that a clause bearing construction (iv) may or **4.23**

---

[25] *Linden Gardens Ltd v Lenesta Ltd* [1994] 1 AC 85, 104 per Browne-Wilkinson LJ.
[26] RM Goode, 'Inalienable Rights?' (1979) 42 MLR 553, 554; B Allcock, 'Restrictions on the Assignment of Contractual Rights' [1983] CLJ 328. For a different view see DM Kloss, 'Assignments Without the Consent of the Debtor' (1979) 43 Conveyancer 133.
[27] [1994] 1 AC 85, 104 per Browne-Wilkinson LJ.
[28] Goode (n 26 above) 554.
[29] ibid.

may not be valid, depending on whether the clause fell foul of the rules of equity governing forfeiture,[30] and that a clause bearing construction (iii) ought not to be countenanced because a provision which sought to restrict the assignor's ability to deal with assets which had by the time of the purported assignment become his property was repugnant to the assignor's ownership and should therefore be rejected.[31]

4.24 The conclusion of this analysis in relation to Figure 4.2 is that it is possible for a depository in his agreement to provide custodial services for the sub-custodian on condition that an assignment by the sub-custodian would be honoured but would constitute a breach of contract which may lead to damages payable by the sub-custodian to the depository. Beyond that, an assignment may actually be barred, in the sense of permitting a depositor to refuse to pass the benefits due to the sub-custodian to any other party. It is likely that such a provision would be upheld by the courts if it did not purport to restrict the rights of the sub-custodian to deal with whatever he received as he likes.[32] Any stipulation that a purported assignment may lead to both the sub-custodian and his assignee, whether investor or lead custodian, forfeiting the rights claimed from the depository is likely to be struck down for offending the rules against forfeiture and a provision suggesting that the sub-custodian may not alienate the substance of whatever benefits are received from the depository is similarly likely to be held invalid.

Orders to the Trustee

4.25 The sub-custodian could direct the depository *qua* trustee to hold whatever he (the sub-custodian) was entitled to on trust for the investor or lead custodian instead. Although different from an assignment, such an order would nonetheless transfer the sub-custodian's equitable interest to the investor or lead custodian.[33]

Sub-Trust

4.26 Even if an assignment is barred, a sub-custodian should find other means of passing on the substance of his equitable interest to the purported 'assignee'. Should the sub-custodian prove reluctant to do this, the purported 'assignee' may be able to enforce the transfer of such benefits by seeking a court declaration of a con-

---

[30] ibid 554, 557. See also *Bysouth v Shire of Blackburn and Mitcham (No 2)* [1928] VLR 562, SC of Victoria, Australia.

[31] Goode (n 26 above) 556. However, although Lord Browne-Wilkinson in *Linden Gardens* had apparently accepted Goode's analysis, he cast doubt on this by deprecating any distinction in practice between the assignment of rights to future performance under a contract and the assignment of fruits of performance, at 105, and by expressing 'no view' on this point at 107; these doubts are reinforced by *Circuit Systems v Zuken-Redac* [1996] 2 BCLC 349, 359–360 per Staughton LJ.

[32] However, this is no longer an assignment because there is no substitution of obligee for the depository. The benefits must first go to the sub-custodian, but may then be further transferred.

[33] *Grey v Inland Revenue Commissioners* [1958] 1 Ch 375, 381 per Upjohn J, at first instance.

structive trust over benefits received by the sub-custodian which should have been transferred. An analogy may be drawn with the transfer of assets to a recipient who has undertaken to pass on or hold after-acquired property to a third party. Although the recipient remains entitled to the benefit, he holds the asset received for the third party, who would have acquired an equitable interest in the benefit once it reached the hands of the recipient.[34]

Whether other means of transfer are barred or not, the voluntary establishment of **4.27** a sub-trust over his entitlements by the beneficiary of a principal trust has long been recognised to be another method of passing on benefits.[35] In Figure 4.3, this requires the sub-custodian to create a sub-trust based on his entitlements from the depository in favour of the lead custodian or investor. There may be a number of tiers of sub-trusts.

Figure 4.3: Tiers of sub-trusts

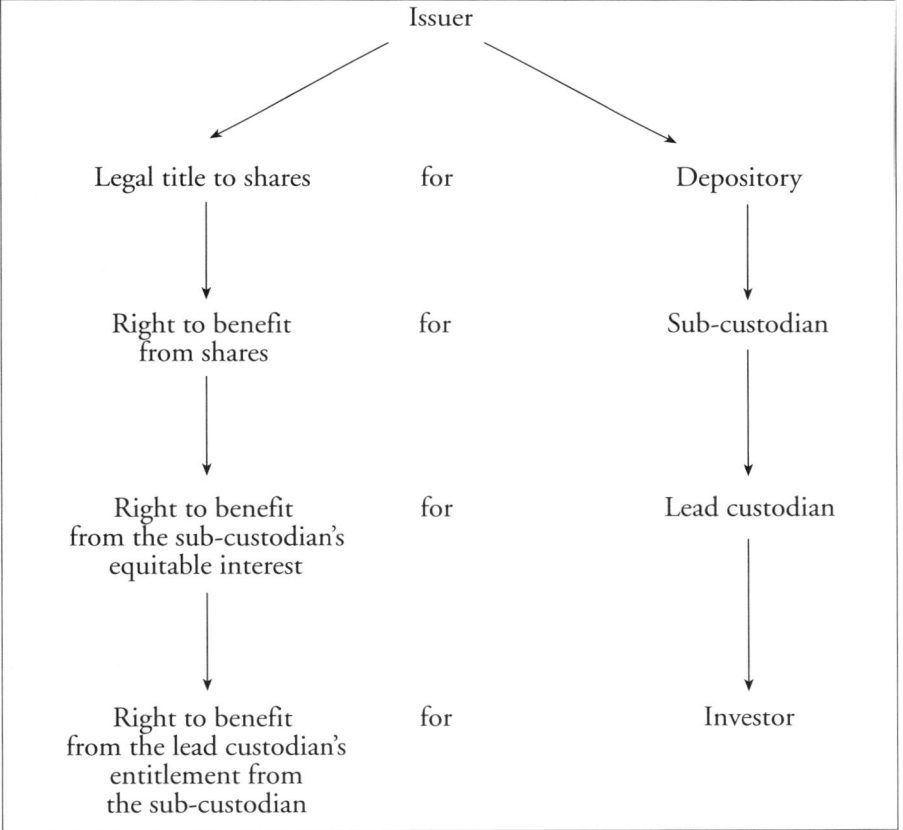

---

[34] *Holroyd v Marshall* (1862) X HLC 191, 209 per Lord Westbury LC, 11 ER 999; *Tailby v Official Receiver* (1888) 13 App Cas 523.
[35] *Re Turcan* (1888) 40 ChD 5, 10–11 per Cotton LJ.

4.28 It has been suggested that whether a beneficiary under an existing trust establishes such a sub-trust or issues orders to his trustee to hold for another, this amounts to 'really indistinguishable methods of operating to transfer the equitable title by way of declaration of trust in contrast to doing so by way of assignment'.[36] The implication of this view is that a head trustee holds directly for the beneficiary of a sub-trust. There is academic support for this.[37] It is suggested that where a sub-trust is a bare trust[38] the sub-trustee is ignored, excluded from the structure, leaving the main trustee (depository) holding the benefit of the asset directly for the ultimate beneficiary (lead custodian or investor). A number of cases are often cited in support of this proposition, including *Re Lashmar, Moody v Penfold*,[39] *Grainge v Wilberforce*,[40] *Onslow v Wallis*[41] and *Head v Lord Teynham*.[42] Since it is likely that at least one amongst tiers of custodian intermediaries may come within the definition of a bare trust, it is essential to determine whether tiers of sub-trusts may be collapsed in this way in order to identify what precisely a beneficiary of intermediary custodial holdings structured as sub-trusts enjoys.

4.29 The essence of a trust is the division between separate parties of a bare title to something and entitlement to the benefit of the thing. In creating a sub-trust over an equitable entitlement, a division would take place in the sub-custodian's equitable interest, such that he is left with a bare equitable title to the securities held by the depository and the further (sub-) beneficiary would take the benefit of the sub-custodian's entitlement.[43] The right to benefit enjoyed under the sub-trust is a new equitable right created by the sub-trustee in relation to the sub-trustee's own subsisting equitable interest, the creation of a subsidiary equitable interest. This subsidiary equitable interest is created out of, and cannot therefore be equated with, the original equitable interest. Further, because this subsidiary title is based

---

[36] *Grey v Inland Revenue Commissioners* [1958] 1 Ch 375, 382 per Upjohn J, at first instance.

[37] For example DJ Hayton, *Hayton and Marshall, Cases and Commentary on the Law of Trusts* (9th edn, 1991) 62; AJ Oakley, *Parker and Mellows: The Modern Law of Trusts* (6th edn, 1994) 36; DJ Hayton, *Underhill and Hayton, Law Relating to Trusts and Trustees* (15th edn, 1995) 208–209; and RA Pearce and J Stevens, *The Law of Equitable Obligations* (1995) 578–579; who cite *Re Lashmar, Moody v Penfold* [1891] 1 Ch 258 and *Grainge v Wilberforce* (1889) 5 TLR 436 in support of this proposition. Hayton in *Cases and Commentary* (above) cites, in addition, *Onslow v Wallis* (1849) 1 Mac & G 506, 41 ER 1361.

   WJ Mowbray, *Lewin on Trusts* (16th edn, 1964) 623 makes the same proposition; as do PV Baker and PStJ Langan, *Snell's Equity* (29th edn, 1990) 103, citing *Head v Lord Teynham* (1783) 1 Cox 57, 29 ER 1061.

[38] A bare trust is defined as one where the trustee has no active duties to perform, *Christie v Ovington* (1875) 1 ChD 279; *Re Cunningham and Frayling* [1891] 2 Ch 567. For another view see *Morgan v Swansea Urban Sanitary Authority* (1878) 9 ChD 582 per Jessel MR.

[39] [1891] 1 Ch 258.

[40] (1889) 5 TLR 436.

[41] (1849) 1 Mac & G 506, 41 ER 1361.

[42] (1783) 1 Cox 57, 29 ER 1061.

[43] B Green, 'Grey, Oughtred and Vandervell: A Contextual Reappraisal' (1984) 47 MLR 384, 396.

on the first equitable title, it must depend for its own existence on the continued existence of the first equitable title. The fact that the sub-trustee has not taken an active role in the process does not mean he has done nothing. He will have performed the precise function for which he was appointed, that of acting as a repository for an entitlement to be received from the head trustee. Particularly in the case of custody, the role of a nominee is an important one that may not be ignored.[44] The fact that the ultimate beneficiary should receive the substance of the entitlements passed down the chain should not cloud the issue that his entitlement is derived from the (sub- or sub-sub-, etc) trustee holding directly for him and not from a trustee holding for another tier above.

Some of the cases cited in support of the proposition that extended trusts may be **4.30** collapsed are simply not relevant.[45] *Onslow v Wallis*[46] is authority for the proposition that a trustee subject to specific instructions is obliged to fulfil them and cannot enquire as to their purpose; *Re Lashmar*[47] merely suggests that where the trust of a one-time trustee has ended he is no longer a trustee and, as such, he is no longer relevant to proceedings in relation to the property which formed the basis of the one-time trust. Although *Grainge v Wilberforce*[48] offers direct support for the theory of collapsing extended trusts, the passage[49] which suggests this does not specifically address bare trustees but suggests that sub-trusts in general are collapsed, whether or not they are bare, a suggestion which would make a nonsense of the position of intermediary trustees with active duties. Indeed, the case is not so much authority for the collapse of extended trusts, but relates to the formalities for dealing with the head legal title where there is a structure of tiers of trusts. It suggests that where an ultimate beneficiary is in a position to direct how his (intermediate) trustee should act, such intermediate trustee is not necessary to dealings by the head trustee agreed to by the ultimate beneficiary. This, of course, does not mean that the intermediate trustee necessarily drops out of the picture, as may be suggested by one passage in Chitty J's first instance judgment, but merely indicates that the intermediate trustee is not a necessary party to the

---

[44] For instance, to allow the investor to enjoy an entitlement where he cannot take legal title directly. See the section on nominees in Chapter 1.

[45] Green (n 43 above) 397–398.

[46] (1849) 1 Mac & G 506, 515–516 per Cottenham LC, 41 ER 1361. 'The ground on which I proceed is this, that there are persons appointed by the owner of the property to whom the property is to be conveyed. They are the only parties having a right to it, and whether or not they have power afterwards to dispose of all beneficial interest in it is a matter with which the Defendant Wallis, as a mere owner of the legal estate, has nothing whatever to do.' Lord Cottenham's distinction between a right of entitlement and alienation of the right to benefit therefrom is inconsistent with the citation of this case as authority for the theory that sub-trusts are collapsed.

[47] [1891] 1 Ch 258, 267 per Lindley LJ: 'William [sic.] Moody . . . is, or rather was, . . . a bare trustee', and 269 per Fry LJ: 'John Moody has no title to claim the conveyance from the trustee of Charles's [sic.] will'.

[48] (1889) 5 TLR 436.

[49] ibid 437.

transaction in relation to the legal title vested in the head trustee. Furthermore, the only case (*Head v Lord Teynham*) cited by Chitty J in *Grainge v Wilberforce* does not support the view that sub-trustees absolutely drop out of the picture. *Head v Lord Teynham*[50] provides that where the ultimate beneficiary agrees with the main trustee to effect a transaction in relation to the legal title held by the main trustee, the sub-trustee is not a necessary party to the transaction. The case is authority for the proposition that a sub-trustee has no interest in lawful dealings with the legal title held and dealt with by a principal trustee. This does not suggest that sub-trustees necessarily drop out of extended trust structures.

4.31 In view of the foregoing, the position taken in this work is that the theory that extended trusts may be collapsed is doubtful. The theory seems to focus on the fact that benefits should ordinarily flow from head trustee to ultimate beneficiary, ignoring strict legal analysis. A stricter legal analysis suggests that each tier in a structure of sub-trusts must be respected, with each (sub-) trustee holding exclusively for his direct beneficiary.

4.32 If this stricter analysis is applied to tiers of (sub-) trusts established by intermediary custodians, it suggests that beneficiaries of lower tier (sub-) trusts established by lead or global custodians may not interact directly with depository or other sub-custodian trustees. Whatever benefits come to an investor must come through the intermediary holding directly for him, not the intermediary holding the underlying assets under a main trust at a different tier. It is only with intermediaries holding directly for them that investors enjoy direct dealings: these will often be their global custodians.

(2) Formalities for Dealing with Equitable Interests

4.33 Section 53(1)(c) of the Law of Property Act 1925 provides that 'a disposition of an equitable interest or trust subsisting at the time of the disposition, must be in writing signed by the person disposing of the same, or by his agent thereunto lawfully authorised in writing or by will'.

4.34 Although the parameters of the word disposition were not defined in *Grey v Inland Revenue Commissioners*,[51] indications were given by the Court of Appeal and the House of Lords as to how the word is to be considered. The view was taken that the word should be given its ordinary and natural meaning. The Oxford Dictionaries suggest that the word, when used in the sense of transferring a thing,

---

[50] (1783) 1 Cox 57, 29 ER 1061. The case relates to the sale of land by the head trustee without involving the sub-trustee. The question was whether the sub-trustee needed to be party to the transaction. The plaintiff claimed that 'as the original trustees . . . who had the legal estate, and all the children who had the beneficial interest were before the court, there was no occasion to make the other trustee a party'. The court agreed.

[51] [1958] 1 Ch 690, CA; [1960] AC 1, 12 and 15 per Viscount Simonds and 15 per Lord Radcliffe, HL.

means 'getting rid of' or 'making over' a thing.[52] On this approach, the question of disposition is principally to be determined from the perspective of the donor, regardless of what the recipient actually receives.[53]

The House of Lords in *Grey v Inland Revenue Commissioners*[54] confirmed that **4.35** even a narrow reading of disposition would encompass the assignment of the entirety of an equitable interest.[55] It also determined that a direction by one entitled to an equitable interest under a trust to his trustee to hold for another would also constitute a disposition within the ordinary meaning of the word.[56]

It is more debatable whether this definition of disposition encompasses the decla- **4.36** ration of a sub-trust by the beneficiary of a trust in relation to his entitlement. If the strict analysis of the mechanics of sub-trusts that is proposed above is accepted, the section may not be applicable. A declaration of sub-trust does not get rid of the existing interest of the sub-trustee; all he does is to carve out of his interest a new and subsidiary interest for the sub-trust's beneficiary. Nevertheless, there are suggestions[57] that the provision should apply to sub-trusts on the grounds that even if the establishment of a sub-trust does not involve an outright disposition, it entails a part-disposal of the equitable interest in relation to which the sub-trust was established. It has also been suggested that the establishment of a sub-trust results in the transfer of the benefit of the equitable interest, a difference of form for a substantially similar transaction to an assignment or order to a trustee to hold for another that is 'equally deserving of formal protection'.[58] This view may be justified on the basis that the House of Lords in *Grey v Inland Revenue Commissioners*[59] seemed to take the view that 'disposition' in section 53(1)(c) should be given an expansive, ordinary construction.

In any event, it is submitted that the practical significance of section 53(1)(c) of **4.37** the Law of Property Act 1925 in the present context remains slight. As a rule, the record-keeping of (sub-) custodians as to who is entitled to which of the assets they hold on their books should amount to sufficient writing to satisfy the requirement.[60] The writing that legally constitutes the disposition may be contained in two or more documents.[61] Further, for transactions covered by regulation 32(5) of

---

[52] *Oxford English Dictionary* (2nd edn, 1989) Vol IV, 822, cols 1–2, sense 4a; *New Shorter Oxford English Dictionary* (1993) Vol 1, 700, col 1, sense 1.
[53] *Grey v Inland Revenue Commissioners* [1958] 1 Ch 690, 723 per Ormerod LJ, CA.
[54] [1960] AC 1.
[55] ibid 13 per Viscount Simonds and 16 per Lord Radcliffe.
[56] ibid 12–13 per Viscount Simonds and 15 per Lord Radcliffe.
[57] Green (n 43 above) 398.
[58] ibid.
[59] [1960] AC 1, 12, 15 per Viscount Simonds and, especially, 15 per Lord Radcliffe.
[60] Interpretation Act 1978, s 5, Sch 1: ' "Writing" includes typing, printing, lithography, photography and other modes of representing or reproducing words in a visible form'.
[61] *Re Danish Bacon Co Ltd* [1971] 1 WLR 248, 254–255 per Megarry J.

the Uncertificated Securities Regulations 1995, SI 1995/3272, the requirements of section 53(1)(c) of the 1925 Act are expressly disapplied. This disapplies the requirement of writing, would it otherwise have applied, from transactions undertaken in CREST.

C. Rights of Investors in Relation to Assets in Sub-Custody

4.38 The above analysis suggests that the interest of an investor using a sub-custodian in relation to the underlying assets depends on whether the sub-custodian is a true intermediary or not and, if an intermediary, the method by which the benefits are passed from tier to tier. Where the sub-custodial structure is non-intermediary, the investor owns the securities in custody, regardless of the location of the token. Where the custody is intermediated, there are various options.

4.39 If benefits are passed by the sub-custodian by way of assignment or by orders to his own intermediary, the lead custodian or investor will be able to step into the shoes of the sub-custodian and be brought into direct contact with the depository. This enables the party in whose favour the assignment or orders are made to enjoy a direct equitable interest in the securities that make up the underlying custody assets. By these two methods the extended tiers of sub-custody are collapsed into a simple trustee-beneficiary trust relationship involving the depository as trustee over the securities in custody with the lead custodian or investor as the new beneficiary. The analysis of this relationship is the same as that of any other single-tier intermediary custody.

4.40 However, as may more typically obtain in practice, the benefit may be passed by the creation of a sub-trust by the sub-custodian over his entitlement. With reference to Figure 4.3, the interests of the various parties may be described as follows: (i) the depository holds a bare legal title to the assets in its care; (ii) the sub-custodian is entitled to the benefit of the interest of the depository in relation to the assets held by the depository for the sub-custodian; (iii) the lead custodian is entitled to the benefit of the interest enjoyed by the sub-custodian; and (iv) the investor is entitled to the benefit of the interest enjoyed by the lead custodian. The important point to note is that the beneficiary of the sub-trust does not enjoy a direct interest in relation to the underlying assets under the main trust and does not enjoy direct relations with the depository.

4.41 It is not inconceivable that tiers of sub-custody may be made up of a mixture of non-intermediary and intermediary custody. Using Figure 4.3 as a model, the depository may be custodian of the token of ownership of registrable securities. In such a case, the depository would be bailee of the certificate. The sub-custodian would be the head trustee, with legal title to the securities, holding the benefit of the securities for the lead custodian who enjoys a direct equitable title in relation thereto. However, such equitable title would be bare, as the lead custodian would be obliged to pass any benefits gained thereby to the investor.

D. Increased Risk to Investors by Sub-Custody

Where the investor enjoys legal title to securities the tokens for which are in sub-custody, the principal risk is that of misfeasance by the custodian with the certificate, but this is unlikely to impact adversely on the investor's entitlement to the underlying securities. In the case of intermediary custody, however, if the custodian wrongfully alienates the securities to a bona fide purchaser, such purchaser will take free of the interest of the investor, leaving the investor with a possibly worthless claim against the custodian. **4.42**

Where there are sub-custodial holdings constituted by more than one tier of intermediaries, the investor must inevitably bear an increased risk, if only by virtue of the fact that there are more custodians in his chain of entitlements. First, it is possible that at one tier the benefit is to be passed by an improperly constituted trust. In such an event, every tier below bears the credit risk of the creditor or obligor at the tier that fails to be constituted as a trust. Inevitably, the more tiers there are, the greater the chances that one tier may have been improperly set up. Even if the chain of intermediaries is properly constituted as sub-trusts, the risk to an investor in these circumstances is increased by the fact that the benefit of the securities is passed from one intermediary to another until the investor is reached, by way of increasingly removed entitlements in tiers of subsidiary interests carved out of the original direct beneficial rights in relation to the securities. A wrongful alienation at any tier in circumstances that enable the alienee to take free of subsidiary equitable interests will necessarily be prejudicial to the rights enjoyed by the investor. **4.43**

E. Privity

Whilst investors generally enjoy contractual and other relations with their custodians, the method by which the benefits of the assets held by sub-custodians are passed to them may also bring them into direct relations with their sub-custodians. The question of privity is important for various reasons; it may determine to whom the sub-custodian owes duties or may have recourse to enforce any indemnities for holding the custody assets. Privity may also determine against whom the investor would have contractual recourse in case of loss. **4.44**

The present analysis indicates that the investor will only enjoy direct relations with the depository, as ultimate sub-custodian, where the custody is **4.45** non-intermediary; or the beneficiary of the depository has assigned his interest to the investor or directed the depository to hold his interest for the investor. In the more likely event of tiers of sub-trusts, the investor will only enjoy direct relations with his own lead custodian.

5

THE NATURE OF THE INVESTOR'S INTEREST

The law governing the offer and operation of custodial services in England is an **5.01** amalgam of the common law of contract, trusts and agency, as supplemented or supplanted by regulatory law. In the USA, the authors of the 1994 version of article 8 of the Uniform Commercial Code (UCC) sought to avoid leaving the determination of the interest of entitlement holders of a securities intermediary to 'common law property concepts' on the basis that those 'concepts do not work for the indirect holding system'.[1] The analysis in the preceding chapters suggests that reliance on those same concepts in England, even if not wholly unworkable, can often be complex.[2]

A. Single Tier

(1) Non-Intermediary Custody

Where there is non-intermediary custody, the investor whose certificates are with **5.02** the custodian remains the legal owner of the securities represented thereby, maintaining a direct link with them. However, this type of custodial holding represents a minority of assets in custody. The vast majority of assets in custody are in

---

[1] Paragraph 1, Comment No 2 to s 8-503, The American Law Institute and National Conference of Commissioners on Uniform States, *Uniform Commercial Code* (14th edn, 1995), Official Text with Comments.

[2] Many of the issues to watch out for are highlighted in the Annex, Checklist of the main legal issues in assessing custodial arrangements.

intermediary custody in order for the beneficiaries of them to take advantage of the value-enhancing services of modern custodial practices.

(2) Intermediary Custody

5.03 Where there is intermediary custody, the investor surrenders his direct rights against the issuer of the securities for an alternative set of rights.

5.04 The investor enjoys personal rights against the custodian for the enjoyment of the benefit of the securities in his care and for delivery of equivalent securities if he calls for this. If restricted to these rights, however, the investor would be left carrying the credit risk of his custodian. In order to avoid this risk, custodial holdings are established as a trust so that the investor also enjoys an equitable interest in the assets in custody which would preclude those assets being claimed by the creditors of the custodian in the event of the custodian's insolvency.

5.05 Therefore, the property of an investor who has transferred assets into intermediary custody is no longer the securities themselves, but a package of rights consisting of rights against the custodian and an equitable interest in the assets held by the custodian for him.

Identification of Interest for Trust

5.06 Where the custodian separates the assets in his care into segregated, client-specific holdings, this achieves the degree of identification necessary for the establishment of a trust. Where client assets are only separated from the custodian's own assets, but otherwise held in a pool without individual designation, this poses some problems of identification. Although the common law has rules for the identification of claims to mixtures that would permit the establishment of trusts in favour of investors, the analysis in Chapter 3 suggests that there remain difficulties. These rules may produce 'fortuitous, arbitrary, and unpredictable results for customers who claim interests in fungible bulks of securities controlled by a common intermediary',[3] such that '[s]imilarly placed claimants may receive very different treatment'.[4] Further, although there are cases which permit the establishment of a trust over part of a pool, where that pool is composed of assets owned by the holder of the pool and assets held for others, this idea has generated much controversy.

5.07 The new article 8 of the UCC avoids the complex and often controversial process of identification required for the establishment of proprietary interests under the common law. Section 8-503(a) simply declares the achievement of the state of

---

[3] CW Mooney, Jr, 'Beyond Negotiability: A New Model for Transfer and Pledge of Interests in Securities Controlled by Intermediaries' (1990) 12 Cardozo Law Review 307, 350.
[4] ibid.

affairs sought by the establishment of a trust,[5] that assets held by the intermediary for clients may not be claimed by the custodian's creditors. In view of the difficulties encountered in a common law analysis of modern custodial practices under English law, consideration may be given to the adoption of a similar provision in England. One attractive feature of such a provision is that it would finally put to rest any controversy as to whether a custodian could constitute himself trustee over part of a pool of assets held by him.

Direct Rights in Underlying Assets

Under English law, by virtue of being beneficiary of a trust over custody assets, **5.08** investors are recognised as enjoying direct equitable rights with respect to the custodial assets. However, since they are not the legal owners of the securities that constitute the custodial holding, investors cannot in ordinary circumstances exercise rights with respect to the securities as against the issuer. The custodian is the legal owner of the custody assets and the investors are the beneficial owners who enjoy the benefit of the securities through the custodian. The direct equitable right is not of any practical significance outside the insolvency of the custodian or the misapplication of custody assets where the custodian cannot make good the error and the assets remain identifiable.

The investor enjoys a package of rights, with different rights applicable in differ- **5.09** ent circumstances. In the ordinary operations of a custodian, the investor has no rights against the issuer for the enjoyment of the benefits of the asset in custody in the custodian's name. To enjoy the benefits, the investor may look only to his custodian. However, in the event of the insolvency of the custodian the investor will be recognised as enjoying direct equitable rights with respect to the custody assets so that they may not be claimed by the custodian's creditors.

The direct proprietary interest in custody assets need not be a clog on the wheel of **5.10** capital market transactions. The discussion of a delegated power of disposition in Chapter 2 suggests that a custodian could, in appropriate circumstances, offer transfers of custody assets that take free of this retained right.

In the ordinary course of events, the investor with assets in intermediary custody **5.11** exchanges his rights against the issuer for new rights against the intermediary for the enjoyment of any benefits which pass to the custodian by virtue of the custodial holding. However, if the investor's rights are ever going to be more than mere personal rights against the custodian, these personal rights will have to be backed

---

[5] 'To the extent necessary for a securities intermediary to satisfy all security entitlements to a particular financial asset, all interests in that financial asset held by the securities intermediary are held by the securities intermediary for the entitlement holders, are not property of the securities intermediary, and are not subject to claims of creditors of the securities intermediary, except as provided in Section 8-511.'

up by direct proprietary rights in the underlying assets, as a protection against the insolvency of the custodian. This much is not in dispute;[6] the question is whether common law property concepts of tracing adequately address the issue, or whether this would be better dealt with by specific regulation.

Proprietary Rights in the Absence of Tracing?

5.12 Under English law the investor's property rights are recognised simply on the basis of the common law rules of tracing. This approach is eschewed in the USA by the drafters of new article 8 in favour of an approach which accords property rights to investors on the basis of four criteria: (i) insolvency of the custodian; (ii) the custodian does not have sufficient assets to meet the legitimate claims of the investor; (iii) the custodian was in breach of his duties when 'transferring the financial asset or interest therein to the purchaser';[7] and (iv) the transferee of the asset either did not give value, did not obtain control or acted in collusion in the breach of duty by the custodian.

5.13 Notwithstanding the attempt in the USA to break from the common law tracing law analysis of investors' interests, the difference in operation between the English common law and article 8 approaches to the recognition of proprietary rights may be described, as recognised in the Official Commentary to new article 8, as slight.[8] As section 8-503(e)(3) of new article 8 apparently concedes, one of the criteria on which proprietary rights are accepted under new article 8 is the fact of wrongful alienation of the investor's assets.[9]

5.14 Indeed, it is difficult to see how proprietary rights could be recognised in an orderly fashion that avoided arbitrariness, without some element of tracing. The fear of tracing as expressed in the Official Commentary to new article 8 seems misplaced. It is stated in the Commentary that '[t]he idea that discrete objects might be traced through the hands of different persons has no place in the Revised Article 8 rules for the indirect holding system'.[10] However, as is demonstrated in Chapter 8 on breach of duty, tracing does not involve following discrete assets. Tracing seeks to reflect how value in original assets is notionally transferred from one repository to another.[11] In undertaking this process, one is freed from the con-

---

[6] In the Official Commentary to article 8 of the UCC, the package of rights enjoyed by an investor with assets in custody under new article 8 of the UCC is said to consist of 'rights and interests that a person has against the person's securities intermediary and the property held by the intermediary': para 1, Comment No 2 to s 8-503 UCC (n 1 above).

[7] Section 8-503(e)(3) UCC (n 1 above).

[8] Paragraph 4, Comment No 2 to s 8-503 UCC (n 1 above).

[9] Paragraph 3, Comment No 2 to s 8-503 UCC (n 1 above). See also JL Schroeder, 'Is Article 8 Finally Ready This Time? The Radical Reform of Secured Lending on Wall Street' [1994] Colum Bus L Rev 291, 373.

[10] Paragraph 1, Comment No 2 to s 8-503 UCC (n 1 above).

[11] LD Smith, *The Law of Tracing* (1997) 248.

straints of following a particular thing and one traces the notional path through various tangible or intangible repositories in which such value passes or abides. The substitute repository in which the value inheres is treated as the claimant's asset.[12]

Nevertheless, there are some clear points of departure between the English **5.15** approach and the approach of new article 8. Whereas the English approach specifies that transferees without notice take free, new article 8 applies the collusion test as set out above. A further difference in emphasis is that whilst the English approach sets limits on the effectiveness of claims by recognising a class of transferees that take free, article 8 sets limits on when a claim against a transferee can be made in the first place.

B. Multi-Tier

(1) Non-Intermediary Custody

As with any other case of non-intermediary custody, the investor retains direct **5.16** rights in his securities which he can exercise against the issuer. As discussed in Chapter 4, these rights are in addition to whatever rights the investor enjoys by virtue of the principles of bailment (including sub- and quasi-bailment) against his custodian or sub-custodian with respect to the chattel in custody.

(2) Intermediary Custody

In a case of multi-tier intermediary custody, there would be at least the investor's **5.17** direct, lead or global, custodian and a sub-custodian holding for the lead custodian. The sub-custodian may simply be a depository where the underlying assets, the securities themselves, are held or an offshore custodian for holding foreign assets.

In the multi-tier scenario, it is the lead custodian, as beneficiary of the sub- **5.18** custodian, that enjoys rights against the sub-custodian and direct equitable rights in the underlying assets, the securities, held by the sub-custodian. The interest of the lead custodian is in turn held for the investor. Therefore, assuming a validly constituted trust by the lead custodian in favour of the investor, the investor enjoys proprietary rights with respect to the lead custodian's interest in the sub-custodian's trust for the lead custodian.

The distinction between rights with respect to the lead custodian's interest and the **5.19** rights which constitute the lead custodian's interest must be emphasised. The interest of the investor with assets in multi-tier custody consists of rights against

---

[12] ibid 119–120.

the lead custodian and proprietary rights with respect to the lead custodian's interest, consisting of rights against the sub-custodian and rights with respect to the securities held by the sub-custodian, together with whatever benefits accrue to the lead custodian thereby. The investor does not enjoy direct rights with respect to the underlying securities. The investor is not substituted for the lead custodian.

5.20   In view of this analysis, a proper assessment of the practical utility or economic value of an investor's interest whose assets are in multi-tier intermediary custody will necessitate at least the following: (i) an appraisal of the rights enjoyed by the beneficiaries of each tier of custody; in the example given above this will involve as a minimum the rights of the lead custodian and the investor; and (ii) assumptions or an assessment of the honesty of each tier of custodian, as to whether the custodian will do what he is meant to do and pass benefits to the next tier. If the sub-custodian were somehow able to alienate benefits which should have been passed to the lead custodian, the investor's interest in the rights of the lead custodian, though valid and subsisting, would be financially worthless.

5.21   Based on the foregoing, Mooney's characterisation of the nature of claim of an investor with assets in multi-tier custody as 'not-quite-property, not-quite-unsecured claim'[13] would seem not to reflect properly all of the features of the interest as it would exist under a chain of trusts in English law. Mooney's assessment seems to confuse the nature of the investor's interest with an appraisal of the likelihood that the investor will receive benefits which should ordinarily accrue to him from underlying securities. It may be the increased risk of benefits being untraceably lost at one of the tiers of custody that suggests elements of an unsecured claim. However, this increased risk does not turn the investor's proprietary claim with respect to the interest of the lead custodian into an unsecured one. Assuming a properly constituted trust relationship between lead custodian and investor, the investor's claim is proprietary. The essential point to note, however, is that the thing to which the proprietary rights fasten is not the underlying securities, but the interests of the lead custodian with respect to a sub-trust established by the sub-custodian.

C. The Need for Legislation

5.22   In the USA, the architects of new article 8 took the view that leaving the analysis of the nature of an investor's interest to common law property principles was unsuited to the practice of modern custody. They therefore drafted new article 8 by which provision the interests of investors with assets in custody are described.

---

[13] CW Mooney, Jr, 'Beyond Negotiability: A New Model for Transfer and Pledge of Interests in Securities Controlled by Intermediaries' (1990) 12 Cardozo Law Review 307, 413.

Whether England should follow suit necessitates an assessment which balances **5.23** the degree of uncertainty and complexity of the common law approach against the benefits to be derived from any clarity which may be brought by legislation, the cost of new legislation and the risk of new problems or uncertainties which may be engendered by the new legislation. The goals of any legislation should be clearly articulated and also assessed on the basis of the likelihood of success.

Legislation would be useful in that it would highlight problem areas and would **5.24** make an attempt to offer solutions, eg whether a trustee can hold part of his assets on trust without segregating them from his own. However, legislation cannot solve all perceived problems. For instance, if the goal of legislation were to eliminate any need for tracing in the assessment of an investor's interest, this goal would be likely to remain unachieved.

In his article, Mooney states that it is unlikely that specially drafted legal rules **5.25** alone will be able to adequately address concerns about the protection of those who receive transfers through intermediaries. He expressed the view that '[f]inancial institutions that serve as securities intermediaries have special roles and characteristics. A prudent regulatory approach to inherent intermediary risk, coordinated with property law, may provide a more feasible route to enhanced safety'.[14] This is what already seems to obtain in England. The assessment of the nature of an investor's rights where his assets are in custody is left to common law property concepts and the Financial Services Act 1986 (Extension of Scope of Act) Order 1996, SI 1996/2958, promotes proper safeguarding and administration of custody assets. In this way, benefits should be passed from tier to tier as anticipated and the investor's interest recognised by common law property concepts will reflect the financial value it is meant to have.

In the event, however, that the decision is taken to undertake a wholesale review **5.26** of the law of England as pertains to the custody of securities, the list of issues in the Annex would serve as a useful starting point for the areas that need to be considered.

---

[14] ibid 414.

6

CUSTODY ASSETS AS SECURITY FOR LENDERS

In the capital and money markets, the availability and/or pricing of loans may **6.01** depend on the borrower's ability to offer some form of security[1] to the lender, especially security that will be effective in the insolvency of the borrower. For many participants in such markets, a large part of their assets are made up of shares, bonds and other securities which may be held by their custodian. For creditors to be willing to accept custody assets as security for the debtor's obligations, at least two conditions need to be met. The custody assets must be of a type satisfactory to the secured lender; and the asset offered must be susceptible to the intended or comparable form of security so that, in the case of real security, the creditor can assert a proprietary right to the assets offered as security and thereby protect itself from the consequences of the debtor's insolvency.

English law distinguishes between the creation of real security, by which security **6.02** interests are conferred on a creditor, and quasi-security, by which other means of

---

[1] Security in general means 'an additional right, which tends to render more certain or probable the discharge of a debt or claim than if satisfaction were dependent only on the person primarily liable'. See *Maddaford v de Vantee* [1951] SASR 259, 267 per Mayo J, SC of South Australia; *Broad v Commissioner of Stamp Duties* [1980] 2 NSWLR 40, 45 per Lee J, SC of New South Wales, Australia.

offering some degree of assurance of repayment to the creditor are employed.[2] One of the principal consequences of this distinction is whether any formalities have to be observed for the validity of the method of security.

6.03 Real security 'is created where a person ("the creditor") to whom an obligation is owed by another ("the debtor") by statute or contract, in addition to the personal promise of the debtor to discharge the obligation, obtains rights exercisable against some property in which the debtor has an interest in order to enforce the discharge of the debtor's obligation to the creditor'.[3] Goode suggests that security in the strict sense involves the acquisition of a *ius in re aliena* and that a right *in re sua* would not qualify.[4] In his view, there are 'only four types of consensual security known to English law: the pledge, the contractual lien, the mortgage and the charge'.[5] Quasi-security involves the granting of rights that produce a security effect without constituting a security at law. The security effect achieved is that the lender enjoys some degree of priority in the insolvency of the borrower, for example, by way of retention of title, contractual set-off, flawed asset and negative pledge.[6]

6.04 Depending on the terms of custody, a custodian may be permitted to trade or lend custody assets. As observed in Chapter 3, such powers make the characterisation of the investor's interest difficult. Since real security must relate to identifiable assets, these powers may also cast doubt on the susceptibility of custody assets to real security.[7] Even if these doubts were overcome, this factor would tend to limit the range of methods by which real security is effected. In view of these limitations to the use of custody assets for real security, as well as the burden of having to observe various formalities to validate the method of real security, quasi-security is often considered instead. However, there arises the risk that a quasi-security

---

[2] WJ Gough, *Company Charges* (2nd edn, 1996) 3–4. Although this has been called into question by AL Diamond, *A Review of Security Interests in Property* (HMSO for DTI, 1989), paras 3.1–3.10 and 9.3.2, this remains the state of the law. See also generally the report of the Crowther Committee on Consumer Credit (Cmnd 4596, 1971) vol 1, Parts 4–5.

[3] *Re Paramount Airways Ltd* [1990] BCC 130, 149 per Browne-Wilkinson V-C.

[4] Goode, *Commercial Law* (2nd edn, 1995) 642.

[5] RM Goode, *Legal Problems of Credit and Security* (2nd edn, 1988) 10. See also Bell, *Modern Law of Personal Property* (1989) 202–203. This may be contrasted with s 1-201(37) of the Uniform Commercial Code which provides that ' "Security interest" means an interest in personal property or fixtures which secures payment or performance of an obligation. The retention or reservation of title by a seller of goods notwithstanding shipment or delivery to the buyer . . . is limited in effect to a reservation of a "security interest". The term also includes any interest of a buyer of accounts or chattel paper which is subject to Article 9': The American Law Institute and National Conference of Commissioners on Uniform States, *Uniform Commercial Code* (14th edn, 1995), Official Text with Comments.

[6] M Phillips and F Oditah, 'Securities over Moveables: An Understanding of the English Position' (1996) Insolvency Lawyer, Special Issue, 11–12.

[7] This is developed in the discussion of particular forms of real security.

may be re-characterised as a real security entailing formalities the failure to observe which may render the security invalid or of inferior priority.[8]

Against this background, this chapter explores how custody assets may be used for **6.05** security. Since the essence of security is the provision of safeguards for the creditor, regardless of the form that such safeguards may take, it seems appropriate for us to consider both real security and quasi-security. Nevertheless, this chapter does not seek to undertake a general survey of security. Only those characteristics that are of particular significance to the use of custody assets for security will be addressed.

A. The Asset Offered as Security

With non-intermediated custody, the investor enjoys original rights in relation to **6.06** the securities. As observed in Chapter 2, this type of structure will generally only arise where the registered owner of securities evidenced by a certificate or who is entitled to negotiable securities which have been indorsed in his favour chooses to keep such certificates in custody. In this case, an investor has two things that he may offer as security, his legal title and/or certificate to his securities.

In the case of intermediated custody, what the investor may offer depends on the **6.07** manner in which the custodial structure is set up. If the investor is the creditor of the custodian, being owed mere personal rights of re-delivery as opposed to enjoying proprietary interests in relation to custody assets, he would only be able to offer the promise of the custodian as security. Some creditors may not be content with security based on such a promise because it would mean running the credit risk of the intermediary promissor.

Difficult analytical problems may also arise in relation to the grant of security over **6.08** pooled fungible securities.[9] Even if the investor of assets in intermediary custody enjoys beneficial rights in relation to assets held by the custodian, what the investor has to offer depends on the number of tiers of intermediation. With single-tier custody, the investor may be recognised by virtue of a validly constituted trust as the beneficial owner of the securities held by the custodian and would be in a position to create security interests directly in relation to the securities. Where, however, there are two or more tiers of intermediary custodians, it is the ultimate sub-custodian who is the holder of record, and the intermediary custodian he holds for is the equitable owner of the securities. The investor only enjoys, and can therefore only offer as collateral, rights with respect to the entitlement of

---

[8] This risk in relation to offshore assets is considered in Chapter 10.

[9] See Chapter 3 where the problem of ascertainment of investors' proprietary interests in pooled fungible securities is discussed. See also C Mercer and D Sandy, 'Security Over Unascertained Shares' (1997) 12(8) BJIBFL 399 and (1997) 11(9) *Corporate Briefing* 3–4.

the custodian holding directly for him. He does not enjoy rights in relation to the underlying securities and is therefore not in a position to offer security interests in relation thereto. Nevertheless, assuming tiers of properly constituted trusts, the benefit of the underlying securities will ultimately be held in an economic sense for the investor through whom the secured creditor claims and this may satisfy the creditor.

6.09 In addition to the fact that a secured creditor may have no direct interest in the underlying securities, there are two further consequences of multi-tier intermediated custody. First, the secured creditor runs the risk that there may be no properly constituted trust in relation to one of the custodial tiers, ie that only a debtor-creditor relationship exists in relation to one of the custodial tiers. The result would be to leave all tiers below, including the secured creditor, bearing the credit risk of the obligor intermediary at that tier in case of that intermediary's insolvency. Secondly, the tiered rights also suggest, since the entitlements at various tiers are different, that separate security interests may be offered in relation to the same underlying securities at different tiers of the custodial chain. Should this occur, difficult priority problems arise which are explored in the section on priorities.

B. Forms of Security

6.10 This section explores some of the methods by which custody assets may be offered as security, beginning with a discussion of the main methods of real security known to English law, followed by a consideration of the principal forms of quasi-security.

(1) Possessory Security

6.11 Modern custodial practices severely restrict the scope of possessory security in relation to assets in custody.

6.12 If the investor's interests relate to wholly dematerialised investments, there would be nothing on which to base a possessory security. Given current trends towards dematerialisation of securities, possessory security is likely to be comparatively rare. Even if securities in custody have a tangible token, where the custody is intermediary, the investor's intangible rights would be incapable of physical possession and therefore unsusceptible to possessory security. This would generally obtain in relation to immobilised securities.

6.13 An investor with registrable securities registered in his name or negotiable securities indorsed in his favour holding the certificate in non-intermediary custody may seek to offer the certificate which he owns by way of possessory security. However, transfer of possession of the certificate to registrable securities cannot properly constitute possessory security over the underlying securities,[10] because such transfers do not pass title to the underlying securities. The transfer of possession of such evidence of title by way of security takes effect, if at all, by way of mortgage or charge.[11]

Pledge

A pledge is a simple method of giving possessory security. It only requires the transfer of possession of a thing, a form of bailment, with the intention that it is held as security.[12] A pledge is said to confer 'the most powerful security interest known to English law'.[13] **6.14**

However, there are some clear problems with any attempt by an investor with assets in custody to offer a security interest by way of pledge. An investor who remained owner of a certificate in custody could attempt to offer the certificate for pledge, but there is limited utility to this as there is authority that only documents of title which transfer title by possession of the document are capable of being the subject of possessory security in relation to the underlying securities in English law.[14] If there is no certificate, or the investor seeks to offer his interest under the custodial structure, this could not form a valid pledge as such interest is intangible and incapable of possession. **6.15**

Lien

In the event that a custodian bank is constituted the investor's financier, it may seek to assert a banker's lien over the investor's certificates in its possession. A banker's lien is particularly wide-ranging; it may be applied to a broad range of commercial paper, including traditional bills of exchange,[15] orders for payment,[16] depository receipts[17] and share certificates.[18] Such a lien arises by law and may arise whenever a customer leaves assets with his banker in the absence of circumstances indicating an intention to the contrary.[19] Where, however, assets are deposited with banks specifically for safe custody, they are ordinarily exempt from a banker's lien.[20] **6.16**

---

[10] *Harrold v Plenty* [1901] 2 Ch 314, 316 per Cozens-Hardy J.
[11] *Carter v Wake* (1877) 4 ChD 605, 606 per Jessel MR.
[12] *Coggs v Bernard* (1703) 2 Ld Raym 909; 92 ER 107; *Donald v Suckling* (1866) LR 1 QB 585 See generally Palmer, *Bailment* (2nd edn, 1991) ch 22.
[13] Goode, *Commercial Law* (n 4 above) 644.
[14] *Carter v Wake* (1877) 4 ChD 605, 606 per Jessel MR.
[15] *Wylde v Radford* (1863) 33 LJR (NS) Ch 51, 53 per Kindersley VC.
[16] *Manuel Misa v Raikes Currie, G Grenfell Glyn* (1876) 1 App Cas 554, 568 per Lord Hatherley.
[17] *Jeffryes v Agra and Masterman's Bank* (1866) LR 2 Eq 674.
[18] *Re United Service Company, Johnston's Claim* (1870) LR 6 Ch App 212, 217 per Sir WM James LJ.
[19] *Wylde v Radford* (1863) 33 LJR (NS) Ch 51, 53 per Kindersley VC.
[20] *Brandao v Barnett* (1846) 12 Clark & Finnelly 787, 808, 8 ER 1622 per Lord Campbell; *Leese v Martin* (1873) LR 17 Eq 224, 234–236. Contrast with *Re United Service Company, Johnston's Claim* (1870) LR 6 Ch App 212, 217 per Sir WM James LJ.

(2) Non-Possessory Security

6.17 In view of the incompatibility of much of modern custody assets and operations with possessory security, the ability to offer non-possessory security becomes more important to investors with assets in custody.

Mortgage

6.18 A mortgage is the transfer of ownership of something to a creditor by way of security on condition that ownership will be re-transferred to the debtor upon discharge of his obligation.[21] Since transfer of possession is not a necessary, but not incompatible, factor of this type of security, it may be better suited to the intangible *res* that may be offered by many investors with assets in custody.

6.19 Investors who enjoy legal title to securities, the certificate of which is in custody, or who are able to direct how the legal title should be dealt with, may effect a legal mortgage. How the transfer of legal title to the securities is effected depends on the nature of the securities to be transferred. For bearer securities, possession should be transferred to the mortgagee. Registrable securities, on the other hand, may have to be surrendered for re-issue in the name of the mortgagee or his nominee. It is not possible to effect a legal mortgage of immobilised securities; by definition legal title to such securities may not be transferred.

6.20 If the title transferred is equitable, the result is an equitable mortgage. An equitable mortgage also arises upon a failed attempt to effect a legal mortgage. One distinction between the position of beneficiaries of legal and equitable mortgages relates to priorities: beneficiaries of the latter may be defeated by bona fide purchasers of the legal interest without notice. Where the equitable title that is mortgaged is based on tiers of holdings, the fact that security interests may be offered at various tiers of the custodial structure may also affect the economic value of the thing mortgaged.[22]

6.21 Where the investor seeks to mortgage his equitable rights under the custodial structure, the fact of pooling by the custodian does not impede this. There is academic support for this view.[23] This is implied by cases such as *Hodson v Tea Company*,[24] where the security was by way of an assignment of a fluctuating pool of assets, and *Sadler v Worley*,[25] where claimants under a debenture which was secured by a pool of fluctuating assets were recognised to enjoy a right of foreclo-

---

[21] Goode, *Legal Problems of Credit* (n 5 above) 14.

[22] This idea is more fully developed in the section on priorities.

[23] Goode, *Legal Problems of Credit* (n 5 above) 15; Gough, *Company Charges* (n 2 above) 100–101.

[24] (1880) 14 ChD 859, 862 per Hall VC.

[25] [1894] 2 Ch 170. However, this case is criticised as anomalous in E Sykes and S Walker, *The Law of Securities* (5th edn, 1993) 960.

sure. Given that foreclosure is a right exclusive to mortgagees,[26] the implication of the granting of this remedy in such circumstances is that the security of the debenture was by way of mortgage. Such mortgages were expressly upheld in *Re Hamilton's Windsor Ironworks*[27] and *Evans v Rival Granite Quarries, Limited*.[28]

The mortgage of an investor's equitable interest of custody securities under single-tier intermediated custody is likely to take effect by way of a transfer to the pledgee/mortgagee on the books of the custodian. **6.22**

Charge

A charge[29] need not involve the transfer of possession of anything and does not **6.23** entail the transfer of ownership of anything. It takes effect by way of an agreement between debtor and creditor to appropriate certain assets to the settlement of a debt not otherwise discharged in priority to the claims of unsecured creditors and junior incumbrancers. The debt is settled out of the proceeds of the sale of the asset. Since a charge is a mere incumbrance, not involving any conveyance or assignment at law, it only exists in equity or by statute. An agreement to confer a charge constitutes a charge.[30]

A charge may be fixed or floating, the principal consequence of the distinction **6.24** between them being the need for a floating charge to be registered under sections 395–396 of the Companies Act 1985, failure to register rendering the charge void in certain circumstances. Although there are suggestions from the Court of Appeal that the labelling of a charge as fixed or floating may be determinative of its nature,[31] this has been criticised[32] and the better view may be that in general for a fixed charge the chargor should have appropriated assets to the charge without retaining autonomous control over them.[33] A fixed charge has been described as 'one that without more fastens on ascertained and definite property or property capable of being ascertained and defined'.[34] Typical characteristics of a floating charge include a charge on present and future assets which, in the ordinary course of the business of the chargor, would change; and it is contemplated that, until

---

[26] *Carter v Wake* (1877) 4 ChD 605; *Harrold v Plenty* [1901] 2 Ch 314.
[27] (1879) 12 ChD 707, 713–714 per Mallins VC.
[28] [1910] 2 KB 979, headnote, 999 per Buckley LJ.
[29] For an exhaustive treatment of this topic see Gough, *Company Charges* (n 2 above).
[30] Goode, *Commercial Law* (n 4 above) 646.
[31] *Re New Bullas Trading Ltd* [1994] BCC 36, 41 per Noursel LJ, 'charge, is a creature of exceptional versatility, malleable to the intention of its creators'; see also *Re Atlantic Medical* [1992] BCC 653.
[32] Goode, *Commercial Law* (n 4 above) 735; Phillips and Oditah (n 6 above) 11.
[33] *Re Cimex Tissues Ltd* [1994] BCC 626, 635 per SJ Burnton QC, sitting as a deputy High Court Judge.
[34] *Illingworth v Houldsworth* [1904] AC 355, 358 per Lord Macnaghten.

some future step is taken by or on behalf of those interested in the charge, the char-gor may use the charged assets in the ordinary course of business.[35]

6.25 Whilst both types of charge constitute immediate security, the difference between the two before crystallisation of the floating charge is in the extent of freedom to deal with the assets afforded to the chargor. It has been suggested that the degree to which a licence to deal with the assets is compatible with a fixed charge is partly a function of the nature of the asset charged. Where the asset is one that is natu-rally fluctuating, a licence to deal will be readily construed to be inconsistent with a fixed charge.[36] Gough has suggested that the hallmark of a fixed charge is the need for specific consent for any dealing with the charged assets.[37]

6.26 As indicated in Chapter 3, the fact of pooling is not in itself incompatible with the establishment, enjoyment and transfer of proprietary rights. However, given the above description of floating charges, there is the risk that a charge in relation to assets kept in fungible custody would be characterised as a floating charge and may therefore need to be registered. If the fungible custody is of a sort where the custodian has to seek specific consent from the investor, or the secured creditor once the security is on foot, prior to any dealing, a charge of assets in these cir-cumstances may be characterised as a fixed charge with a licence to deal. The fast-moving nature of trading on capital markets would make this wholly impractical, and blanket consent to deal in these circumstances would probably lead to the characterisation of the charge as floating. Although the requirements of the Bills of Sale Acts ordinarily preclude individuals from giving floating security over their chattels,[38] this restriction is not applicable where the assets encompassed by the security relate only to securities and choses in action.[39]

6.27 As with a mortgage, the secured creditor will need to satisfy himself with the asset offered by way of charge. An investor with assets in non-intermediated custody could charge the securities themselves, giving the creditor a security interest in the securities in custody. An investor with assets in intermediated custody would have one of two types of equitable interest to offer. A beneficiary of single-tier interme-diated custody would have beneficial interests in relation to the securities in cus-tody and could therefore offer the secured creditor a security interest in the

---

[35] *Re Yorkshire Woolcombers Association Limited* [1903] 2 Ch 284, 295 per Romer LJ.
[36] *Re Cimex Tissues Ltd* [1994] BCC 626, 635 per SJ Burnton QC, sitting as a deputy High Court Judge.
[37] Gough, *Company Charges* (n 2 above) 90–92, 366–369.
[38] Bills of Sale Act 1878, s 10(2) and Bills of Sale Act (1878) Amendment Act 1882, s 4.
[39] By s 4 of the Bills of Sale Act 1878 ' "bill of sale" shall include . . . licences to take possession of personal chattels as security for any debt, and also any agreement . . . by which a right in equity to any personal chattels, or to any charge or security thereon, shall be conferred . . . "personal chattels" shall mean goods, furniture, and other articles capable of complete transfer by delivery, . . . but shall not include . . . shares or interests in the stock, funds, or securities of any government, or in the capital or property of incorporated or joint stock companies, nor choses in action'.

securities. However, a beneficiary of multi-tier intermediated custody will not enjoy such rights and so will not be able to offer a security interest in the securities. Such an investor would only be in a position to charge the rights he enjoys with respect to his direct custodian's entitlement. Secured creditors may exist at various tiers based on one set of underlying securities; the implications of this for the priority of the various secured creditors is explored in a later section on priorities.

(3) Quasi-Security

The validity of these forms of security does not depend on the observance of registration and other perfection formalities required for real non-possessory security.[40] They would also be outside the ambit of negative pledge clauses which sought to restrict the creation by a debtor of subsequent real security. In the case of two-way collateral transfers, such as for repos and stock-loans, the assets taken by the lender can be utilised for whatever purposes he chooses since they belong to or are held for him.   **6.28**

Sale and Repurchase (Repo) and Stock-Lending

The sale and repurchase (repo) transaction is a popular means of quasi-security. In such transactions the investor-borrower sells certain assets to a buyer with an accompanying undertaking to repurchase identical assets at a future date; the repurchase price reflects a measure of interest for the use of the buyer-lender's money. Typically, a repo transaction will permit margin to be called for upon the rise in value of the securities sold and repricing if the value of the securities falls. In case of the insolvency of either party, provision is usually made for the close-out of the transaction and netting of the respective obligations of the parties.   **6.29**

Stock-lending is an analogous transaction. In this case, the investor-lender transfers his ABC securities to the borrower on the undertaking by the borrower to return identical ABC securities at a future date. Not only is a fee paid to the lender for this loan, but the borrower also effects a collateral transfer of XYZ securities or cash of equivalent value in favour of the lender. The typical stock-lending transaction will contain an obligation to mark to market, so that the amount of collateral is adjusted according to the prevailing value of the securities lent. As a rule, in case of default by either party, the other party can set off the defaulting party's obligations against the assets it is holding.   **6.30**

Even if transactions such as these are labelled repo or stock-loan, ie two two-way outright transfers, the foregoing indicates that in each case the buyer/lender is in substance a super-priority creditor. Economically, there is little distinction   **6.31**

---

[40] For other considerations see PR Wood, *Title Finance, Derivatives, Securitisations, Set-off and Netting* (1995) ch 2.

between his position and the position he could have enjoyed as the beneficiary of real security. This raises the risk that the transaction may be re-characterised as conferring real security, a consequence of which may be that the security of the lender is invalidated for want of observance of any formalities.[41]

6.32 Fortunately, from the point of view of reducing the risk of re-characterisation, English courts adopt an approach that permits a degree of predictability in this area. As long as a transaction is of a clear legal structure on the face of the documentation, it is likely that it will be respected for what it is without consideration to the motivation for choosing that legal form.[42] Choosing to structure one's transactions in order to avoid the scope of legislation on real security will not lead to its re-characterisation. Re-characterisation will generally only occur if it can be demonstrated that the document being construed is a sham, that it does not represent the agreement of the parties; or that the substance of the transaction does not correspond to the label attached to it.[43] Terms in agreements that tend to restrict the autonomy of the parties to deal with the assets when received may increase this risk.

6.33 However, if there is scrupulous adherence to the labelling of the parties as buyer and seller in a repo, and there is nothing that suggests an equity of redemption remaining in the seller, it is unlikely that the transaction will be re-characterised as an attempt to confer real security. Similarly, if in a stock-lending transaction the parties are seen to take outright assignments of the transferred assets, it is unlikely that the transaction will be unfavourably re-characterised.

6.34 As with assignments for mortgages, what the investor transfers depends on whether the custody is intermediated or not, and on the number of tiers between him and the underlying securities where custody is intermediated. It is only where there is non-intermediated custody or single-tier intermediated custody that he can assign interests in relation to the underlying custody assets. The interest of a beneficiary of multi-tier intermediated custody is only linked to the entitlement of his custodian. In common with other forms of security created by an investor, notwithstanding the outright nature of the transfers for such transactions, transferees of an equitable interest based on assets held in custody may yet be defeated by transferees of interests at upper tiers of a custodial structure in relation to the same underlying assets. This issue is more fully explored in the section on priorities.

---

[41] *Chase Manhattan Asia v Official Receiver* [1990] 1 WLR 1181.

[42] *Re George Inglefield Limited* [1933] Ch 1, 23 per Lawrence LJ, 26 per Romer LJ; *Welsh Development v Export Finance* [1992] BCLC 148, 185–188 per Staughton LJ; *Orion Finance v Crown Financial Management* [1996] 2 BCLC 78, 85 per Millett LJ. For a fuller exploration of these issues see, for example, F Oditah, 'Financing Trade Credit: Welsh Development Agency v Exfinco' [1992] JBL 541, especially 546–551; Gough, *Company Charges* (n 2 above) 521–525; and the cases cited therein.

[43] *Welsh Development v Export Finance* [1992] BCLC 148, 186 per Staughton LJ; *Orion Finance v Crown Financial Management* [1996] 2 BCLC 78, 84 per Millett LJ.

Negative Pledge

An investor may seek to offer security by way of a free-standing negative pledge. **6.35**
Where this is nothing more than an undertaking by the investor not to encumber
his assets, this is unlikely to be construed as providing the beneficiary of the pledge
with a security interest because it does not purport to confer on the beneficiary of
the pledge any rights in relation to the investor-debtor's assets.

The more difficult question is where the 'negative' pledge is construed as an affir- **6.36**
mative promise to confer a security interest on the first creditor if a security interest is granted to a subsequent creditor. Clearly, if there is no identification of the
assets on which the negative pledge should bite there can be no question of the creation of a security interest thereby. However, if assets by which this special obligation should be met are identified, there is a chance of such a provision being
characterised as conferring real security, at least from the time at which the contingency occurs which brings the provisions of the negative pledge to life.[44] The
rationale for suggesting that a negative pledge may give rise to real security is based
on the view that where there is an obligation to confer an interest in relation to
something for the breach of which damages would be an inadequate remedy, the
obligations will be specifically enforceable and, as such, 'give rise to an equitable
charge upon the subject matter'.[45]

If a negative pledge is construed to provide real security, depending on the assets **6.37**
to which it is meant to attach, the provision may need to be registered as a floating
security under companies legislation. It may also be necessary, if the pledge constitutes dealing with an equitable interest, for the agreement to be in writing.

As with other forms of security, the beneficiary of a negative pledge which confers **6.38**
interests in relation to the debtor's assets will need to pay close attention to whatever it is he is receiving. The creditor may receive an interest in relation to securities by way of the legal or equitable title of the investor, or may receive only rights
linked to the entitlements of the investor's custodian. The implications of this for
priorities generally are developed in a later section.

If it is accepted to be possible, the granting of real security by way of negative **6.39**
pledge raises peculiar problems of priority. Ordinarily, an interest conferred on
the occurrence of a contingency must rank in time, and therefore priority, after
the contingency. If the contingency that makes the negative pledge bite is the
granting of real security to another creditor, it is obvious that the real security of
that other creditor will enjoy priority over that brought into being by the negative
pledge. If it is intended to grant real security by way of negative pledge which

---

[44] This is persuasively argued by P Gabriel, *Legal Aspects of Syndicated Loans* (1996) 86–90; and
Phillips and Oditah (n 6 above) 20–22.
[45] *Swiss Bank v Lloyds Bank* [1982] AC 584, 595, see generally 595–596 per Buckley LJ.

ranks ahead of the granting of real security subsequent to the pledge, the contingency which makes the pledge bite will need to be an action which occurs prior to the establishment of the subsequent (real) security, such as a resolution or formal decision to confer the latter security.

(4) Provision for Security by Settlement Systems

6.40 Where investors' assets are kept in a settlement system such as CGO, CMO or CREST, it may be possible to confer security interests by complying with the specific provisions for so doing which are established by the management of the system. This would be relevant if both the investor and the secured creditor or their custodians are account-holders in the settlement system.

6.41 However, where inter-account transfers are considered absolute,[46] this may be inconsistent with the retention by investors of an equity of redemption. The rationalisation of this apparent inconsistency may be that whilst as between any account-holder and the settlement system transfers are considered absolute, as between account-holders party to a security agreement the equity of redemption remains valid.

6.42 Settlement systems may also provide for charging, whereby assets within a member's account are transferred into an escrow balance held to the order of a third party.[47] This form of collateral remains in the name of the chargor. Given that such an investor would not be able to deal with the assets in that balance without the consent of the chargee it is likely that such a charge would be characterised as fixed, without the need for registration under companies legislation.

6.43 The absolute nature of transfers within settlement systems is well suited to repos and stock-loans, which we have characterised as two two-way transfers of securities or value. Indeed, some settlement systems have elaborated specific stock-lending and repo functionality which, beyond providing for the exchange of securities or value, provide for the co-ordination of the various stages of the transactions, the constant valuation of transferred assets and the taking of margin.[48]

---

[46] *Central Moneymarkets Office Reference Manual,* version No 2 (updated May 1997) F.1.5, I.2.2, K.1.2 and K.1.4. In F.1.5 the following words appear: 'the Bank of England does not recognise any proprietary or equitable interest, or any other right in respect of any instrument, other than an absolute right to the entirety of the instrument in the CMO member to whose account the instrument is credited'.

[47] CREST, *CREST Reference Manual* (May 1996) 105; and *Central Gilts Office Reference Manual,* version No 1 (October 1997) 7.3.1.

[48] CREST, *CREST Reference Manual* (May 1996) 100; and *Central Gilts Office Reference Manual,* version No 1 (October 1997) 7.1.1.

C. Perfection and Formalities

Perfection involves taking steps to ensure that third parties are made aware of, or **6.44** otherwise barred from access to, the security interest of a secured creditor in certain subject-matter. Perfection may affect the validity and/or priority of the security interest. The idea is that if a third party chooses to have dealings in relation to the asset he does so fully informed, at his peril and subject to interests in relation to the asset that already subsist. Perfection does not ensure that one's security interest will always prevail over all third parties; other parties may have their own perfected security or other interests which rank ahead of that of the creditor. In such circumstances, the resolution of who takes first is a question of priorities, the rules of which are considered below.

(1) Quasi-Security

Where legal title is transferred by way of quasi-security in the form of a sale, eg **6.45** repo, this should not require perfection, although for registrable securities this will involve the issuer registering the transferee as legally entitled to the securities. Perfection is not necessary for the validity of quasi-security because there is no security interest to validate. Yet, where the transfer is of an equitable title, it may be necessary for the secured party to inform the custodian holding the legal or other title via which the investor/assignor claims in order to preserve the priority of his (the secured party's) claim.[49] This requirement should not prove unduly onerous.

Where equitable title is transferred as quasi-security in a settlement system, the **6.46** formality of notice will automatically have been met. Likewise, where the custodian is the transferee. Any suggestion that the custodian has to inform himself of an assignment in his favour is nonsense; it may be taken that the custodian is automatically aware. Where quasi-security of an equitable interest is given outside the context of settlement systems, it may be advisable for the creditor to inform the custodian of the investor.

A further formality that may need to be observed for assignment of equitable **6.47** interests is the need for writing under section 53 of the Law of Property Act 1925. However, as indicated in Chapter 4, this is a formality that either may have been excluded by legislation or may be automatically conformed to by the records of the assignor, his custodian and the assignee.

(2) Real Security

Perfection of real security is achieved in one of two principal ways: by taking such **6.48** control of the asset as should not leave a third party with access to the assets used

---

[49] *Dearle v Hall* (1823) 3 Russ 1, 12–13, 20–21, 38 ER 475 per Sir Thomas Plumer MR.

for collateral, or by informing third parties of the establishment of the security interest, such as by way of notice, filing or registration with a view to third parties forbearing from entering into dealings in relation to the charged assets.

6.49 The most effective method of ensuring that a security interest will be respected by third parties is for the creditor to take such control over the asset that he will not need the co-operation of the debtor to enforce his security. The secured creditor may become registered as legal owner of the underlying assets or come into possession, actual or constructive,[50] of the underlying assets. However, because of the formalities that may be necessary to be complied with for this to be validated and/or the remoteness of the investor from the actual custodian of the underlying assets, this may not be the option of choice. Assuming intermediary custody, and that the investor wishes to offer his interest thereunder as collateral, the secured creditor could be registered as entitled under the custodial structure in place of the investor or the custodian be made to agree to not act without the agreement of the secured creditor. In the alternative, steps may simply be taken to put the assets out of reach of anyone but the creditor, as is effected by the escrow balance system in CREST. In all such cases, third parties are denied access to the asset subject to the security interest unless they go through the secured creditor.

6.50 Where an intermediary custodian is the creditor of the investor, its security interest will automatically be perfected because the custodian will always already be in control of the subject-matter of the security interest, whether by way of possession or title.[51] It must be taken as given that, if the custodian advances credit to the investor based on assets in custody, the custodian will have the intention of perfecting. The appropriation of certain assets to the security would be sufficient for both attachment and perfection. If this results in a misappropriation of assets that should be held to the order of others, then appropriate remedies may be pursued.

6.51 Filing or registration obligations may be imposed where custody assets are used as security for credit. However, by virtue of the fact that shares and other choses in action do not come within the definition of a personal chattel,[52] the registration obligations of the Bills of Sale Act 1878 do not apply. Whilst this may exempt private individuals, custodians or investors that are companies which create security interests may yet be caught by the registration obligations of section 396 of the Companies Act 1985. In particular, it may be felt that the provision requiring reg-

---

[50] ibid 12. This requires the consent of the custodian and there is no certainty that this would be forthcoming. The custodian may not want to have dealings with any other party, especially with respect to possibly contentious security interests. This right of refusal is enshrined for American custodians in section 8-106(g) UCC: The American Law Institute and National Conference of Commissioners on Uniform States, *Uniform Commercial Code* (14th edn, 1995), Official Text with Comments.
[51] This is provided for American custodians by section 8-106(e) UCC (n 50 above).
[52] Bills of Sale Act 1878, s 4.

istration of charges on book debts[53] may apply to the intangible entitlements that constitute the core of custody. The better view may be that because book debts are 'debts arising in a business in which it is the proper and usual course to keep books, and which ought to be entered in such books',[54] the term broadly only 'includes business receivables, but probably does not include debt securities held as investments'.[55] This is particularly true of the custodial industry where the benefits anticipated are not for the custodian's account. Notwithstanding the foregoing, section 396 makes it explicit that if a security interest is established by a company with a view to 'securing any issue of debentures'[56] or as a floating charge,[57] such security interest will need to be registered.

Failure to register a registrable charge renders the charge void against any admin- **6.52** istrator, liquidator or secured creditor of the company.[58] It is neither invalid as against the company nor as against purchasers and does not extinguish the company's personal obligation to settle the debt. Registration is a perfection requirement; it has no direct implications for priorities.[59] However, since notice may be a deciding factor in the ordering of priorities, the degree to which registration under any relevant regime constitutes notice is critical. Two questions that arise are to whom does registration constitute notice and of what does registration constitute notice.

There is authority that registration of a charge constitutes notice at least of the **6.53** existence of the charge.[60] The question that arises is whether notice is restricted to the existence of the charge *ipso facto* or whether registration constitutes notice of the terms of the charge as well. The issue should not be of importance where the first charge is fixed because the chargor is not at liberty to deal with the charged asset in the normal course of business[61] and so subsequent chargees should not be afforded access to the asset. The question is important to subsequent chargees where the first charge is a floating charge, which by definition permits the chargor to deal with the asset, and which may include a negative pledge or other conditions as to action which may be taken by the chargor. The absence of notice or knowledge on the part of the subsequent chargee may be grounds for enabling them to take free of the restrictive provisions.

---

[53] Companies Act 1985, s 396(1)(e).
[54] *The Official Receiver v Tailby* (1887) 18 QBD 25, 29 per Lord Esher.
[55] PR Wood, *Comparative Law of Security and Guarantees* (1995) 9–36.
[56] Companies Act 1985, s 396(1)(a).
[57] ibid s 396(1)(f).
[58] ibid s 395(1).
[59] Goode, *Commercial Law* (n 4 above) 715.
[60] *Re Standard Rotary Machine Company Limited* (1906) 95 LT 829, 834 per Kekewich J (affirmed in *Wilson v Kelland* [1910] 2 Ch 306, 313 per Eve J); and *G and T Earle Limited v Hemsworth RDC* (1928) 44 TLR 605, 608 per Wright J.
[61] Note should be taken that powers of substitution may permit the chargor limited dealing powers even under a fixed charge.

6.54 With regard to the question of to whom registration constitutes notice, at least one case has suggested that registration constitutes notice to all persons dealing with the charged property who could reasonably be expected to search the register of all matters for which registration is prescribed.[62] If at all, notice of the provisions of the charge should be restricted to this limited group. It does not matter that a particular provision may be commonly inserted in the type of charge; if details of the provision are not required to be registered, registration of the charge should not constitute notice of the provision.[63] However, it has been argued that notice of a charge should lead to inferred knowledge of the terms of the charge because one should be put on inquiry by notice of the existence of the charge and failure to act on the inquiry may lead to inferred knowledge.[64] There are criticisms of this line of reasoning. Courts have chosen not to extend notice or knowledge in this way. In *Siebe Gorman & Co Ltd v Barclays Bank Ltd*, Slade J expressed his opposition to stretching 'the doctrine of constructive notice too far'.[65] Further, if inferred knowledge involves wilfully shutting one's eyes to facts of which one is aware,[66] inferred knowledge based on provisions of which one is not conscious would seem contrary to reason. The concept of inferred knowledge based on constructive notice is not a development that businessmen are likely to welcome.

6.55 Another method of perfection, for choses in action, is for a creditor to give notice to the obligor of the chose in action to which his security interest attaches, the rule in *Dearle v Hall*.[67] This enables subsequent creditors of the investor to check whether they may confidently deal with the investor in relation to his entitlement. This form of perfection is relevant whenever the security given will require the secured creditor to claim the investor's entitlement via the investor's custodian. The rule is not applicable to registered securities.[68]

6.56 A number of criticisms of this system of perfection may be made. Where the rule in *Dearle v Hall* is applicable, the administrative burdens on custodians would be increased. For instance, custodians would have to keep track of the security interests established by their various customers, oversee issues of release, and may be called upon to make a determination as to who is properly entitled to the benefit

---

[62] *Siebe Gorman & Co Ltd v Barclays Bank Ltd* [1979] 2 Lloyd's Rep 142, 159–160 per Slade J.

[63] *G and T Earle Limited v Hemsworth RDC* (1928) 44 TLR 605, 608 per Wright J. Contrast with the view of David Neuberger QC, sitting as a deputy judge of the High Court in *Ian Chisholm Textiles Ltd v Griffiths* [1994] 2 BCLC 291, 304, where he came to the 'tentative' view, albeit not having 'heard full argument on the subject, and it is not necessary for my decision', that where a subsequent transferee of property has notice of an incumbrance to that property he will have constructive notice of the provisions of the agreement of incumbrance.

[64] JH Farrar, 'Floating Charges and Priorities' (1974) 38 The Conveyancer 315, 320, n 32, 322.

[65] [1979] 2 Lloyd's Rep 142, 160 per Slade J.

[66] *The English and Scottish Mercantile Investment Company Limited v Brunton* [1892] 2 QB 700, 707–708 per Lord Esher MR.

[67] (1823) 3 Russ 1, 38 ER 475.

[68] *Macmillan v Bishopsgate Investment Trust plc (No 3)* [1996] 1 WLR 387, 411 per Auld LJ.

in the event of dispute. These are obligations that it is unlikely that custodians would wish to undertake, and even if they could be so persuaded, they may seek extra remuneration for doing this. Furthermore, the rule is effectively displaced for registrable real security that is properly registered. Registration of the relevant interest would constitute notice to subsequent assignees.

Perfection of a security based on an investor's entitlement does not address the issues raised by multi-tiered intermediated custody. Whilst perfection may offer effective notice to other parties who subsequently deal with the investor, it does not account for the actions of intermediaries at other tiers in relation to the same underlying assets. As will be developed in the section on priorities, whilst the interest of an investor's creditor's security is in principle secure, it may be jeopardised in substance by the action of intermediaries at tiers closer to the underlying assets.   **6.57**

The solution to this may be for the creditor to take control of the underlying asset. However, as already mentioned, this option may not be possible or practical. Immobilisation does not permit this and there may be formalities involved in taking control that would make this approach unattractive. Further, the investor could no longer trade the constituent assets of his portfolio to optimise its value. With respect to tiered holdings, there are obvious difficulties with an investor issuing orders to an intermediary, that he may not know and who is unlikely to know him, with respect to a transaction that the intermediary knows nothing about.   **6.58**

Aside from perfection, there may be formalities to be observed to give the granting of security legal validity. According to section 53 of the Law of Property Act 1925, assignments of equitable interests ordinarily need to be in writing.[69] However, as indicated in Chapter 4, this is a formality that either may have been excluded by legislation or may be automatically conformed to by the records of the assignor, his custodian and the assignee. Another possible formality, for registrable securities, is that an assignment or transfer will not be given legal validity unless the issuer is informed and the necessary steps for transfer have been taken.   **6.59**

D. Enforcement

Upon default of the terms of repayment of credit, a creditor may sue on personal covenants or undertakings for repayment given by the person to whom credit was advanced or any other person, such as a guarantor or surety, who has undertaken the obligation of repayment. This type of enforcement may not be the strategy of choice as it entails running the credit risk of the relevant party. Enforcement of a   **6.60**

---

[69] This provision is more fully discussed in Chapter 4 on the formalities for dealing with equitable interests.

security may also be achieved by one or a combination of: possession, sale, or fore-closure of assets to which a security interest attaches. These property-based methods of enforcement are likely to be the most effective in the insolvency of a debtor.

6.61   It is vital in the custodial scenario, where one is dealing with assets of highly volatile value, that secured creditors can enforce rapidly. The right to enforce arises or is exercisable with varying degrees of ease. A right of self-help may be implied by the nature of the security or otherwise recognised at common law, as is the case with possessory securities, for the creditor to retain possession[70] and/or sell the asset.[71] Where security takes the form of title being transferred to the cred-itor at the outset, he may come into or retain possession of[72] or sell the asset.[73] A right of self-help is an inherent part of quasi-security, usually by way of outright transfer with a contractual right to set-off. Where there is no right of self-help, application may be made to court.[74] Indeed, the right of foreclosure is only exer-cisable following an application to court.[75]

6.62   Notwithstanding the existence of a right to self-help, one may seek a court order before enforcement, possibly in order to insulate the enforcement exercise from later challenge. This will only be granted in exceptional circumstances.[76] The right to enforce may also be provided by statute. For instance, the right of a legal mortgagee or chargee by deed to sell the asset in the absence of a contractual right is provided by section 101(1)(i) of the Law of Property Act 1925. However, the statutory right of sale is subject to extensive notice periods, at the end of which there may be nothing left to sell. Applications to court may be drawn out by debtors seeking to frustrate the attempt at enforcement. One way of resolving this difficulty may be for creditors to provide for contractual rights of enforcement in the security agreement.

(1) Possession

6.63   Possession is likely to be of restricted application in security over custodial assets because of the combined effect of the trend towards dematerialisation of invest-ments and the nature of assets offered by investors with assets in multi-tier inter-mediated custody. Furthermore, possession *ipso facto* is of limited use. Whilst possession may put pressure on the debtor to pay up, it does not provide a direct

---

[70]   *Clark v Gilbert* (1835) 2 Bing (NC) 343, 132 ER 135.
[71]   *Ex p Official Receiver, Re Morritt* (1886) 18 QBD 222, 232 per Cotton LJ; *The Odessa, The Woolston* [1916] 1 AC 145, 159 per Lord Mersey.
[72]   *Four-Maids Ltd v Dudley Marshall (Properties) Ltd* [1957] Ch 317, 320 per Harman J.
[73]   *Deverges v Sandeman, Clark & Co* [1902] 1 Ch 579, the headnote, 596 per Cozens-Hardy LJ; *Stubbs v Slater* [1910] 1 Ch 632, 641 per Cozens-Hardy MR, 647 per Buckley LJ.
[74]   *The Odessa, The Woolston* [1916] 1 AC 145, 159 per Lord Mersey.
[75]   *Ness v O'Neill* [1916] 1 KB 706, 709 per Swinfen Eady LJ.
[76]   *Arab Bank plc v Merchantile Holdings Ltd* [1994] 2 All ER 74, 89 per Millett J.

means of the creditor getting his money back. The right to possession does not of itself enable a creditor to keep the asset as his own or sell it. For example, it is said of a pledgee who enjoys an implied power of sale that he does so, 'not with a new title of his own . . . the right of sale is exercisable by virtue of an implied authority from the pledgor'.[77]

(2) Sale or Foreclosure

In relation to sale or foreclosure, the asset that may be sold or foreclosed on by the secured creditor depends on the asset to which his security interest attached. Because of intermediation, this means of enforcement will often not relate to the underlying custody assets but to the investor's rights linked to his custodian's entitlement. Nevertheless, the fact that the rights should reflect the economic value of the underlying assets should make this a distinction of little importance. The secured creditor's overriding concern will ordinarily be to realise sufficient value to liquidate the sums owed. **6.64**

In any event, due to a number of factors, foreclosure is infrequently encountered.[78] This may be because foreclosure is only properly exercisable by mortgagees on application to court.[79] Although foreclosure has been applied to charges in some cases, including by one judge who recognised that his judgment amounted to 'an order the like of which has never been made before',[80] it is unclear whether there are many instances of foreclosure other than for a mortgagee.[81] Other reasons why foreclosure is rarely encountered may include the reluctance of judges to allow mortgagees to reap windfalls, as well as the resistance from debtors that applications for such may engender. **6.65**

(3) Restrictions on Enforcement

The attitude of English courts is facilitative of the right of creditors to enforce security. This attitude is exemplified by the dictum of Blackburn J in *Brighty v Norton*, where he stated that 'a debtor who is required to pay money on demand, or at a stated time, must have it ready, and is not entitled to further time to look **6.66**

---

[77] *The Odessa, The Woolston* [1916] 1 AC 145, 159 per Lord Mersey.

[78] *Palk v Mortgage Services Funding plc* [1993] 2 WLR 415, 419 per Sir Donald Nicholls VC.

[79] *Sampson v Pattison* (1842) 1 Hare 533, 535 per Sir James Wigram VC, 66 ER 1143; *Jenkin v Row* (1851) 5 De G & Sm 106, 110 per Sir James Parker VC, 64 ER 1039; *Re Owen* [1894] 3 Ch 220, 227 per Stirling J.

[80] *Sadler v Worley* [1894] 2 Ch 170, 176 per Kekewich J; see also *Re Continental Oxygen* [1897] 1 Ch 511, 514 where he stated that since he was unable to ascertain how far his previous judgment had been criticised or approved by his peers, he did not see any reason to revise his earlier dictum on this point.

[81] Cases such as *Re George Inglefield Limited* [1933] Ch 1, 27 where Romer LJ, in discussing the distinction between a sale and a mortgage or charge, stated that 'in the case of a mortgage or charge, the mortgagor is entitled, until he has been foreclosed, to get back the subject-matter of the mortgage or charge by returning to the mortgagee the money that has passed between them', may be dismissed as examples of a loose usage of the term 'charge'.

for it'.[82] Nevertheless, the right to enforce is not unbridled. Both the common law and equity impose safeguards on the manner of enforcement.[83] Where a creditor takes possession of assets subject to the security, he may owe the debtor certain duties.[84] There are also a number of restrictions on the ability of the creditor to exercise his power of sale. A creditor is obliged to give the debtor reasonable notice of the sale.[85] Further, he must not only account to the debtor for any sum actually realised from the sale,[86] he is obliged to act in good faith in order to realise the full market value that the asset sold ought to achieve.[87] In view of the fact that custody assets will ordinarily have a publicly quoted market price, there should be little difficulty in obtaining the proper price upon sale.

6.67 There are also some legislative controls on the manner of enforcement. For instance, if the transaction relates to sums of less than £5,000 and the debtor is an individual, the ability to enforce at all would be subject to the restrictions of the Consumer Credit Act 1974. By sections 76(1) and 87(1) of this Act, a creditor is not permitted to enforce unless he has given the debtor seven days' notice. Similarly, section 103 of the Law of Property Act 1925 restricts the exercise of a statutory power of sale until the debtor has been in default of a request for payment of mortgage money for three months; or interest payments are in arrears or unpaid for two months after becoming due; or there has been a breach of the terms of the mortgage deed or of the Act, other than the requirement to pay. Whilst the restrictions of the Consumer Credit Act 1974 are mandatory, the restrictions on statutory powers of sale contained in the Law of Property Act 1925 may be, and often are, excluded by deed.

E. Priorities

6.68 The question of priorities determines, perhaps more than any other factor, the practical efficacy of one's security interest. One may validly establish a security

---

[32] (1862) 3 B & S 305, 312, 122 ER 116. See also, for example, *Frederick Henry Moore v Rowland Mansfield Shelley* (1883) 8 App Cas 285, 293 per Sir Barnes Peacock; *Cripps (Pharmaceuticals) Ltd v Wickenden* [1973] 2 All ER 606, 616–617 per Goff J; *Sheppard & Cooper Ltd v TSB Bank plc* [1996] 2 All ER 654, 657–658 per Blackburne J.

[33] *Palk v Mortgage Services Funding plc* [1993] Ch 330, 337 per Sir Donald Nicholls VC.

[34] ibid 337–338; *Downsview Nominees Ltd v First City Corporation Ltd* [1993] AC 295, 315 per Lord Templeman.

[35] *William Wilson v James Tooker* (1714) V Brown 193, 2 ER 622; *Deverges v Sandeman, Clark & Co* [1902] 1 Ch 579, 596 per Cozens-Hardy LJ.

[36] *William Wilson v James Tooker* (1714) V Brown 193, 2 ER 622; *Stubbs v Slater* [1910] 1 Ch 632, 641 per Cozens-Hardy MR, 647 per Buckley LJ.

[37] *Polak v Everett* (1876) 1 QBD 669, 675–676 per Blackburn J; *Cuckmere Brick Co Ltd v Mutual Finance Ltd* [1971] Ch 949, 966 per Salmon LJ, 978 per Cairns LJ; *Palk v Mortgage Services Funding plc* [1993] Ch 330, 337–338 per Sir Donald Nicholls VC; *Downsview Nominees Ltd v First City Corporation Ltd* [1993] AC 295, 315 per Lord Templeman.

interest that is perfected and capable of enforcement, but this may be true of any number of competing claimants, especially in relation to floating charges. Where the available resources are insufficient to satisfy all secured creditors, their ability to settle their claims will be determined according to applicable rules of priority. The question of priorities in the custodial context is particularly important because of the multiplicity of interests, security or otherwise, in relation to any set of underlying custody assets. There will be at least a beneficial owner, his custodian and an issuer. Added to this may be security interests issued at the level of the custodian or the owner. There may also be interests that arise by virtue of the operational mechanics of settlement in the particular market in which the underlying custody assets are kept or traded. Given that various interests may arise where the various beneficiaries of the interests are blameless, creating a competition between a number of innocent parties, it is the role of the rules on priorities to establish a rational order in which the competing claims will be met.

Modern custodial practice necessitates a distinction to be drawn between differ- **6.69** ent types of priority contests. A priority contest may take place between parties on the same tier, intra-tier, and this will be resolved by the application of the traditional rules of priorities. Where the contestants are on different tiers, inter-tier, one will need to have regard to the nature of the custodial structure to determine whose claim is more likely to be satisfied. The question arises whether claimants on different tiers in relation to the same underlying asset may be termed rivals when the thing claimed by each party is analytically distinct.

(1) Intra-Tier Priority

As between rivals on the same tier, priority is determined according to the general **6.70** principles of priorities.[88] For successive dealings in relation to the same title, the basic rule is that the first in time has priority. This is a rule of logic. One cannot give out what one no longer has. Priority is therefore generally determined by chronology. However, this general rule permits numerous exceptions. Priority according to chronology may be modified by filing or registration of interests, notwithstanding the difficulties, as set out in the section on perfection, that arise with respect to determining who is affected by filing or registration and to what degree. Priority based on chronology may also be modified by estoppel of the first secured creditor. There are other exceptions, some of the most relevant of which are briefly examined below.

An exception is made as between successive dealings in relation to a chose in **6.71** action, the rule in *Dearle v Hall*.[89] By this rule, priority is determined according to

---

[88] See, for example, *Snell's Equity* (29th edn, 1990) ch 4; F Oditah, *Legal Aspects of Receivables Financing* (1991) ch 6; Goode, *Commercial Law* (n 4 above) chs 24 and 25; PR Wood, *Comparative Law of Security and Guarantees* (1995) ch 12.
[89] (1823) 3 Russ 1, 38 ER 475.

the order in which assignees of the chose notify the obligor of the chose of their acquired interests. This exception will not apply where the subsequent assignee that notifies the obligor has prior notice of the first one. In view of our earlier comments as to the effect of registration of registrable secured interests giving notice automatically to subsequent creditors, it is likely that this exception to the general rule on priorities will be of restricted scope. Further, where the priority dispute is as between a legal assignment and an equitable assignment, the equitable assignment is overreached by a subsequent disposition of the legal title to a bona fide purchaser for value without notice.

6.72 Another exception is that of a purchase-money security interest, which may be established by a creditor who provides credit by which custody assets are acquired. This is relevant to settlement systems where transfers are undertaken on the basis of short-term, maybe intra-day, credit from a settlement system's operator on the basis of the security of the assets transferred. Where a purchase-money security interest is established subsequent to an all assets security, how are they to be ranked? In *Church of England Building Society v Piskor*[90] the Court of Appeal decided that an after-acquired property clause should enjoy priority on the basis that for the investor to be able to give out any kind of security interest, whether to the financier of the particular assets or the earlier creditor, the investor would first have had to obtain the asset free of any other interests. In the *scintilla temporis* before giving out any kind of interest he would be estopped by the after-acquired property clause from giving any interest to anyone else, including to the financier of the later acquisition. This reasoning was rejected by the House of Lords in *Abbey National Building Society v Cann*[91] where it was determined that there is no *scintilla temporis* before the purchase-money security attaches, the financier's interest is contemporaneous to that of the investor.[92] As such, the purchase-money security must take priority over an after-acquired clause. Since it is solely by virtue of money advanced and on the condition of the purchase-money security that the investor is able to acquire the asset, it seems appropriate that any interest claiming the asset through him must do so subject to the conditions on which the asset was acquired.[93]

6.73 A creditor may seek to enhance his priority ranking by entering into a subordination agreement with other creditors, by which priority of earlier creditors is voluntarily ceded. This may take effect by direct or indirect means. The indirect

---

[90] [1954] 1 Ch 533.

[91] [1991] 1 AC 56.

[92] ibid 92. Lord Oliver of Aylmerton stated that an argument to the contrary 'flies in the face of reality' and that the purchase of the thing and the charge 'are not only precisely simultaneous but indissolubly bound together'.

[93] ibid 102. Lord Jauncey of Tullichettle stated that '[s]ince no one can grant what he does not have it follows that such a purchaser could never grant an interest which was not subject to the limitations of his own interest'.

method of achieving this is where the first creditor undertakes to account for any receipts from the investor to the second or other creditor before retaining anything in satisfaction of his own claim. In the event that this merely constitutes a contractual undertaking, nothing more is required. In the event, however, that the terms of the agreement constitute the first recipient a trustee of the receipts, the transaction may amount to a charge on the book debts of the first recipient requiring registration under section 396(1)(e) of the Companies Act 1985 or else be void for non-regulation.[94]

In *Re Maxwell Communications Corporation plc*,[95] Vinelott J stated that 'a loan can **6.74** be effectively subordinated if the creditor constitutes himself a trustee for other unsecured creditors . . . or he may contract to assign the benefit of his debt to other unsecured creditors without in either case affecting the ordinary process of proof in the liquidation or the application of the company's assets pari passu amongst creditors whose proofs have been submitted. However, . . . to recognise subordination by these means, and not by a direct contract between the company and the creditor, would represent a triumph of form over substance'.[96] He 'reached the clear conclusion that such a clause is valid and effective and is not avoided by any consideration of public policy'.[97]

Given the ability of parties to alter the normal scheme of priorities, problems of **6.75** circularity may arise. For example, creditor A may agree to subordinate his claims to those of creditor C in circumstances where creditor C should ordinarily take after creditor B and creditor A take before creditor B. Creditor A may be a fixed chargee, creditor C a floating chargee and creditor B a preferred creditor, such as the Inland Revenue. The problem of circularity stems from the fact that creditor A agrees to come after creditor C, but creditor A should come before creditor B who ranks ahead of creditor C. At least two solutions are possible. If the agreement between A and C amounts to giving C rights of subrogation to A's rights, there would be no problem. C and A would simply exchange roles to the maximum extent of A's rights or C's claim, whichever is the lesser.[98] However, if all the agreement between A and C amounts to is that A will simply take after C, then this will be enforced with the result that B takes first because he ranks before C, C ranks second because he now ranks ahead of A, and A ranks last because this is the implication of his agreement.[99]

---

[94] Companies Act 1985, s 395.
[95] [1993] 1 WLR 1402.
[96] ibid 1416–1417.
[97] ibid 1420.
[98] *Woodroffes (Musical Instruments) Ltd* [1986] Ch 366.
[99] *Re Portbase Clothing Ltd* [1993] Ch 388. See also *Waters v Widdows* [1984] VR 503, 513–514, SC of Victoria, Australia.

6.76 Although priority based on chronology appears simple, the numerous exceptions to this greatly reduce the ease with which the rule is applied. Matters are further complicated by the uncertain scope of some of the exceptions, notably the effect of filing or registration. It is against this background that the Drafting Committee of article 8 of the Uniform Commercial Code of the USA sought to inject 'needed clarity'[100] to the rules on priorities. Their solution was to abandon the traditional schema in favour of priority based on control as defined in the provisions. By section 9-115(5) of the UCC, a party in control ranks ahead of a party who is not in control. Where there are two parties in control, they rank equally unless one of them is the intermediary through whom the other claimant will have to claim, in which case the intermediary ranks ahead. This approach may be justified on at least two grounds. This order of priority seeks to reflect the reality of who will actually be best able to enforce their security interest. It also seeks to reward a secured creditor that has made the most efforts to guard his position and who has sought to minimise the risk that his assets will be alienated unlawfully.

(2) Inter-Tier Priority

6.77 There may be an apparent priority dispute between claimants of security interests on different tiers of a custodial structure.[101] The logic of multi-tier custody is that the *res* which may be owned, and therefore the thing to which the security interest may attach, on different tiers of an intermediary custodial structure are necessarily distinct, because they are based at each tier on new and different entitlements. This would seem to make a priority contest inappropriate. Even if secured creditors at different tiers of one custodial structure may be viewed as rivals in substance, because they enjoy security based on the same underlying asset, the fact that the security interests are established on different tiers means that the separate secured creditors are technically not rivals because their interests attach to different things. A security interest attaching to the interest of an investor is not legally in contest with a security interest established by a sub-custodian tier above. Claimants on one tier of intermediary custody do not have direct proprietary claims to the underlying assets, their claims are restricted to their intermediary.

6.78 Notwithstanding the foregoing, given that secured creditors on different tiers may be rivals in substance, the question arises of how this so-called priority dispute should be resolved. For the proper answer to this, we revert to the earlier analysis of interests at different tiers of intermediary custody. That analysis suggests that it

---

[100] CW Mooney, Jr, SM Rocks and RS Schwartz, 'An Introduction to the Revised UCC Article 8 and Review of Other Recent Developments with Investment Securities' (1994) 49 The Business Lawyer 1891, 1900.

[101] This should not ordinarily arise. However, in the event of mistaken, fraudulent or other misapplication of custody assets by custodian intermediaries such a dispute may arise.

is a logical consequence of the nature of claims on different tiers that the claim of the upper tier, the tier closer to the underlying assets, will ordinarily win. Of course, if the secured creditor at the upper tier is aware of the interests of the beneficiary of the intermediary who grants the security interest to him, he will not be able to take free and overreach all those who claim via the beneficiary. However, assuming that the secured creditors of both the intermediary and the investor are bona fide purchasers, the logic of modern custodial structures determines that it is the claimant at the upper tier who will win. As the stream of benefits flow downwards through the tiers, the upper tier claimant will be satisfied before the lower tier claimant. This is effectively a simple application of the *nemo dat* principle. The lower tier claimant through whom his secured creditor claims will not have any more to give his secured creditor than any residue remitted by the upper tier.

In view of the nature of claims through intermediaries in a multi-tier custodial **6.79** scenario, chronology is simply not relevant to the resolution of a multi-tier priority dispute. Even if the upper tier security interest is established subsequent to that of the lower tier, assuming that both security interests are bona fide and for value, it is that of the upper tier that will ordinarily prevail. Bona fides and the proximity to the underlying assets appear to be the determining factors. A secured creditor who takes security from the investor runs greater risks of his security being reduced in value through no fault of his own or that of the investor when there are numerous tiers of custody than one who takes security from an intermediary at a tier closer to the underlying assets.

The idea of multi-tier priority disputes being determined by proximity to the **6.80** underlying assets is not without support. In his seminal article[102] on the nature of modern intermediary securities holdings, Mooney advocates what he terms the Upper Tier Principle (UTP), an idea which greatly influenced the drafting of the new article 8 of the Uniform Commercial Code. However, starting with the premise that an intermediary custodian in the USA would not be constituted a trustee of the securities held for customers,[103] Mooney did not base UTP on bona fides and taking free. He based UTP on economic efficiencies to be gained by the principle and the fact that analogies for the idea existed in other parts of the UCC. Nevertheless, in accepting that non-innocent upper tier beneficiaries of security

---

[102] CW Mooney, Jr, 'Beyond Negotiability: A New Model for Transfer and Pledge of Interests in Securities Controlled by Intermediaries' (1990) 12 Cardozo Law Review 307, especially at sections IV, V and the conclusion. For other American perspectives on multi-tier disputes between secured lenders see, for example: JL Schroeder, 'Is Article 8 Finally Ready This Time? The Radical Reform of Secured Lending on Wall Street' [1994] Columbia Business Law Review 291; CW Mooney, Jr, SM Rocks and RS Schwartz, 'An Introduction to the Revised UCC Article 8 and Review of Other Recent Developments with Investment Securities' (1994) 49 The Business Lawyer 1891; and an unattributed note in the Harvard Law Review, 'Super-Priority of Securities Intermediaries under the new Section 9-115(5)(c) of the Uniform Commercial Code' (1995) 108 Harvard Law Review 1937.
[103] Mooney, 'Beyond Negotiability' (n 102 above) 376–377.

interests should not take free, Mooney's UTP does not seem to differ substantially in practice from the approach taken in this work.

6.81 In view of the position taken in this work as to priorities, it may seem appropriate for secured creditors of investors to seek undertakings from the investor's intermediaries to respect the security by not taking action which may jeopardise the substance of benefits which flow from upper tiers to the investor. Such undertakings would raise certain difficulties. To be effective, it would be necessary to take irrevocable undertakings from intermediaries at every tier of a custodial structure above an investor. As mere contractual provisions, if such undertakings were breached or improperly revoked, this could provide the aggrieved creditor with personal rights of action against the intermediary. Although the credit risk of many intermediaries would not ordinarily be great, because they are often banks or bank-funded depositories with deep pockets, it may be that it is precisely those intermediaries who are already in financial difficulty that would breach or revoke such an undertaking,[104] rendering a personal action by the creditor of little economic value. It is unclear whether such an undertaking would justify a custodian refusing to take action ordered by the party (an intermediary custodian) he holds for and is accountable to, on the speculation that this may harm another party (the investor) he has undertaken to protect. The need for intermediaries to make such judgements makes it unlikely that they would be willing to enter such undertakings.

---

[104] J Franks and C Mayer, *Risk, Regulation and Investor Protection: The Case of Investment Management* (1989) 2.9.

7

CUSTODIAN'S DUTIES

Duties owed by custodians to investors form part of the package of rights that **7.01** investors with assets in custody enjoy.[1] An analysis of these duties provides investors with a better idea of what their package of rights consists of. This analysis serves two further purposes. It confirms what is expected of a custodian, including the degree of care and skill that should be brought to bear. Further, in case of dispute between custodian and investor, the question of whether a duty has been breached may serve as a basis for investors obtaining a remedy for loss suffered.

There are different types of custodians, ranging from bare nominees to custodians **7.02** who offer a wide variety of additional services, including valuation, tax and corporate action. The service offered may also encompass the use of sub-custodians domestically or, more likely, in order to hold offshore assets for the investor. In view of the endless possibilities regarding the precise duties to be performed by any custodian, the present analysis does not seek to provide an enumeration of the duties that any custodian will be obliged to perform, but rather to suggest principles by which such duties may be identified.

---

[1] See J Benjamin, *The Law of Global Custody* (1996), ch 8.

A. Sources of Duties

7.03 Parties to a custodial relationship will ordinarily have entered into some form of agreement setting out the terms on which the service is offered, including the duties expected of the custodian. Beyond this, the terms of the relationship may be characterised under general law in a manner that results in the imposition of additional, default, duties on the custodian by general law. The applicability and extent of such additional duties is examined in the following section on scope of duties.

7.04 A custodian may also be subject to duties imposed by regulatory provisions relevant to the terms of the custodial service. In particular, duties are imposed on custodians by the application of the Financial Services Act 1986 (Extension of Scope of Act) Order 1996[2] and by the Financial Services Act 1986.[3] Regulatory provisions relevant to the custodial service are considered in Chapter 9 on regulation.

B. Scope of Duties

(1) Terms of the Contract

7.05 The offer and use of a custodial service is essentially a consensual affair between custodian and investor or other intermediaries. Ordinarily, therefore, a custodial relationship will have been established on the basis of a contract between investor and custodian. This contract will set out the custodian's duties. Generally, these will be to look after the investor's assets on whatever terms have been negotiated and to provide whatever other value added services have been agreed.

(2) General Law

7.06 The characterisation of the custodial relationship under general law may also lead to default duties being imposed on the custodian by general law. Nevertheless, it is increasingly clear that if duties are imposed because of the status of the custodian under general law, such duties will apply only to the extent that the custodian acts within the parameters of such status. For example, the fact that a custodian is recognised as trustee or fiduciary of the investor will not necessarily govern all aspects of their relationship. To the extent that the trust relationship is not strictly relevant to their dealings in a particular commercial setting the trust will not be recognised.[4] Similarly, a fiduciary tag will only apply to the extent of fiduciary dealings and not necessarily to other action undertaken in relation to or on behalf

---

[2] SI 1996/2958.
[3] 1986 c 60.
[4] *Target Holdings Ltd v Redferns* [1996] 1 AC 421, 436A–E per Lord Browne-Wilkinson.

of the investor.[5] One difficulty with this approach is that it requires the drawing of bright lines between a custodian acting as trustee or fiduciary and when he acts as ordinary contractual counter-party.

Custodian Bailee

For a custodian as bailee, since the conceptual basis of bailment is the voluntary **7.07** assumption of possession of another's property,[6] the scope of duties as bailee essentially falls to be determined by the terms on which the assets were received. It is therefore unlikely that the characterisation of the custodian as bailee will lead to the imposition by general law of default duties beyond those contemplated in the agreement between investor and custodian or other party from whom the assets were received.

Custodian Trustee

Although many of the default rules of the laws of trusts evolved in the context of **7.08** family or succession trusts over the course of the last century, there is authority that they are of application to modern commercial trusts,[7] presumably including custodians as trustees. However, there is a growing trend to restrict the general application of these rules. Lord Browne-Wilkinson has stated that 'it is in any event wrong to lift wholesale the detailed rules developed in the context of traditional trusts and then seek to apply them to trusts of quite a different kind'.[8] He suggested that although the fundamental principles of equity would remain applicable to any trust, the extent to which the detailed rules of the law of trusts apply is a function of the context of the trust, taking into particular consideration the commercial purposes to which it was being put.[9] There is support for this from at least one American case,[10] as well as American academic commentary.[11] This development does not of itself make the scope of trustees' duties more certain. The question remains of where precisely the lines between detailed rules and fundamental principles will be drawn. Although the results of such an inquiry cannot

---

[5] *Re Coomber* [1911] 1 Ch 723, 728 per Fletcher Moulton LJ; *Bristol and West BS v Mothew* [1996] 4 All ER 698, 710 per Millett LJ. See also P Finn, 'Fiduciary Law and the Modern Commercial World' in E McKendrick (ed), *Commercial Aspects of Trusts and Fiduciary Obligations* (1992) 37; L Sealy, 'Fiduciary Obligations, Forty Years On' (1995) 9 Journal of Contract Law 37, 41; and RP Austin, 'Moulding the Content of Fiduciary Duties' in AJ Oakley (ed), *Trends in Contemporary Trust Law* (1996) 155, 174.

[6] *The Pioneer Container* [1994] 2 AC 324, 342.

[7] *Cowan v Scargill* [1985] Ch 270, 292 per Sir Robert Megarry VC; see also *Wilson v Law Debenture Trust Corp* [1995] 2 All ER 337, 347 per Rattee J.

[8] *Target Holdings Ltd v Redferns* [1996] 1 AC 421, 435 per Lord Browne-Wilkinson; see also *Henderson v Merrett Syndicates Ltd* [1995] 2 AC 145, 206 per Lord Browne-Wilkinson.

[9] *Target* 436.

[10] *Meckel v Continental Resources Co* 758 F2d 811, 816 per Cardamone CJ (US Court of Appeals, Second Circuit, 1985).

[11] JH Langbein, 'The Contractarian Basis of the Law of Trusts' (1995) 105(2) Yale LJ 625, 631.

be predicted with certainty, it may be suggested, given recent pronouncements, that the scope of duties of a custodian trustee will be determined more by the context of the trust and the terms of any agreement between custodian and trustee than by reference to the general law of trusts.

Custodian *Qua* Fiduciary

7.09 Unalloyed altruism may be demanded of custodians as fiduciaries,[12] in order to procure their loyalty in service.[13] The duties imposed on fiduciaries are most often proscriptive,[14] seeking to prevent actual misuse of office and potential conflicts of duty.[15] Thus, fiduciaries were traditionally prevented from deriving any profit from their office, including recompense for labour and skill;[16] and obliged to not permit situations to arise where the interests of the beneficiary came into conflict with their own[17] or a third party's[18] interests. There are suggestions that certain prescriptive obligations also ensue including, inter alia, duties of loyalty or good faith and disclosure.[19] However, Finn has countered that good faith may be an independent principle of law[20] and that a duty of disclosure may simply inhere in the type of undertaking to which the fiduciary is subject, an argument applicable to other detailed prescriptive duties.[21] He also warns against the undue recognition of additional prescriptive duties because this 'has the potential if unrestrained to outflank the law of professional negligence'.[22] For these reasons, the better approach may be to recognise that fiduciary duties are only proscriptive.

7.10 Whether proscriptive or prescriptive, the absolute nature of traditional fiduciary duties may be criticised as excessive. It is unrealistic to expect, as a general rule,

---

[12] *Keech v Sandford* (1726) Sel Cas T King 61, 62 per Lord Chancellor King, 25 ER 223; *Meinhard v Salmon* 164 NE 545, 546 per Cardozo J (1928).

[13] See P Finn, 'Fiduciary Law and the Modern Commercial World' in E McKendrick (ed), *Commercial Aspects of Trusts and Fiduciary Obligations* (1992) 9; and EJ Weinrib, 'The Fiduciary Obligation' (1975) 25 University of Toronto Law Journal 1.

[14] *Chan v Zacharia* (1983) 53 ALR 417, 433 per Deane J, HC of Australia; *Warman International Ltd v Dwyer* (1995) 69 ALJR 362, 366.

[15] P Finn, 'Fiduciary Law and the Modern Commercial World' in E McKendrick (ed), *Commercial Aspects of Trusts and Fiduciary Obligations* (1992) 9; C Harpum, 'Fiduciary Obligations and Fiduciary Powers: Where Are We Going?', a paper delivered at SPTL Seminars for 1996, 'Pressing Problems in the Law XI' 4; and J Glover, *Commercial Equity: Fiduciary Relationships* (1995) 135.

[16] *Robinson v Pett* (1734) 3 P Wms 249, 251 per Lord Chancellor Talbot; 24 ER 1049.

[17] *Spector v Ageda* [1973] Ch 30, 47 per Megarry J.

[18] *Moody v Cox* [1917] 2 Ch 71, 81 per Lord Cozens-Hardy MR.

[19] RP Austin, 'Moulding the Content of Fiduciary Duties' in AJ Oakley (ed), *Trends in Contemporary Trust Law* (1996); and Law Commission, *Fiduciary Duties and Regulatory Rules* (Law Com No 236, 1995) 1.4. See also *Bristol and West BS v Mothew* [1996] 4 All ER 698, 712 per Millett LJ.

[20] PD Finn, 'The Fiduciary Principle' in TG Youdan (ed), *Equity, Fiduciaries and Trusts* (1989) 10–24.

[21] ibid 25.

[22] ibid 26.

people to deploy skill and effort wholly altruistically, possibly to the detriment of their own fortunes. Further pressure on the purity of the traditional fiduciary principle derives from the perception that its indiscriminate nature could be inimical to market efficiency[23] and to the interests of the beneficiary.[24] By the early eighteenth century, therefore, the purity of the fiduciary principle had begun to give way to the extent of the terms on which the fiduciary took office.[25] More recently, the Privy Council has stated that the scope of duties of a fiduciary 'depends upon the terms on which they are acting. . . . the scope of the fiduciary duties owed . . . are to be defined by the terms of the contract'.[26] In view of this development, it is unlikely that unintended default rules will come into play.

Duty of Care

A custodian may be under a general duty of care in relation to the services he offers. Where custodial services are established by contract, this general duty may arise by express or implied contract terms.[27] A duty of care may also be imposed by statute. For example, section 13 of the Supply of Goods and Services Act 1982 provides that in a contract for the supply of services by a supplier acting in the course of his business there will be 'an implied term that the supplier will carry out the service with reasonable care and skill'.   **7.11**

A general duty of care may also be imposed by general law. Whether there is a general duty of care between one party and another depends on whether they are in a position of proximity in circumstances that warrant recognition of such a duty. The courts have approached the determination of this question in relation to the provision of services in a number of ways. Although some of the cases which are considered relate to the provision of information or advice, it is clear that the House of Lords considers them applicable to other areas, including the provision of services.[28] Under general law, where one party with a skill undertakes to deploy that skill in favour of another and that other relies on that skill, a duty of care will   **7.12**

---

[23] W Bishop and DD Prentice, 'Some Legal and Economic Aspects of Fiduciary Remuneration' (1983) 46 MLR 289, 296. Productive inefficiency will arise where innocent economic opportunities must be foregone due to the restrictions.

[24] For example, if the increased efforts of the fiduciary would also result in increased benefit to the beneficiary, such as by seeking out stock-lending opportunities for the investor in circumstances where the custodian receives a commission.

[25] *Robinson v Pett* (1734) 3 P Wms 249, 251 per Lord Chancellor Talbot, 24 ER 1049; *Ellison v Airey* (1748) 1 Ves Sen 111, 115, 27 ER 924.

[26] *Kelly v Cooper* [1993] AC 205, 214–215. See also *Hospital Products Ltd v United States Surgical Operation* (1984) 156 CLR 41, 97 per Mason J, HC of Australia; *Clark Boyce v Mouat* [1994] 1 AC 428, 437 per Lord Jauncey of Tullichettle; *Henderson v Merrett Syndicates Ltd* [1995] 2 AC 145, 206 per Lord Browne-Wilkinson; and Law Commission, *Fiduciary Duties and Regulatory Rules* (Law Com No 236, 1995) 3.29.

[27] *Henderson v Merrett Syndicates Ltd* [1995] 2 AC 145, 193 per Lord Goff; *Banque Bruxelles SA v Eagle Star* [1997] AC 191, 211 per Lord Hoffmann.

[28] *Henderson v Merrett Syndicates Ltd* [1995] 2 AC 145, 180 per Lord Goff.

arise.[29] Some recent cases have suggested that the assumption of responsibility where one knows or ought to know that one's skill or advice will be relied upon is sufficient, without the need for actual reliance by the beneficiary of the responsibility.[30] A duty of care may also arise if between the parties there is foreseeability of damage from the actions of the actor, sufficient proximity between them and it is just and reasonable in the circumstances to impose a duty of care.[31] The facts of custody of assets will generally fall within these approaches to the recognition of a duty of care. The duty is to employ 'reasonable care and skill'[32] as judged against the ordinary standards of people exercising like skill.[33]

7.13 A duty of care imposed by general law may exist concurrently with contractual duties of care.[34] Although it has been suggested that where these duties of care exist concurrently the scope of the general law duty of care is not limited by the terms of the contract,[35] the House of Lords has expressed the view that the scope of the general law duty of care may in such circumstances be restricted by the terms of the contract.[36] As such the two types of duty of care will be substantively 'no different'[37] from one another. However, because of the different forms of the duties, ie contract or tort, issues of privity and limitation periods may make one form of the duty more strategically advantageous in a dispute than the other.

Duty of Care to One Party on the Basis of Services Rendered in Favour of Another Party

7.14 Where there are extended tiers of custody, the question arises whether the ultimate custodian owes a duty of care to the ultimate beneficiary or other intermediary with whom he (the ultimate custodian) is not in direct contact for services provided to his own counter-party. A similar question also arises where the custodian is instructed by a third party, such as a fund-manager, to act for the investor.

---

[29] *Hedley Byrne & Co Ltd v Heller & Partners Ltd* [1964] AC 465, 502–503 per Lord Morris; *Henderson v Merrett Syndicates Ltd* [1995] 2 AC 145, 181–182 per Lord Goff; *White v Jones* [1995] 2 AC 207, 268 per Lord Goff, 271 per Lord Browne-Wilkinson; *Aiken v Stewart Wrightson Members Agency Ltd* [1995] 1 WLR 1281, 1300 per Potter J.

[30] *White v Jones* [1995] 2 AC 207, 275 per Lord Browne-Wilkinson; *Penn v Bristol and West Building Society* [1995] 2 FLR 938, 949 per Kolbert J.

[31] *Caparo Plc v Dickman* [1990] 2 AC 605, 633 per Lord Oliver; *Marc Rich & Co v Bishop Rock Ltd* [1996] 1 AC 211, 235 per Lord Steyn; *Possfund Ltd v Diamond* [1996] 1 WLR 1351, 1359–1360 per Lightman J; *Banque Bruxelles SA v Eagle Star* [1997] AC 191, 211 per Lord Hoffmann.

[32] *Hedley Byrne & Co Ltd v Heller & Partners Ltd* [1964] AC 465, 502–503 per Lord Morris; *Henderson v Merrett Syndicates Ltd* [1995] 2 AC 145, 174 per Lord Goff.

[33] *Bolam v Friern Hospital Management Committee* [1957] 1 WLR 582, 586 per McNair J.

[34] *Henderson v Merrett Syndicates Ltd* [1995] 2 AC 145, 194 per Lord Goff, 206 per Lord Browne-Wilkinson.

[35] *Aiken v Stewart Wrightson Members Agency Ltd* [1995] 1 WLR 1281, 1300 per Potter J.

[36] *Banque Bruxelles SA v Eagle Star* [1997] AC 191, 211 per Lord Hoffmann. See also *Henderson v Merrett Syndicates Ltd* [1995] 2 AC 145, 206 per Lord Browne-Wilkinson.

[37] *Henderson v Merrett Syndicates Ltd* [1995] 2 AC 145, 194 per Lord Goff.

Lord Morris stated in *Hedley Byrne* that '[i]n the absence of any direct dealings between one person and another, there are many and varied situations in which a duty is owed by one person to another'.[38] This has recently been affirmed by Lords Goff and Browne-Wilkinson in the House of Lords, based on the principle of 'assumption of responsibility'.[39] '[T]he fact that the defendant assumed to act in the plaintiff's affairs pursuant to a contract with a third party is not necessarily incompatible with the finding that, by so acting, the defendant also entered into a special relationship with the plaintiff with whom he had no contract.'[40]

Although *White v Jones* was a case in which the third party with whom the defen- **7.15** dant had contracted was dead and the court appears to have been motivated by a desire to achieve practical justice,[41] it is clear that such a duty may be imposed for *inter vivos* transactions.[42] It may be recalled that but for the express disclaimer in *Hedley Byrne*,[43] the negligent provision of a reference by one bank (defendant) to the plaintiff's bank (third party) would have resulted in liability to the plaintiff. Similarly, in *Henderson v Merrett Syndicates Ltd*[44] the House of Lords applied the concept of assumption of responsibility to recognise a duty where the defendant (managing) agent had, pursuant to a contract with the third party (member's agent), undertaken the management of the plaintiff's affairs.[45]

In view of the numerous parties and tiers of transactions often involved in custo- **7.16** dial transactions, the fact that Lord Browne-Wilkinson[46] seemed willing to permit claims from parties unascertained when responsibility for the task was assumed may raise fears of limitless claims. However, Lord Browne-Wilkinson's comment relates to unascertained parties amongst an identified class of beneficiaries under an existing trust, not wholly unascertained parties. Fears of indeterminate suits are further allayed by Lord Goff who stated that liability in these circumstances will not extend to an indeterminate class, but that in the ordinary case it will only extend to 'a small number of identified people'.[47] However, these matters are not entirely free from doubt because he stated that the precise limits would be determined in a pragmatic way as more complicated cases arose.[48] Nevertheless, since this type of duty is based on assumption of responsibility, it is unlikely that the

---

[38] *Hedley Byrne & Co Ltd v Heller & Partners Ltd* [1964] AC 465, 495.

[39] *White v Jones* [1995] 2 AC 207 at 268 and 270 respectively; Lord Nolan agreed at 276 and 295.

[40] ibid 274 per Lord Browne-Wilkinson.

[41] ibid 260, 268 per Lord Goff; Lords Browne-Wilkinson and Nolan agreed at 276 and 295 respectively.

[42] *Spring v Guardian Assurance Plc* [1995] 2 AC 296.

[43] [1964] AC 465.

[44] [1995] 2 AC 145.

[45] Acknowledged by Lord Browne-Wilkinson in *White v Jones* [1995] 2 AC 207, 274.

[46] ibid 271.

[47] ibid 269.

[48] ibid.

class of people to whom such a duty will be owed will be extended beyond those who are somehow identifiable, even if unascertained, at the time the duty was undertaken.

C. Delegation of Duties

7.17 The immobilisation of investment assets, greater interest in offshore investments and increased practice of white-labelling of custodial services will give questions regarding the delegation of duties a heightened prominence. The principal question is the effect that a delegation of duties has on the primary duties of the custodian. Does the fact that the lead custodian has properly delegated the work absolve him of his original duty, or does he remain responsible for the proper execution of the tasks?

7.18 'A sub-bailee is one to whom actual possession of goods is transferred by someone who is not himself the owner of the goods but has a present right to possession of them as bailee of the owner.'[49] The implication of this statement is that the sub-bailment does not cancel the principal bailment. Although the sub-bailment brings the head bailor and sub-bailee into a direct relationship of bailment as well, the two relationships co-exist. This sub-bailment relationship is collateral to the main one between head bailor and bailee.[50] If the bailee delegates possession of the assets to another in circumstances that remove him from the chain between investor and assets, he does not establish a sub-bailment, this amounts to a substituted bailment. It is a question of fact to be determined in any circumstances whether it is the intention of the bailee to determine his involvement in the chain of bailments or to continue therein.[51]

7.19 The fact that a bailee may delegate performance of his obligations does not necessarily lead to the conclusion that he may delegate responsibility for the obligations as well.[52] A bailee that undertakes a task may be made liable for the manner in which it is executed, whether by his own efforts or those of other parties he chooses to rely upon. If, on the other hand, the bailee's duty is simply to assist the bailor in finding a substitute bailee, whereupon his duty is discharged, there seems to be little reason for holding the bailee accountable for the action of the substitute bailee. Even with these more limited obligations, however, if the bailee is negligent in his choice of sub- or substitute bailee, he may be open to an action in tort.

---

[49]   *China Pacific v Food Corpn* [1982] AC 939, 959 per Lord Diplock.
[50]   *The Pioneer Container* [1994] 2 AC 324, 338.
[51]   Pollock and Wright, *An Essay on Possession in the Common Law* (1888) 169; Palmer, *Bailment* (2nd edn, 1991) 1348.
[52]   An argument successfully advanced in analogous circumstances, master-servant, in *Morris v CW Martin & Sons Ltd* [1966] 1 QB 716, 719.

To the extent that a custodian is constituted trustee, there are legislative provisions **7.20** that affect delegation.[53] He is required to act in good faith in employing an agent and, as a rule, is not responsible for the default of the agent so employed.[54] Does this absolve him from the duty to act with care? Is it enough for the custodian to be honest but negligent in the process of delegation? There are suggestions of affirmative answers to these questions by Hoffmann J in *Steel v Wellcome Trustees Ltd.*[55] However, the better view may be that implied by Maugham J in *Re Vickery*,[56] that although the trustee must use good faith in employing an agent, this does not absolve him from employing due diligence as well.[57]

A further provision seeks to relieve trustees of liability for the actions of their **7.21** agents by indicating that a trustee is generally only accountable for his own acts unless loss via a third party arises from 'wilful default' on his own part.[58] Although wilful default used to be taken to mean a lack of reasonable care,[59] Maugham J in *Re Vickery* took it to mean a 'consciousness of negligence, or breach of duty, or recklessness'.[60] It has also been suggested by Millett LJ, in *Armitage v Nurse*,[61] that wilful default means a 'deliberate breach of trust', and that there is no reason why a trustee acting in good faith should not be permitted to benefit from the provision.[62] This development may be criticised on a number of grounds. The provision formed part of a consolidating Act and should therefore not be interpreted in a manner that alters standards of care existing at the time, nor should it be given an interpretation that deviates from what formerly obtained. Secondly, the authorities purportedly relied upon by Maugham J were cases where the phrase was considered in the context of company law, not the law of trusts.[63] Nevertheless, the approach of *Re Vickery* has been welcomed[64] for being consistent with the ordinary meaning of the words. It was also suggested that the analogy of trustees with company directors from the company law cases is apt because early consideration of directors' duties was based on those of trustees. Although the interpretation of Maugham J was recently affirmed in *Armitage v Nurse*,[65] the fact

---

[53] See, generally, Law Commission, *The Law of Trusts: Delegation by Individual Trustees* (Law Com No 220, 1994).
[54] Trustee Act 1925, s 23(1).
[55] [1988] 1 WLR 167, 174.
[56] [1931] 1 Ch 572, 581 per Maugham J.
[57] A view shared by GH Jones, 'Delegation by Trustees: A Reappraisal' (1959) 22 MLR 381; and Hayton, *Underhill and Hayton, Law Relating to Trusts and Trustees* (15th edn, 1995) 623.
[58] Trustee Act 1925, s 30.
[59] *Re Brier* (1881) 26 ChD 238, 243 per Earl of Selborne LC; *Re Chapman* [1896] 2 Ch 763, 776 per Lindley LJ.
[60] [1931] 1 Ch 572 at 584.
[61] [1997] 2 All ER 705, 711.
[62] See *Parker and Mellows, The Modern Law of Trusts* (6th edn, 1994) 405.
[63] *Re City Equitable Fire Insurance Co* [1925] Ch 407, on winding-up; *Re Trusts of Leeds City Brewery Limited's Debenture Stock Deed* [1925] Ch 532, on a debenture trust deed.
[64] R Ham, QC, 'Trustees' Liability' (1994) 61 BPL (November) 1, 5.
[65] [1997] 2 All ER 705, 711–712.

that at least one case subsequent to *Re Vickery* has suggested that the omission of something which a prudent trustee ought to have done may constitute wilful default[66] suggests that a trustee delegating work should ensure that he employs at least ordinary prudence and not rely on the lower standards suggested by Maugham J and Millett LJ. It cannot be taken for granted that the argument of honest incompetence will win the sympathy of a court.[67]

7.22   Having properly delegated work, is that the end of the trustee's duty of care? The manner in which the courts have approached the interpretation of wilful default would suggest not. In cases pre- and post-dating the legislation of 1925 which used the phrase, it was taken for granted that the delegating trustee was obliged to undertake some degree of supervision.[68] The implication of this is that neither the legislative recognition of the right of trustees to delegate work in good faith nor the purported diminution in standards required of trustees relieves trustees of their duty to exercise common prudence in the supervision of people to whom they delegate work.

D. Restriction of Duty or Liability

7.23   Since the offer and use of custodial services is essentially a consensual affair between investor and custodian there may be efforts to circumscribe strictly the scope of the custodian's duties. The effect of any restriction is a question of construction, but substantially takes one of three basic forms: (a) define a finite list of duties, leaving out unwanted duties, so that only what is encompassed by the definition will be regarded as a duty of the custodian; (b) expressly negate a duty that would otherwise apply; or (c) accept the application of a duty but limit liability therefor, such as by offering an indemnity or otherwise insulating the beneficiary of the clause (custodian) from the consequence of breach.

7.24   With forms (a) and (b) the restriction takes effect by avoiding the imposition of the duty altogether, in the former by not including it in the finite list of duties to be performed and in the latter by negating it. With (c) a breach of duty will subsist, although the custodian is absolved of liability for the breach to the extent provided for by the restriction. Therefore, with (c) unanticipated consequences which flow *ipso facto* from the breach that have not been provided for will still take

---

[66]   *Bartlett v Barclays Trust Co (Nos 1 and 2)* [1980] Ch 515, 546 per Brightman LJ.

[67]   See J Getzler, 'Gentlemen do not Collect Rents: Fiduciary Obligations and Principal/Agency Problems', a paper delivered at the W.G. Hart Legal Workshop 1995 (5 July 1995) on 'Liability, Regulation and Risk Management: Reorienting the Legal Debate' at the Institute of Advanced Legal Studies of the University of London. See also *Armitage v Nurse* [1997] 2 All ER 705, 715 per Millett LJ.

[68]   *Re Brier* (1881) 26 ChD 238, 244 per Earl of Selborne LC; *Re Vickery* [1931] 1 Ch 572, 584–585 per Maugham J.

effect. One example of legislative provision for restriction comes in the shape of section 61 of the Trustee Act 1925 by which a trustee may be exonerated, wholly or partly, by a court from liability for benign breach of trust if the trustee acted honestly and reasonably and ought fairly to be excused, a type (c) restriction.[69]

As indicated above in the section on custodian bailees, the essence of a bailment is **7.25** the voluntary assumption of possession of the bailor's thing. If the terms of the bailment are the terms on which possession is undertaken, it must be within the bailee's power to restrict the duties that he undertakes to perform. In relation to trustees it is well accepted that a settlor directing his trustee is 'at liberty to say, "[y]our duty shall require no more of you than this". The Court could not extend the office, or invest it with greater obligation'.[70] The Privy Council in *Kelly v Cooper* has also established that fiduciary duties may be circumscribed by agreement between fiduciary and beneficiary.[71]

(1) Justification of Restriction of Duty or Liability

The decision in *Kelly v Cooper* has been criticised for allowing 'the tail of contract **7.26** to wag the dog of duty'.[72] This reproach could be made in relation to general law trustee and bailee duties as well. One answer to this criticism is that the essence of these general law duties is to ensure that particular acts or relationships are carried out according to the intention or expectation of the relevant parties; and that general law in this context may be facilitative of consensual relationships, not the other way round. If this is right, to adapt the metaphor, it would seem appropriate that the dog of contract wags the tail of general law duties. The criticism that the case provides *carte blanche* to persons acting in potentially inconsistent capacities in the area of financial services[73] is, it is submitted, equally misplaced. Bailees, trustees and fiduciaries are not given *carte blanche*, they only enjoy freedom to the extent agreed by both parties, subject to overriding regulation.

(2) Limitations on the Ability to Restrict Duty or Liability

It has been suggested that since 'it is often the personal shortcomings or limita- **7.27** tions of the property owners that account for the employment of others to manage their affairs, it would be unrealistic in the extreme to expect that they could protect their own interests by some suitable contractual arrangement. It follows, therefore, that this type of relationship cannot of necessity be dealt with by private ordering. Inevitably there will be a need for the legal system to address itself to this

---

[69] Although courts may be slow to relieve paid trustees whose interests may conflict with those of the trust, it remains a possibility, see *Re Pauling's Settlement Trusts* [1964] 1 Ch 303, 339 per Willmer LJ.

[70] *Wilkins v Hogg* (1861) 31 LJCh 41, 43 per Lord Westbury LC.

[71] [1993] AC 205, 214.

[72] I Brown, 'Divided Loyalties in the Law of Agency' (1993) 109 LQR 206, 209.

[73] FMB Reynolds, 'Annotating Bowstead on Agency (15th edn)' [1994] JBL 144, 149.

problem'.[74] In relation to custody business, this assumption may be challenged. Negotiation and assessment of the counter-party and services offered are the stuff of the marketplace, of which custody is an ancillary service. The use of custodians is generally not an act of weakness or desperation, but forms part of a sophisticated strategy in pursuit of profit.

7.28 Nevertheless, there will always be situations that call for the intervention of the legal system. Some who use custodians may not be capable of undertaking the careful risk assessment suggested above. It is also impossible to provide contractually for every eventuality. The fact that the contractual approach is accepted as a basic principle does not lead inevitably to the abandonment of concern for impropriety. An alternative system of controlling the possibility of misfeasance by the fiduciary may be evolved in tandem with general law. A case is therefore made for some degree of regulation. However, for society to justify regulation it will be necessary to demonstrate that the increased costs of regulation, such as the cost of monitoring the fiduciary, do not outweigh the value of any benefits.[75]

Legislative Limitations on the Ability to Restrict Duty or Liability

7.29 If the restriction is by way of a contract term, the provision's validity may fall to be assessed under section 3 of the Unfair Contract Terms Act 1977 (UCTA), which subjects exclusion clauses to a reasonableness test. In spite of the fact that doubts have been expressed as to whether UCTA applies where the contract relates to the restriction of trustee duties, because such duties derive from 'the settlor's power to direct how his property should be dealt with',[76] these doubts would seem to be misplaced. UCTA should apply to a contract setting out custodial arrangements[77] because, notwithstanding the fact that such arrangements also constitute a trust, the agreement is no less a contract. If the custody arrangements do not constitute a trust, and to the extent that services offered do not relate to a trust, such as certain value added services, there should be little dispute that UCTA is applicable.

---

[74] W Bishop and DD Prentice, 'Some Legal and Economic Aspects of Fiduciary Remuneration' (1983) 46 MLR 289. Although these comments were not made with custodians in mind, similar arguments may be made in this context.

[75] Such an exercise has been conducted, see SIB, *Consultative Paper 90: Custody* (August 1995).

[76] *Re Duke of Norfolk's Settlement Trusts* [1982] Ch 61, 77 per Fox LJ.

An early suggestion that UCTA may be applicable to professional trustees may be found in W Goodhart, QC, 'Trustee Exemption Clauses and the Unfair Contract Terms Act 1977' [1980] Conveyancer 333. This was subsequently rejected by the Court of Appeal in the above case; and doubted by P Matthews, 'The Efficacy of Trustee Exemption Clauses in English Law' [1989] Conveyancer 42, 52; by C Harpum, 'Fiduciary Obligations and Fiduciary Powers: Where Are We Going?', a paper delivered at SPTL Seminars for 1996, 'Pressing Problems in the Law XI', 6, n 45 and by Goodhart himself in 'Trust Law for the Twenty-First Century' in AJ Oakley (ed), *Trends in Contemporary Trust Law* (1996) 270.

[77] Hayton, *Underhill and Hayton, Law Relating to Trusts and Trustees* (15th edn, 1995) 559, 562.

Where UCTA applies, an exclusion clause may yet be exempt from the Act by **7.30**
virtue of paragraph 1(e) of Schedule 1 to the Act which provides, inter alia, that
section 3 of the Act will not apply to 'any contract so far as it relates to the creation
or transfer of securities or of any right or interest in securities'. This provision
applies 'not merely to contracts for the creation or transfer of securities. It is
worded to apply to *any* contract *so far as* it relates' to the expressed action.[78]
Examples of where this may be relevant in the present context would include a
contract for single-tier intermediated custody which involves transfer of securities
to a custodian, as well as the creation of interests in the transferred securities in
favour of the transferor investor; if the beneficiary of an equitable interest in securities, possibly of an offshore custodial holding by way of trust, transferred his
interest to a local (English) custodian as his global custodian; and the settlement
of securities or interests therein. Exclusion clauses relating to the safe-keeping and
value added services portions of such contracts should not be exempt from the
scrutiny of UCTA by virtue of paragraph 1(e) of Schedule 1; and exclusion
clauses in relation to interests under multiple tiers of intermediary custody should
also not qualify for the exemption under paragraph 1(e) because they do not relate
to securities or direct interests therein.

Even if exempt from UCTA, an exclusion clause relating to a consumer may yet **7.31**
have to be assessed for unfairness under the Unfair Terms in Consumer Contracts
Regulations 1994.[79] A consumer is defined as a natural person who in making the
contract is acting outside his business.[80] These regulations may, therefore, apply
only to retail investors. Contracts entered into by professional investors and custodians with one another as intermediaries should be exempt. The regulations
apply to contracts entered into by consumers that are made up of standard terms
or terms that have not been individually negotiated.[81] Terms that are unfair
according to the criteria set out in regulation 4 are not binding on consumers.[82]
However, terms that are individually negotiated or which, in plain intelligible lan-
guage, relate to the main subject matter of the contract or the terms of payment
are exempt from the scrutiny of the Regulations,[83] as are terms incorporated in
order to comply with or reflect statutory or regulatory provisions in the United
Kingdom or the provisions of an international convention to which member
states are party.[84]

---

[78] *Micklefield v SAC Technology Ltd* [1991] 1 All ER 275, 281 per John Mowbray QC, sitting as
a Deputy Judge of the High Court.
[79] SI 1994/3159. See R Thomas and D Sabalot, 'Unfair Terms in Consumer Contracts
Regulations: The Impact on the Financial Services Industry' (1995) 10 BJIBFL 214.
[80] SI 1994/3159, reg 2(1).
[81] ibid reg 3(1).
[82] ibid reg 5.
[83] ibid reg 3(2).
[84] ibid Sch 1, para (e).

General Law Limitations on the Ability to Restrict Duty or Liability

7.32   If an exclusion clause satisfies or escapes the scrutiny of legislative provisions, the clause may yet offend common law limitations on what may be excluded. For instance, if there is misrepresentation in the process of contract formation an exclusion clause contained therein may not be relied upon,[85] though there is authority that this will only obtain if the misrepresentation induced the contract.[86] Similarly, no one may rely on a clause to exclude liability for his own fraud,[87] though whether such a clause can validly exclude liability for the fraud of the person's agent is more arguable.[88]

(a)   Limitation on Restricting Duty of Care

7.33   *Hedley Byrne v Heller*[89] is authority for the proposition that a general duty of care may be excluded by a contractual provision; this was affirmed in *Henderson v Merrett Syndicates Ltd.*[90] A provision in a contract restricting an actor's liability in tort to a third party is also likely to be effective as against the third party.[91] Where the restrictive provision is in a contract between the beneficiary of the duty of care and a third party, the fact that the actor/defendant is not party to it will not bar him from relying on the exclusion clause.[92]

(b)   Limitation on Restricting Duties Under a Bailment

7.34   Express terms that exclude a duty under a bailment will be effective. It is enough to exclude liability that the term is merely inconsistent with the duties owed at common law.[93] Since bailment does not arise by virtue of what the bailor or intermediary does or thinks, but by the voluntary assumption of possession by the (ultimate) bailee, in order to establish a valid exclusion clause effective on the bailee it is essential that the restriction forms part of the terms on which the bailee assumes possession of the assets. Given that bailment and contract are distinct, it is immaterial that the restriction is not contained in an agreement to which both

---

[85] *Curtis v Chemical Cleaning and Dyeing Co* [1951] 1 KB 805, 809 per Denning LJ.

[86] *Horry v Tate & Lyle* [1982] 2 Lloyd's Rep 416, 422 per Peter Pain J.

[87] *S Pearson & Son, Limited v Dublin Corporation* [1907] AC 351, 353–354 per Lord Loreburn LC, 362 per Lord James; see also *Thomas Witter v TBP Industries* (1994) [1996] 2 All ER 573, 598 per Jacob J.

[88] *S Pearson & Son Limited v Dublin Corporation* [1907] AC 351, 353–354 per Lord Loreburn LC.

[89] [1964] AC 465.

[90] [1995] 2 AC 145, 194 per Lord Goff, 206 per Lord Browne-Wilkinson.

[91] *Clerk & Lindsell on Torts* (17th edn, 1995) 7-87. *Leigh and Sillivan Ltd v Aliakmon Ltd* [1985] QB 350, 399 per Goff LJ; *Muirhead v Industrial Tank Ltd* [1986] QB 507, 530.

[92] *Clerk & Lindsell on Torts* (17th edn, 1995) 7-87. *Pacific Associates v Baxter* [1990] 1 QB 993, 1022–1023 per Purchas LJ, 1039 per Russell LJ.

[93] *Union Transport Finance v British Car Auctions* [1978] 2 All ER 385, 390 per Roskill LJ; *Yasuda Ltd v Orion Underwriting Ltd* [1995] QB 174, 186 per Colman J.

bailor and bailee are privy, or that there is no consideration flowing from one party to the other.

In a sub/quasi-bailment, if the head bailor consents (expressly or impliedly) to **7.35** more limited duties for the ultimate bailee than that bailee would otherwise have had to observe, and the ultimate (sub/quasi-) bailee accepts the bailment on such terms, it is such more limited duties that will apply to the ultimate bailee.[94] Thus, if, as in *The Pioneer Container*, the head bailor has given the bailee/sub-bailor a wide discretion as to the terms on which to establish the sub-bailment, the head bailor will be bound by restrictions in such sub- (collateral) bailment. Where, however, the head bailor has only consented to restricted terms of bailment between himself and the bailee, *The Mahkutai*[95] makes clear that a sub-bailee will not necessarily be able to bind the bailor to similar terms as those on which the main bailment was established. The difficulty for the sub-bailee in such a case is to demonstrate that he accepted possession on similar terms as contained in the principal bailment. He is not party to the principal bailment and so cannot rely on the fact that the restricted terms are in that main bailment.

In *The Mahkutai* a sub-bailment was demonstrably established on terms which **7.36** did not include the restrictions that existed in the main bailment. The document setting out the terms of the sub-bailment was construed by the court not to incorporate the restriction (from the main bailment) which the sub-bailee thought had been incorporated and upon which the sub-bailee purported to place reliance. In such a case, there is no room for an implied term that the sub-bailee established the sub-bailment on terms he thought were in the document.[96] The sub-bailment was expressly established on terms that were actually contained in the document and not what he thought was incorporated. It is a question of fact whether the bailee/sub-bailor incorporated restrictive terms in the sub-bailment. If incorporated, the sub-bailee may rely on the restrictions, not because there were similar ones in a principal bailment, but because the restrictions form part of the terms on which he took possession.

(c) Limitation on Restricting Fiduciary Duties

Given what was said earlier about the validity and efficacy of duty-defining **7.37** clauses, it is logical that any fiduciary obligations may be excluded by a suitably worded contract or appropriate circumstances. Cases such as *Kelly v Cooper* that were cited as authority for that position would bear this out.[97]

---

[94] *The Pioneer Container* [1994] 2 AC 324, 341.
[95] [1996] AC 650.
[96] ibid 668.
[97] See Law Commission, *Fiduciary Duties and Regulatory Rules* (Law Com No 236, 1995) 14.20.

(d) Limitation on Restricting Duties under a Trust

7.38   For trusts, there is authority that liability for any act, including negligence but short of fraud, may be excluded.[98] It would also seem to be the position that a trustee can exclude liability for the acts of his agents, such as sub-custodians, as long as the agent was appointed in good faith and the custodian himself was not culpable of wilful default.[99] Is it possible to relieve the trustee of the duty to act in good faith or to do anything at all? In *Hayim v Citibank*[100] Lord Templeman stated that a settlor can 'relieve the trustee of his will of any responsibility or duty in respect of trust property, . . . a testator may do as he pleases'.

7.39   A court faced with the construction of an exemption clause of this type has two options. The court may be governed by the desire to give effect to the intention of the parties to establish a trust, assuming such intention is clear; or the court may simply follow the totality of the specific wishes of the investor without regard to the type of structure which ultimately emerges. Whether explicitly or implicitly, the approach adopted by the court will involve balancing the parties' terms of engagement against what may be perceived to be their overriding wishes.

7.40   If a court perceives an intention to create a trust, it could, to give effect to this overriding intent, determine that a trust consists of an 'irreducible core' and that any clause repugnant to this intent should be struck down and the trust otherwise upheld. This argument readily lends itself to application in the custodial context because of the importance of the trust structure in ensuring that custody assets will be protected for the investor in case of the custodian's insolvency. Some support for this approach may be derived by analogy from the consideration of exclusion clauses in other contexts. In one case Brudnel CJ agreed with the submission that a provision inconsistent with the appointment of executors of a will would be void.[101] There are also cases considering the effect of this type of exclusion clause on a contract, in one of which Devlin J stated that '[i]t might be necessary to consider whether it is so repugnant that . . . it should not be rejected altogether'.[102] It is this approach which Hayton believes to be 'more likely, . . . so that the lengthy trust document is not a futile sham'.[103]

---

[98]   *Wilkins v Hogg* (1861) 31 LJ Ch 41, 43 per Lord Westbury LC; *Pass v Dundas* (1880) 43 LT 665, 666 per Bacon VC; *Armitage v Nurse* [1997] 2 All ER 705, 713–714 per Millett J.

[99]   See the earlier discussion of the Trustee Act 1925, ss 23 and 30.

[100]   [1987] 1 AC 730, 744.

[101]   *Anon* (1527) 1 Dyer, 3b, 4a, 73 ER 8.

[102]   *Firestone Tyre & Rubber Co Ltd v Vokins & Co Ltd* [1951] 1 Lloyd's Rep 32, 39. See also *Mendelsohn v Normand Ltd* [1970] 1 QB 177, 184 per Lord Denning MR, 186 per Phillimore LJ, who both affirmed *Firestone Tyre & Rubber* on this point. *Mendelsohn* was itself affirmed in cases such as *Gallaher Ltd v BRS Ltd* [1974] 2 Lloyd's Rep 440, 446–447 and *Evans (J) Ltd v Andrea Merzario Ltd* [1976] 1 WLR 1078, 1082. The analysis of these cases seems to be approved by Treitel on the basis of a doctrine of overriding undertaking, see GH Treitel, *The Law of Contract* (9th edn, 1995) 222–223.

[103]   Hayton, *Underhill and Hayton, Law Relating to Trusts and Trustees* (15th edn, 1995) 560. See

If it is accepted that a trust consists of a minimum set of obligations owed by **7.41** trustee to beneficiary, what does this core consist of? In a recent judgment, Millett LJ stated that '[t]he duty of the trustees to perform the trusts honestly and in good faith for the benefit of the beneficiaries is the minimum necessary to give substance to the trusts, . . . in my opinion it is sufficient'.[104] Hayton has stated, however, that there may be duties ancillary to the fundamental core duty of good faith, in order to enable the beneficiary to take advantage of his rights.[105] Assuming that the doctrine of repugnancy were to be applied, this lack of unanimity as to the precise scope of the core set of obligations of a trust makes it an unsuitable criterion for determining which clauses should be upheld or struck down, because of the uncertainty that would arise.

As it is, it seems unlikely that the doctrine of repugnancy will be applied. In **7.42** *Armitage v Nurse*, Millett LJ appeared unreceptive to the use of the doctrine of repugnancy to strike down a clause excluding liability for negligence.[106] He suggested that intentions inconsistent with a trust would simply negate the existence of a trust. 'If the beneficiaries have no rights enforceable against the trustees there are no trusts.'[107] This may be the better approach in that it would concentrate the minds of those in the business of establishing relationships which are intended to constitute a trust to do so in a manner that would not render it liable to be struck down; and does not call into question the principle that the courts will recognise the rights of parties to restrict the duties of trustees. The principle of repugnancy has also been sharply criticised by Glanville Williams as 'irrational'[108] and 'a useless piece of medieval lumber'.[109]

(3) Construction of Provisions Restricting Duty or Liability

It has been suggested that the exclusion of contractual liability 'must be most **7.43** clearly and unambiguously expressed, and . . . must be construed contra proferentem'.[110] Such exclusion, it is said, will be judged by 'specially exacting standards' because of 'the inherent improbability that the other party to a contract including such a clause intended to release the profererens from a liability that would

---

also R Ham, QC, 'Trustees' Liability' (1964) 61 BPL (November) 1, 6, where he expresses similar sentiments.

[104] *Armitage v Nurse* [1997] 2 All ER 705, 713.

[105] D Hayton, 'The Irreducible Core Content of Trusteeship' in AJ Oakley (ed), *Trends in Contemporary Trust Law* (1996).

[106] *Armitage v Nurse* [1997] 2 All ER 705, 713 per Millett LJ.

[107] ibid.

[108] 'The Doctrine of Repugnancy—I: Conditions in Gifts' (1943) 59 LQR 343.

[109] 'The Doctrine of Repugnancy—III: "Clogging the Equity" and Miscellaneous Applications' (1944) 60 LQR 190, 194.

[110] *Ailsa Craig Fishing v Malvern Fishing* [1983] 1 WLR 964, 966 per Lord Wilberforce.

otherwise fall on him'.[111] Such clauses are said to be regarded with 'hostility'.[112] There is authority to similar effect in relation to exclusion of duties under a bailment.[113] The Law Commission suggests that a similar position obtains in relation to exemption clauses in favour of trustees.[114] It takes the view that where the trustee is remunerated, as most custodians would be, there is a marked reluctance on the part of the courts to recognise an exoneration clause.[115]

7.44 Although the foregoing represents the traditional approach to exemption clauses, it is not certain that this approach continues to prevail. One leading practitioner has stated that the interpretation of an exemption clause 'is all a matter of construction: if the draftsman has expressed himself sufficiently unambiguously to cover the breach in question the clause will be effective'.[116] According to one leading academic, English courts 'have failed to apply anything like a doctrine of *contra proferentem*'.[117] In *Re Imperial Foods Limited Pension Scheme* an exemption clause was given its natural meaning.[118] In *Galmerrow Securities Ltd v National Westminster Bank plc,*[119] the application of the doctrine of *contra proferentem* in relation to exemption clauses for trustees was explicitly rejected by Harman J. He stated that he did not 'consider that the proposition that the Court leans against giving the advantage of an indemnity clause to a trustee . . . is made out'. This is supported by the Court of Appeal decision in *Armitage v Nurse*, in which Millett LJ gave one such clause its 'plain and unambiguous'[120] meaning, interpreting the clause on the basis that it 'means what it says'.[121]

7.45 Under general law, the balance between the protection of investors' interests and the right of custodians to avoid liability seems firmly to favour custodians. The desire to redress this imbalance is seen to be one of the grounds for intervention in the otherwise consensual relations between investors and their intermediaries in the area of financial services.[122] Such intervention, however, is felt not to be a

---

[111] ibid 970 per Lord Fraser. See also *Geo Mitchell v Finney Lock* [1983] AC 803, 814 per Lord Bridge.

[112] ibid 966.

[113] *Union Transport Finance v British Car Auctions* [1978] 2 All ER 385, 390 per Roskill LJ.

[114] Law Commission, *Fiduciary Duties and Regulatory Rules* (Law Com No 236, 1995) 15.10.

[115] Cases cited as authority for this include *National Trustees Company of Australasia v General Finance Company of Australasia* [1905] AC 373, 381; *Re Pauling's Settlements Trusts* [1964] Ch 303, 338–339.

[116] R Ham, QC, 'Trustees' Liability' (1994) 61 BPL (November) 1, 6.

[117] R Nobles, 'Trustees' Exclusion Clauses in Jersey and England' (1996) 10(3) TLI 66, 67.

[118] Unreported on this point, but the relevant extract is set out in N Inglis-Jones, *The Law of Occupational Pension Schemes*, Vol 2 (1996) Part V, 18-01. The case is generally reported in [1986] 1 WLR 717.

[119] Unreported, ChD, 20 December 1993.

[120] *Armitage v Nurse* [1997] 2 All ER 705, 709.

[121] ibid 710.

[122] AC Page and RB Ferguson, *Investor Protection* (1992) 17.

proper function of the courts,[123] but for Parliament.[124] The degree of regulatory intervention in custody business is examined in Chapter 9.

---

[123] *Armitage v Nurse* [1997] 2 All ER 705, 715 per Millett LJ.

[124] For example, the purported exclusion of liability for negligence by the manager or trustee of a unit trust scheme in respect to the discharge of his functions is void, see the Financial Services Act 1986, s 84. See also, in relation to trustees for bondholders, Companies Act 1985, s 192.

8

BREACH OF DUTY

This chapter considers the implications of breach of duty by a custodian under **8.01** general law and examines some of the criteria that an investor would need to satisfy to obtain redress. It has been suggested that the cost and complexity of these types of action constitute one of the motives for enacting financial services regulation, not least to provide alternative avenues of recovery.[1] The avenues for redress under regulation are examined in the chapter on regulation.

It is admitted that much of the content of this chapter is not peculiar to custody **8.02** business and risks trespassing on territory which is addressed more exhaustively in specialist works on obligations, remedies and restitution. Yet, a proper review of the law relating to custody business would be incomplete without a discussion of the remedies available to investors with assets in custody. Although the heart of this work, in Chapters 2 to 5, is dedicated to an analysis of the interests of

---

[1] AC Page and RB Ferguson, *Investor Protection* (1992) 16, 106; AI Ogus, *Regulation: Legal Form and Economic Theory* (1994) 27, 217.

investors, this analysis becomes of greatest importance in the event of breach by and/or insolvency of the custodian. It may be recalled that one of the principal motives for undertaking this analysis was to identify if and when custody assets would be insulated from claims by the general creditors of an insolvent custodian. It therefore seems appropriate that this work should include a detailed discussion of the different personal and proprietary remedies that may be open to an investor with assets in custody.

A. Breach

8.03   The role of fault in the establishment of breach is not great. A custodian may be in breach of contract if he 'without lawful excuse fails or refuses to perform what is due from him under the contract, performs defectively or incapacitates himself from performing'.[2] He may also be in 'breach of bailment independent of any liability in tort or contract',[3] irrespective of fault on his part.[4]

8.04   As a trustee any 'act or neglect on the part of a trustee which is not authorised or excused by the terms of the trust instrument, or by law, is called a breach of trust'.[5] By this view, even an unimpeachable breach of trust remains a breach.[6] Yet, Millett LJ has expressed an unwillingness to treat an unconscious (negligent or unknowing) breach of trust as a breach, and ruled that he was not compelled by principle or authority to do so.[7] However, the foregoing demonstrates that the introduction of this subjective element into an assessment of breach of trust is contrary to earlier authority; and although Millett LJ states that an unconscious breach of trust should not be treated as a breach, his analysis suggests that it is not so much breach but liability that he had in mind.[8]

8.05   Until recently it seemed settled that fiduciary duties were strict. However, this has again been questioned by Millett LJ, who stated that '[b]reach of fiduciary obligation, . . . connotes disloyalty or infidelity',[9] and that 'there can be no justification for treating an unconscious failure as demonstrating a want of fidelity'.[10] This is again contrary to authority and principle. The House of Lords has stated that

---

[2]   GH Treitel, *The Law of Contract* (9th edn, 1995) 746, see generally 746–751.
[3]   *Sutcliffe v Chief Constable of West Yorkshire* [1996] RTR 86, 90 per Otton LJ.
[4]   *Davis v Garrett* (1830) 6 Bing 716, 723–724 per Tindal CJ, 130 ER 1456.
[5]   *Underhill's Law of Trusts and Trustees* (10th edn) 3, approved in *Green v Russell McCarthy* [1959] 2 QB 226, 241 per Romer LJ. See *Underhill's Law of Trusts and Trustees* (15th edn, 1995) 3.
[6]   *Target Holdings v Redferns* [1996] 1 AC 421, 432 per Lord Browne-Wilkinson.
[7]   *Bristol and West BS v Mothew* [1996] 4 All ER 698, 709–710, 715–717.
[8]   ibid 717.
[9]   *Bristol and West BS v Mothew* [1996] 4 All ER 698, 712.
[10]   ibid 715.

mala fides is not a necessary constituent of breach of fiduciary duty.[11] 'A man of integrity can be a defaulting fiduciary without ceasing to be honest.'[12]

Breach of a duty of care turns upon whether the obligor of the duty has exercised the requisite degree of skill and care in the performance of his tasks. In consider- **8.06** ing this question the obligor's 'state of mind is irrelevant. It is his conduct that has to be judged'.[13] Nevertheless, the question remains whether the index should be the conduct that is normally achieved in the profession that offers the service[14] or conduct that in the opinion of the court ought to be achieved.[15] Given that a profession may habitually perform to lax standards, the latter approach would seem to be preferable. This latter view has been taken by courts in some cases,[16] as well as by leading commentators[17] in this area of the law. The fact that the obligor possessed inadequate skills when performing the service is no defence,[18] especially where the service provider is a corporation which should have, and properly deploy, appropriate skills and resources for any service offered.[19]

Standards are dynamic and a service-provider is expected to keep abreast of developments in his field.[20] If this appears unduly onerous, it is mitigated by the fact **8.07** that courts will generally not be astute to assume that an error of judgement constitutes a breach of duty of care. The onus of proving professional negligence over and above errors of judgement is a heavy one.[21] In the event that express standards have been adopted and set out by a profession's responsible body, although this does not necessarily remove from a court the determination of whether there is negligence or not, it is unlikely that a person meeting such standards will be liable for negligence.[22]

---

[11] *Keech v Sandford* (1726) Sel Cas T King 61, 62 per Lord Chancellor King, 25 ER 223; *Regal (Hastings) Ltd v Gulliver* (1942) [1967] 2 AC 134, 137, 143, 153; *Boardman v Phipps* [1967] 2 AC 46, 104, 105, 112.

[12] Glover J, *Commercial Equity: Fiduciary Relationships* (1995) 5.24.

[13] *Westway Homes Ltd v Gore Wood & Co* [1991] TLR 331 per Beldam LJ. The quotation is from Lexis. See also *Charlesworth & Percy on Negligence* (9th edn, 1997) 1–16.

[14] *Smith v Bush* [1990] 1 AC 831, 851 per Lord Templeman; *Luxmore-May v Messenger May Baverstock* [1990] 1 WLR 1009, 1020 per Slade LJ. See also *Halsbury's Laws of England* (4th edn) Vol 34, para 12.

[15] *Midland Bank v Hett, Stubbs & Kemp* [1979] 1 Ch 384, 402 per Oliver J; affirmed in *Bown v Gould & Swayne* [1996] PNLR 130.

[16] For example, *Deeny v Gooda Walker* [1996] LRLR 183, 207 per Phillips J; *Henderson v Merrett Syndicates Ltd (No 2)* [1996] 1 PNLR 32, 36–37 per Cresswell J.

[17] *Jackson & Powell on Professional Negligence* (4th edn, 1997) 1-95/96.

[18] *Wilsher v Essex AHA* [1987] QB 730, 750 per Mustill LJ.

[19] ibid 751.

[20] *Henderson v Merrett Syndicates Ltd (No 2)* [1996] 1 PNLR 32, 37 per Cresswell J.

[21] *Rondel v Worsley* [1969] 1 AC 191, 230 per Lord Reid.

[22] *Henderson v Merrett Syndicates Ltd (No 2)* [1996] 1 PNLR 32, 38 per Cresswell J.

B. Consequences of Breach

8.08 A breach may entail various consequences. In the first place, it may cause injury, which in the context of investments and capital market operations will normally be by way of economic loss alone. Beyond that, breach may attract criminal sanction[23] or lead to one or more forms of civil action by the injured investor in order to obtain one or more remedies. The remedy of injunction is not considered here because, given the extent of delegated powers, it is unlikely that the investor will be aware of potential wrongdoing sufficiently early to make the remedy useful. Likewise, specific performance is not addressed because most investments are fungible and, even if not, are principally held for the value they represent. Investors will generally not demand specific performance if the custodian or another party otherwise makes good his loss.

C. Investor's Options upon Breach by Custodian

8.09 An investor may pursue one or a combination of three broad strategies. He may seek compensation for injury due to such breach, and such injury is likely to be by way of economic loss. In the event that the breach involves a misapplication of custody assets, he may adopt two other strategies, ie recover the assets or their substitutes from the party holding them; or seek restitution from a party enriched by, or otherwise implicated in, the misapplication of his assets. The choice of which strategy to pursue depends on whether the claimant can satisfy the conditions for pursuit of the claim. Other considerations would include the value of the assets at the time of claim, the solvency of the parties linked to the custodial arrangement or transfer of assets, as well as the existence or not of limitation periods.

D. Damages or Compensation

(1) Kinds of Loss for which Damages or Compensation may be Recovered

8.10 In *Banque Bruxelles SA v Eagle Star*,[24] Lord Hoffmann stated that in an action for recovery it is first necessary to decide for what kind of loss the plaintiff may obtain recovery.[25] The type of loss for which a defendant may be liable is ascertained by examining the scope of the duty of which he is accused of being in breach. For instance, the scope of duty in tort depends on the purpose of the rule imposing the duty,[26] whilst that of an implied contractual duty is determined by the 'term which

---

[23] This is beyond the scope of this work.
[24] [1997] AC 191.
[25] ibid 211.
[26] ibid 212.

the law implies . . . the process is one of construction of the agreement as a whole in its commercial setting'.[27] The scope of an express contractual term is 'that which the law best regards as giving effect to the express obligations assumed'.[28] Recovery for breach of trust is consistent with this approach. In *Target Holdings Ltd v Redferns*[29] Lord Browne-Wilkinson stated that 'only if some relevant right has been infringed so as to give rise to a loss is it necessary to consider the extent of the trustee's liability to compensate for such loss'.[30]

(2) Measure of Recovery

Given that losses will generally relate to assets with an objective market price, any injury should be readily quantifiable. Nevertheless, the measure of damages may depend on the cause of action pleaded. There is little doubt that reliance losses can generally be recovered. However, since investments are undertaken with anticipated returns in mind, it is of singular importance that such losses should be recoverable.   **8.11**

For breach of contract the measure of recovery is the amount of damages that will place the plaintiff 'so far as money can do it . . . in the same situation . . . as if the contract had been performed'.[31] In relation to actions for negligence, Lord Goff in *Henderson v Merrett Syndicates Ltd*[32] confirmed that *Hedley Byrne* is authority for the recovery of economic loss in general and in *White v Jones*[33] suggested that this included economic expectation loss. The general rule for breach of bailment is that recovery should put the bailor in the position as if no property was lost or injured.[34] Where the bailee's duties are specific, and he is aware of the purpose of the bailment, he may be liable for the consequences of his breach.[35] The guiding principle for equitable compensation for breach of trust[36] or fiduciary duty,[37] which are dealt with in similar fashion,[38] is pragmatism. This involves an   **8.12**

---

[27] ibid.

[28] ibid.

[29] [1996] 1 AC 421.

[30] ibid 433–434.

[31] *Robinson v Harman* (1848) 1 Ex 850, 855 per Parke B, 154 ER 363.

[32] [1995] 2 AC 145, 178.

[33] [1995] 2 AC 207, 268, agreed with by Lord Browne-Wilkinson at 274–276, and Lord Nolan at 295. See also *Banque Bruxelles SA v Eagle Star* [1997] AC 191, 211, 214 per Lord Hoffmann.

[34] *Anderson v North-Eastern Railway Company* (1861) 4 LT 216. See also *Building and Civil Engineering Holidays Scheme Management Ltd v Post Office* [1966] 1 QB 247, 261–262 per Lord Denning MR; *Morris v CW Martin & Sons* [1966] 1 QB 716, 726 per Lord Denning MR; *Swiss Bank v Brink's-Mat* [1986] 2 Lloyd's Rep 79, 84–85 per Bingham J.

[35] *Anderson v North-Eastern Railway Company* (1861) 4 LT 216. See also Palmer, *Bailment* (2nd edn, 1991) 79–80.

[36] *Target Holdings Ltd v Redferns* [1996] 1 AC 421, 435 per Lord Browne-Wilkinson.

[37] *Mahoney v Purnell* [1996] 3 All ER 61, 90 per May J; *Bristol and West BS v Mothew* [1996] 4 All ER 698, 711 per Millett LJ.

[38] *Re Dawson* [1966] 2 NSWR 211, 216 per Street J, SC of NSW; *Canson Enterprises Ltd v Boughton & Co* (1991) 85 DLR 4th 129, 162 per McLachlin J, SC of Canada; *Target Holdings Ltd v Redferns* [1996] 1 AC 421, by implication of Lord Browne-Wilkinson at 438–439.

assessment, in a common sense way with the benefit of hindsight,[39] of whether the loss would have occurred if there had been no breach.[40] Damages for fraud compensates 'the plaintiff for all the loss he has suffered . . . for all the actual damages directly flowing' from the fraud.[41] Lord Hoffmann stated that 'the whole risk of loss which would not have been suffered if the plaintiff had not' been subjected to the fraud 'is transferred to the defendant'.[42]

(3) Causation

8.13   It is not an ineluctable conclusion that breach of duty followed by economic loss to the investor leads to compensation. Upon breach of contract, negligence or fraud recovery will only follow if on a robust view of cause, informed by common sense,[43] the breach constitutes the effective cause of loss.[44] The House of Lords is of the view that for compensation for breach of trust 'common law rules of . . . causation do not apply. However there does have to be some causal connection between the breach of trust and the loss'.[45] If causation is assessed according to 'common sense',[46] the difference from the common law approach is not great.[47] Likewise, although it was once felt that causation had no role in compensation for breach of fiduciary obligations,[48] this is now rejected by the House of Lords.[49] Loss due to breach of bailment does offer a plaintiff an easier path to recovery because the mere fact of loss in relation to bailed assets puts the onus on the bailee to prove 'that the loss or damage is not due to any fault on his part'.[50] The breach need not

---

[39]   *Target Holdings Ltd v Redferns* [1996] 1 AC 421, 439 per Lord Browne-Wilkinson.

[40]   *Re Dawson (deceased)* [1966] 2 NSWR 211, 215 per Street J, SC of NSW; affirmed in *Target Holdings Ltd v Redferns* [1996] 1 AC 421, 434 per Lord Browne-Wilkinson.

[41]   *Doyle v Olby Ltd* [1969] 2 QB 158, 167 per Lord Denning MR; affirmed in *Smith New Court Ltd v Scrimgeour Vickers* [1997] AC 254, 263–267 per Lord Browne-Wilkinson.

[42]   *Banque Bruxelles SA v Eagle Star* [1997] AC 191, 215.

[43]   For contract see *Galoo Ltd v Bright Grahame Murray* [1994] 1 WLR 1360, 1375 per Glidewell LJ; for negligence see *Stapley v Gypsum Mines Ltd* [1953] AC 663, 681 per Lord Reid; *Banque Bruxelles SA v Eagle Star* [1997] AC 191, 214 per Lord Hoffmann; for fraud see *Smith New Court Ltd v Scrimgeour Vickers* [1997] AC 254, 285 per Lord Steyn.

[44]   For contract see *Monarch Steamship Co v Karlshamns Oljefabriker (A/B)* [1949] AC 196, 212 per Lord Porter, 227 per Lord Wright; for negligence see *Norris v W Moss & Sons Ltd* [1954] 1 WLR 346, 351 per Vaisey J; *Banque Bruxelles SA v Eagle Star* [1997] AC 191, 213 per Lord Hoffmann; for fraud see *Smith New Court Ltd v Scrimgeour Vickers* [1997] AC 254, 267 per Lord Browne-Wilkinson.

[45]   *Target Holdings Ltd v Redferns* [1996] 1 AC 421, 433–434 per Lord Browne-Wilkinson.

[46]   ibid 439.

[47]   D Capper, 'Compensation for Breach of Trust' [1997] Conveyancer 14, 23.

[48]   *Brickenden v London Loan & Savings Co* [1934] 3 DLR 465, 469, PC.

[49]   *Target Holdings Ltd v Redferns* [1996] 1 AC 421 by implication of Lord Browne-Wilkinson treating compensation for breach of fiduciary obligations in the same fashion as breach of trust at 438–439 and declaring at 434 that compensation breach of trust requires causation to be established; followed in *Swindle v Harrison* [1997] TLR 197, CA.

[50]   *Building and Civil Engineering Holidays Scheme Management Ltd v Post Office* [1966] 1 QB 247, 261 per Lord Denning MR; *Morris v CW Martin & Sons* [1966] 1 QB 716, 726 per Lord Denning MR; and *Swiss Bank v Brink's-Mat* [1986] 2 Lloyd's Rep 79, 85 per Bingham J.

be the sole, primary or even equal cause of loss. It is sufficient that the breach has 'any' role in causing the loss.

Even in common sense terms, proof of causation in the present context will not **8.14** always be straightforward. There is an inherent difficulty in demonstrating a chain of cause leading to non-physical harm. Of course, where loss is due to theft, causation is easy to establish. Where, however, wrongful advice or information leads to a diminution in the value of the custody assets, matters become more complex. Further, in view of the susceptibility of custody assets to different market forces and the actions of parties who do not owe the investor a duty, especially if there are tiers of intermediary custodians, the fact of breach may not be the only cause of loss.

Where there is more than one cause of loss, if a breach of contract is of equal **8.15** importance to the other causes,[51] the negligence more than a mere trifle[52] or the fraud a substantial cause of the loss,[53] such action may still form the basis for liability for the loss. Nevertheless, if, subsequent to breach of contract or negligence, loss is caused by an extraneous supervening event, then even if the breach might have partly or wholly caused similar loss, the party in breach will not be liable for the loss.[54] In this respect causation for breach of trust differs from the common law approach because even if the immediate cause of loss can be ascribed to a third party, where the loss could not have occurred but for the breach of trust, the errant trustee will remain liable for the loss.[55] The same result obtains for breach of contract where the intervention by the third party was a natural, probable or foreseeable consequence of the breach. For example, if in breach of a contractual duty of care to recommend a broker a custodian recommends one without exercising due care and the broker commits theft, the custodian would be liable for losses arising therefrom.[56]

(4) Contributory Negligence

A custodian accused of breach of duty may seek to limit his liability by pleading **8.16** contributory negligence on the part of the investor. This could arise if an investor has insisted that the custodian use further intermediaries who have contributed to the loss; or where the investor has insisted on operating in markets where it is

---

[51] *Heskell v Continental Express Ltd* [1950] 1 All ER 1033, 1048 per Devlin J; *Clarkson v Modern Foundries Ltd* [1958] 1 All ER 33, 36 per Donovan J; also by implication in *Reay v British Nuclear Fuels* [1994] 5 Med LR 1, 53 per French J.

[52] *Bonnington Castings Ltd v Wardlaw* [1956] AC 613, 621 per Lord Reid; see also *Norris v W Moss & Sons Ltd* [1954] 1 WLR 346, 351 per Vaisey J.

[53] *Smith New Court Ltd v Scrimgeour Vickers* [1997] AC 254, 285 per Lord Steyn.

[54] For contract *Beoco Ltd v Alfa Laval Co Ltd* [1994] 4 All ER 464, 475, 477 per Stuart-Smith LJ; for negligence see *Weld-Blundell v Stephens* [1920] AC 956, 986 per Lord Sumner; *The Oropesa* [1943] P 32, 39 per Lord Wright.

[55] *Target Holdings Ltd v Redferns* [1996] 1 AC 421, 434 per Lord Browne-Wilkinson.

[56] *De la Bere v Pearson Limited* [1908] 1 KB 280.

impossible for the custodian to observe all of his duties. Whilst such a plea may be difficult to establish in practice, there is some scope for applying it in the present circumstances.

8.17   There is statutory provision for a defendant to raise contributory negligence in response to a claim for negligence on his part.[57] Even in response to contractual liability, if the contractual liability gives rise to concurrent independent non-contractual duties of care which are the same whether in contract or tort, there is authority that the fact of contractual liability is immaterial and that the defendant may assert negligence on the part of the plaintiff, and thereby reduce his own liability by winning an apportionment of damages.[58] This does not apply if the duty breached did not require the application of care[59] or was one of strict liability.[60] Palmer suggests that the plea may be invoked in response to breach of bailment as well.[61] In view of the position of English courts that contributory negligence applies strictly to tortious liability,[62] this seems likely to succeed only if an action for breach of bailment is framed in terms of negligence,[63] but not if the charge is one of conversion.[64]

8.18   It has been suggested[65] that although negligent breach of trust does not constitute a tort, the plea of contributory negligence should nevertheless be available because it is a 'mere historical accident' that negligent breach of trust does not constitute a tort. However, contributory negligence should not be applicable to claims for breach of trust or fiduciary obligation because a beneficiary should be entitled to trust his fiduciary and not be 'under a duty to check up on the person he is entitled to expect to be acting loyally in his own best interests'.[66] Likewise, there is generally no scope for contributory negligence for fraud because 'in this field the court does not allow an examination into the relative importance of contributory

---

[57]   Law Reform (Contributory Negligence) Act 1945, s 1.

[58]   *Forsikringsaktieselskapet Vesta v Butcher* [1986] 2 All ER 488, 510, [1989] AC 852, 879 per Sir Roger Ormrod; *Barclays Bank plc v Fairclough Building Ltd* [1994] 3 WLR 1057, 1073 per Simon Brown LJ. See also A Porat, 'The Contributory Negligence Defence and the Ability to Rely on the Contract' (1995) 111 LQR 228.

[59]   *Bristol and West Building Society v Kramer & Co* [1995] TLR 57.

[60]   *Barclays Bank plc v Fairclough Building Ltd* [1994] 3 WLR 1057.

[61]   Palmer, *Bailment* (2nd edn, 1991) 69–71.

[62]   *Barclays Bank plc v Fairclough Building Ltd* [1994] 3 WLR 1057, 1072.

[63]   See the illustration provided by G Williams, *Joint Torts and Contributory Negligence: A Study of Concurrent Faults* (1951) 328, §80.

[64]   Torts (Interference with Goods) Act 1977, s 11(1). This may be rationalised on the basis that the proprietary nature of an action for conversion bars a defendant claiming for contributory negligence, see Williams, *Joint Torts and Contributory Negligence* (n 63 above) §57.

[65]   ibid §80.

[66]   Hayton, *Underhill and Hayton, Law Relating to Trusts and Trustees* (15th edn, 1995) 837, n 4, 838. Support for this view may be derived from KR Handley, 'Reduction of Damages Awards' in PD Finn (ed), *Essays on Damages* (1992) 127; and J Glover, *Commercial Equity: Fiduciary Relationships* (1995) 6.128. Contrast with *Day v Mead* [1987] 2 NZLR 443, CA of NZ; and *Canson Enterprises Ltd v Boughton & Co* (1991) 85 DLR 4th 129, SC of Canada.

causes'.[67] Contributory negligence is 'a device of the common law to control the incidence of liability for negligence',[68] strictly only applicable to tortious liability,[69] and therefore not relevant to fraud. However, once one is aware of the fraud[70] or untrustworthiness[71] of the person owing duties, reasonable steps to mitigate loss ought to be taken.

E. Remedies Based on Misapplied Assets

An investor may base his action for recovery on the fact of misapplied assets. If the assets or their substitutes remain in existence, he could seek to reclaim them from the holder. In the alternative, he could seek restitution from anyone who has been enriched by receipt of the assets; seek an account of profits from anyone who has otherwise made a wrongful profit from the misapplication of the assets; or seek compensation from anyone implicated in the misapplication of the assets. **8.19**

(1) The Process of Identification

To succeed in a claim for recovery, enrichment or complicity in the misapplication of assets that belong(ed) to the claimant, logic dictates that he will need to demonstrate his former or continuing interest in the assets. This issue is fully explored in Chapters 2 to 5. He will then need to demonstrate that this interest existed until the happening of the events that form the basis of his claim, ie that he had an undestroyed proprietary base. **8.20**

Following

One method of identification is to follow the assets in relation to which the claim is to be brought: following is 'the movement of things in time and space'.[72] However, this method of identification is only open to investors with discrete documentary intangibles in non-intermediary or single-tier custody, where the investor enjoys a direct legal or equitable interest in the custody assets. The increasing dematerialisation of assets and extended tiers of intermediary custody, which leave investors with intangible interests only, means that this process will often be unsuitable for many users of modern custodial services. By the definition of following that is set out above, it is impossible to 'follow' things that have no **8.21**

---

[67] *Barton v Armstrong* [1976] AC 104, 118 per Lord Cross of Chelsea.
[68] The Hon. Mr Justice Gummow, 'Compensation for Breach of Fiduciary Duty' in TG Youdan (ed), *Equity, Fiduciaries and Trusts* (1989) 86.
[69] *Barclays Bank plc v Fairclough Building Ltd* [1994] 3 WLR 1057, 1072.
[70] *Smith New Court Ltd v Scrimgeour Vickers* [1997] AC 254, 266–267 per Lord Browne-Wilkinson.
[71] *Lipkin Gorman v Karpnale Ltd* [1987] 1 WLR 987, 1019 per Alliott J.
[72] LD Smith, *The Law of Tracing* (1997) 6.

physical existence. In the present context, a transfer of intangible things may take effect by the extinction of the rights of the transferor and the establishment of new rights in favour of the transferee.[73]

Tracing

8.22 Following as a means of identification may also become impossible or impracticable where the original asset is exchanged for a new thing in circumstances where the original thing no longer exists or is no longer attractive to base a claim on.[74] In such a case, the owner of the original thing may wish instead to base his claim on a substitute of the original thing. A suitable substitute for the purposes of such a claim is identifiable by the rules of tracing.[75] With tracing, the investor is freed from the constraints of following a particular thing, and is permitted to trace value through various tangible or intangible repositories in which such value inheres. The repository in which the value inheres is treated as the claimant's asset.[76] The process does not depend on intent; it merely seeks to reflect how value in original assets is notionally transferred from one repository to another.[77]

8.23 Where the notional transfer of value is direct, or if the original asset is the subject of a clean exchange between two parties, tracing is straightforward. The 'transferred' or substitute asset is readily identifiable. Examples of this are where securities or interests are exchanged by the custodian for another asset, or if within a book entry securities settlement system assets are alienated to an identifiable party. The numbering or other form of earmarking of assets would be of great assistance in such circumstances, permitting what may confusingly be described as 'intangible following'.[78]

8.24 However, it may be necessary to undertake tracing in a multiple party scenario. This may arise, for example, where the wrongful alienation of the claimant's assets is to one party, such as the transferee's custodian, and the substitutes received from another institution, such as the transferee's other custodian or bank (for funds transferred). The difficulty which the claimant faces is to link his lost assets, which went to one party, with assets which were received from another party; to prove that assets received by the custodian from one party are the substitute for assets alienated by the custodian in favour of another party. If such exchanges or transfers are effected within individual settlement exchanges or in parallel transactions, the process of tracing may remain relatively uncomplicated. However, some mar-

---

[73] Support for this view may be derived from *R v Preddy* [1996] AC 815, 834 per Lord Goff, and Lords Mackay, Jauncey, Slynn and Hoffmann at 826, 841, 842 and 842 respectively.

[74] Such as if the original asset is of reduced value.

[75] Smith, *The Law of Tracing* (n 72 above) 6, see generally for an exhaustive analysis of this method of identification.

[76] ibid 119–120.

[77] ibid 248.

[78] ibid 69.

ket operations, such as settlement by netting, can complicate the process of tracing. These practices are examined below.

To perform tracing via several intermediaries, 'what is needed is tracing in transit',[79] identifying substitutions that occur in the hands of intermediaries. The investor will need to demonstrate that his thing was exchanged for some new thing with the intermediary and that that new thing was further exchanged with another intermediary until the thing received by the ultimate beneficiary is linked in the chain of exchanges. **8.25**

Exchange-Product Theory

Tracing via numerous intermediaries may be tedious. If the substitute is obvious, is it still necessary to undertake tracing? In relation to banking systems, Birks stated that 'rules of tracing are rules of convenience which penetrate evidential impasses. They do not need to be called into play at all when it is clear that a series of banking movements, however complex, has been motivated by a well evidenced intent that A should be enabled to make a payment to Z'.[80] This process of identification may be described as the exchange-product theory.[81] Although the validity of the exchange-product theory has been challenged,[82] on the grounds of a lack of authority for it, the theory has been affirmed by the Court of Appeal[83] citing *Lipkin Gorman v Karpnale Ltd*.[84] **8.26**

Whilst the exchange-product theory has been described as a form of tracing,[85] this may be misconceived. Exchange-product theory is not concerned with tracing value,[86] and it is immaterial that the exchange-product may also be identifiable by tracing. The theory merely seeks, in a common sense way, to identify a substitute regardless of how the substitute has come about. The theory is better rationalised by the intention of the recipient[87] or a fictional presumption of **8.27**

---

[79] ibid 243–262, especially at 248.

[80] PBH Birks, 'Overview: Tracing, Claiming and Defences' in PBH Birks (ed), *Laundering and Tracing* (1995) 304.

[81] This is more fully discussed in LD Smith, 'Tracing in Taylor v Plummer: Equity in the Court of King's Bench' [1995] LMCLQ 240, 263–265; PBH Birks, 'Overview: Tracing, Claiming and Defences' in PBH Birks (ed), *Laundering and Tracing* (1995) 302–305; and NH Andrews and J Beatson, 'Common Law Tracing: Springboard or Swan-Song' (1997) 113 LQR 21, 23–25.

[82] *Bank Tejrat v HK & SBC* [1995] 1 Lloyd's Rep 239, 245–246 per Tuckey J.

[83] *Jones & Sons (Trustee) v Jones* [1996] 3 WLR 703, 711 per Millett LJ.

[84] [1991] 2 AC 548, 573–574 per Lord Goff.

[85] *Jones & Sons (Trustee) v Jones* [1996] 3 WLR 703, 711. See also LD Smith, 'Tracing in Taylor v Plummer: Equity in the Court of King's Bench' [1995] LMCLQ 240, 266–267; Andrews and Beatson, 'Common Law Tracing: Springboard or Swan-Song' (1997) 113 LQR 21, 23.

[86] This seems to be accepted by PBH Birks, 'Overview: Tracing, Claiming and Defences' in PBH Birks (ed), *Laundering and Tracing* (1995) 304; and LD Smith, 'Constructive Fiduciaries?', a paper delivered at SPTL Seminars for 1996, 'Pressing Problems in the Law XI' 6–7.

[87] S Khurshid and P Matthews, 'Tracing Confusion' (1979) 95 LQR 78, 85; LD Smith, 'Tracing in Taylor v Plummer: Equity in the Court of King's Bench' [1995] LMCLQ 240, 263–264; Andrews and Beatson (n 81 above) 21, 24; and Birks (n 80 above) 304.

equity.[88] If this view is accepted, it becomes obvious why the exchange-product theory does not render tracing redundant. For example, if the recipient or intermediary effecting the transfer of exchanged goods is fraudulent, denying that the received assets are the substitute of the investor's original assets, the investor may yet have to resort to tracing to make his case.

Operational Factors which Complicate the Process of Identification

8.28 A number of operational practices may render identification more difficult. Chief amongst these are the practices of settlement by netting and trading for various parties from an omnibus account.

(a) Settlement by Netting

8.29 Where the settlement of transferred assets is by netting, it is not obvious how particular assets are applied. Netting is the simultaneous settling of numerous transactions or accounts, and 'a settlement of account cannot be followed'.[89] Although each transaction is accounted for individually, they are mixed in the process of set-off.

8.30 Nevertheless, netting need not constitute an insurmountable hurdle to identifying how assets are applied. Netting may be analysed as a mixed substitution,[90] where assets on two sides are separately pooled, subsequently exchanged, and then unbundled at the other side for allocation to various parties. As demonstrated in Chapter 3, pooling is not incompatible with the retention of interests in the pool by a contributor. The claimant need only demonstrate his contribution to the pool used to acquire the substitute pool. His ability to identify anything in the substitute assets is explained by tracing.

8.31 Given that netting can properly only take effect if the inputs to the mixture for substitution correspond, all contributors should ordinarily be satisfied to the extent that netting takes place. If problems do arise, records of the inputs should indicate reasons for this. Difficulties of identification after netting due to unclear or non-existent records are a function of poor record-keeping and not due to netting per se.

(b) Actively Traded Omnibus Accounts

8.32 If assets are traced to an actively traded account, a claimant may seek to demonstrate that his assets remain in or have been withdrawn from the account. Traditionally, this was done according to the rule in *Clayton's Case*;[91] transactions

---

[38] *Taylor v Plummer* (1815) 3 M & S 562, 574 per Lord Ellenborough CJ, 105 ER 721.
[39] *Re Hallett & Co ex p Blane* [1894] 2 QB 237, 244 per Lord Esher MR.
[90] Smith, *The Law of Tracing* (n 72 above) 239.
[31] *Devayne v Noble, Clayton's Case* (1816) 1 Mer 572, 608 per Sir William Grant MR, 35 ER 781.

in an account with more than one contributor are appropriated to contributors on the basis that the first assets in are the first assets out. However, the Court of Appeal has held that although the rule is a convenient way of resolving competing claims to assets in a fund, if the rule would be impractical to apply, work injustice or run against the implied or express intention of the contributors to the fund, then the rule may be rejected in favour of an alternative method of distribution.[92] An example of where this rule would be unjust is where, because a few early contributors made large inputs to the fund, a relatively small number of claimants are entitled to recover the lion's share of available assets in the fund. In any event, the Court of Appeal has suggested that where claimants have suffered the common misfortune of their assets being misapplied and mixed in a fund, then as unwitting contributors to the fund it may be implied that it is their intention to disapply the rule.[93]

Where the rule in *Clayton's Case* is rejected for resolving multiple claims to an insufficient fund in an actively traded account, the lowest intermediate balance rule[94] may restrict the ability of any claimant to succeed. The lowest intermediate balance rule states that one may not claim in excess of the lowest amount in an account between the time one contributed thereto and the time at which one makes one's claim. The idea is that if an account has been so depleted in the interim as to leave less than one's contribution to the account, then one's assets must have been at least in part alienated leaving a reduced amount, or nothing, to claim. If, however, it can be demonstrated that assets subsequently allocated to the account were intended to substitute the assets identified by the claimant which were removed, then the claimant will be able to claim those substitute assets.[95] **8.33**

For the lowest intermediate balance rule to be applied, the order in which transactions concerning the account were made is indispensable.[96] If there is real time settlement in relation to the account, there is no difficulty. No matter how many transactions there are, all that needs to be done to apply the lowest intermediate balance rule is to reconstruct the records and apply the rule. If the record of transactions does not tally with the demonstrable order in which transactions actually occurred, that evidence should be relied upon in applying the lowest intermediate balance rule.[97] With netting, however, it is not obvious when transactions take place. One solution where the precise chronology of a group of transactions is **8.34**

---

[92] *Barlow Clowes International Ltd v Vaughan* [1992] 4 All ER 22.
[93] ibid.
[94] *Roscoe v Winder* [1915] 1 Ch 62.
[95] ibid 69 per Sargant J.
[96] *Republic Supply Co of California v Richfield Oil Co* 79 F (2d) 375, 379 per St Sure DJ (Circuit Court of Appeals, 1935).
[97] *Re Seneca Oil Co* 906 F (2d) 1445, 1452 per Ebel CJ (US Court of Appeals 10th Circuit, 1990).

unclear, but which are known to have occurred within a specific period, is that they be treated as occurring simultaneously.[98]

8.35 By a rigid application of the lowest intermediate balance rule any alienation from the account only affects those who had contributed at the time of that alienation. This is known as the rolling charge[99] or pro rata sharing.[100] Where there are numerous transactions involving numerous parties, the complexities of calculating the shares of the various contributors to the account at any moment in time and factoring in further transactions as they occur is obvious. In *Re Diplock*[101] Lord Greene stated that this approach would lead to 'the greatest difficulty and complication in practice and might in many cases raise questions incapable of solution'. In *Barlow Clowes v Vaughan*[102] the Court of Appeal also avoided this approach because of its complexity; all losses were shared rateably amongst the contributors, as if the mixture consisting of all contributions had suffered one single loss.

8.36 However, since the rolling charge is perceived to provide the fairest result[103] it should not readily be discarded. The fears of complexity expressed in England seem to be overstated. As the rolling charge is the favoured approach for allocating losses to mixtures in North America,[104] it cannot be unworkable. Where records are readily to hand, no matter how many transactions there are, the application of the rolling charge becomes a question of applying formulae and, given the availability, speed and capacity of modern computers, this should not be too onerous. Of course, if the value being traced does not justify the necessary time or resources for the rolling charge, one could take the *Barlow Clowes* approach and treat the fund as if constituted at one time only and suffering one loss.[105] This may also be the only viable option if the records of transactions are incomplete.

---

[98] *Republic Supply Co of California v Richfield Oil Co* 79 F (2d) 375, 380 per St Sure DJ (Circuit Court of Appeals, 1935), affirmed in *Re Seneca Oil Co* 906 F (2d) 1445, 1452 per Ebel CJ (US Court of Appeals 10th Circuit, 1990); *Re Ararimu Holdings Ltd* [1989] 3 NZLR 487, 499 per Wylie J, HC of NZ.

Contrast with *Re Brown* 193 F 24, 29 per Lacombe CJ (Circuit Court of Appeals, 2nd Circuit, 1912), affirmed in *First Nat Bank v Littlefield* 226 US 110, 112 per White CJ, 57 L Ed 145 (SC, 1912) and *Schuyler v Littlefield* 232 US 707, 58 L Ed 806 (SC, 1914), which insist that the plaintiff seeking to trace must establish the precise sequence of events, and that a failure to do so would mean a failure to discharge the necessary onus of proof.

[99] *Barlow Clowes v Vaughan* [1992] 4 All ER 22, 35 per Woolf LJ.

[100] *Re Ontario Securities Com'n and Greymac Credit Corp* (1986) 55 OR (2d) 673, 687 per Morden JA, Ontario CA.

[101] [1948] Ch 465, 554.

[102] [1992] 4 All ER 22.

[103] ibid, a concession by Walker QC, noted by Dillon LJ at 32, echoed by Woolf LJ at 35.

[104] Canada: *Re Ontario Securities Com'n and Greymac Credit Corp* (1986) 55 OR (2d) 673, 688–690, 695 per Morden JA, Ontario CA; affirmed by the Supreme Court [1988] 2 SCR 172, 173; USA: *Re Walter J Schmidt & Co* 298 F 314, 316, 320 per Learned Hand DJ (District Court SD New York, 1923), where he expressed the preference for the rolling charge but felt bound by precedent to apply *Clayton's Case*; *Gibbs v Gerberich* 203 NE 2d 851, 856 per Doyle J.

[105] [1992] 4 All ER 22, 35 per Woolf LJ.

(2) Recovery

If the investor enjoys only personal rights against the custodian for equivalent re-delivery, from any source, of assets deposited in custody, and the custodian is unable to discharge this obligation, then the investor's recourse will be limited to a personal action against the custodian. The custodian's obligation to effect re-delivery is not tied to any assets, so the investor's remedy cannot be based thereon.[106] **8.37**

If the investor enjoyed a proprietary interest in misapplied custody assets which have been identified, unless the holder or another party has a rival claim to the asset, eg a valid security interest, 'the court will treat the defendant as holding the property on a constructive trust for the plaintiff and will order the defendant to transfer it in specie to the plaintiff'.[107] **8.38**

In the case of intermediary custody, an investor may pursue at least two strate-gies.[108] He may seek to have his status as beneficial owner of the alienated assets recognised, so that he becomes beneficial owner under a newly declared trust over the misapplied asset or its substitute, with the transferor as the new trustee. Alternatively, he may choose to have the assets transferred to him directly, ending the custody. **8.39**

In many cases, by virtue of tracing, the identified asset will not be the same asset as was misapplied but a substitute, and it is to this that the claimant's claim will fasten. Where custody assets are applied to acquire a substitute thing, it is appro-priate that the beneficiaries of the misapplied assets be able to claim a pro rata share of the substitute, to the extent that their misapplied assets represent a con-tribution to the substitute. Where, however, misapplied assets are only used to maintain something that has already been acquired by the wrongdoing trustee, such as an insurance policy[109] or a futures contract, it may be more appropriate for the claimant investor to obtain a charge over the thing maintained as security for his reimbursement. **8.40**

Since breach of duty may be a direct consequence of financial difficulty faced by the custodian,[110] it is likely that actions for compensation will often be an ineffec-tive remedy for investors to pursue. The ability to recover misapplied assets or their substitutes is therefore an important remedy where the circumstances per-mit. **8.41**

---

[106] *Re Goldcorp Exchange Ltd* [1995] 1 AC 74, 98–100.
[107] *Boscawen v Bajwa and another* [1996] 1 WLR 328, 334–335 per Millet LJ.
[108] *Re Hallett's Estate* (1880) 13 ChD 696, 708–709 per Jessel MR; *Re Tilley's Will Trusts* [1967] 2 All ER 303, 313 per Ungoed-Thomas J.
[109] *Foskett v McKeown* [1997] 3 All ER 392.
[110] CP Kindleberger, *Manias, Panics and Crashes* (2nd edn, 1989) 91, 95; J Franks and C Meyer, *Risk, Regulation and Investor Protection* (1989) 2.9.

(3) Remedy from those Enriched by, or Implicated in, a Misapplication
of Custody Assets

8.42   A claimant may seek to show that his custody assets were received by someone who has been enriched by the receipt or were used to derive an unlawful profit, notwithstanding that the assets may have been returned or never alienated, in order to claim restitution. He may adopt this strategy where the assets are no longer identifiable or subsisting, or where the assets have depreciated in value, so that recovery of the amount by which the person was enriched would recoup more than simply getting the thing back.

Enrichment from Receipt

8.43   A plaintiff may pursue this by different causes of action, including money had and received or knowing receipt. Given that the essence of the claim is receipt of his custody assets, an investor would need to go through the process of identification outlined earlier. Beyond that, depending on the cause of action pleaded, he may need to prove a particular mental state of the defendant at a point in time. However, the investor avoids having to prove causation of loss. Indeed, actions for unjust enrichment do not strictly address loss, they address enrichment by the defendant. Nevertheless, in linking the investor to the enrichment by the defendant, these causes of action indirectly address loss from the other end of the wrongful transaction.

(a) Money Had and Received

8.44   A claim for money had and received 'lies for money paid by mistake; or upon a consideration which happens to fail; or for money got through imposition, (express, or implied); or extortion; or oppression; or an undue advantage taken of the plaintiff's situation, contrary to laws made for the protection of persons under those circumstances'.[11] Whilst there are suggestions that this necessitates proof of fault,[12] there is copious authority that the claim lies by virtue of receipt of the claimant's money[13] and that it is not necessary to establish wrongdoing by the recipient in order to succeed.[14] Indeed, the money received need not remain in the hands of the recipient, nor remain identifiable, for the bringing of a claim.[15] If the investor is able to prove that his money was received by a string of recipients,

---

[11]   *Moses v Macferlan* (1760) 2 Burr 1005, 1012 per Lord Mansfield, 97 ER 676.

[12]   *Marsh v Keating* (1834) 1 Bing (NC) 198, 220, 131 ER 1094; *Jones & Sons (Trustee) v Jones* [1996] 3 WLR 703, 714 per Nourse LJ.

[13]   *Hudson v Robinson* (1816) 4 M & S 475, 478 per Lord Ellenborough, 105 ER 910; *Banque Belge pour l'Etranger v Hambrouck* [1921] 1 KB 321, 327 per Bankes LJ, 335–336 per Lord Atkin; *Agip (Africa) Ltd v Jackson* [1990] Ch 265, 285 per Millett J; [1991] Ch 547, 563 per Fox LJ.

[14]   *Lipkin Gorman v Karpnale Ltd* [1991] 2 AC 548, 574 per Lord Goff.

[15]   *Agip (Africa) Ltd v Jackson* [1990] Ch 265, 285 per Millett J.

he need not bring the claim against the first recipient, he may proceed against a subsequent recipient.[116]

(b) Knowing Receipt

A claim for knowing receipt involves various elements that must be established by **8.45** the claimant,[117] including that there was a trust[118] or fiduciary[119] relationship. This requirement is likely to be met by the facts of typical custodial operations, but if the custodial structure results in a debtor-creditor relationship, an investor will be deprived of this remedy. It is also necessary to demonstrate that the defendant received trust property or its substitute in breach of trust, as well as the appropriate mental state on the part of the defendant.

Beyond receipt by the defendant, the capacity in which the receipt was made must **8.46** be established. Although there are suggestions that ministerial receipt should suffice,[120] there are doubts about this[121] and, on the contrary, there is authority that beneficial receipt is necessary.[122] Whether a recipient receives securities or entitlements for clients or itself is a matter of fact that should be resolved according to the recipient's intention. However, receipt of cash by a custodian or third party bank raises peculiar difficulties because money paid to a bank is technically loaned to the bank, taken beneficially with a personal obligation to effect repayment.[123] Any bank receiving funds into an account for its customers would seem to be vulnerable to a claim for knowing receipt. Nevertheless, although the law on whether a bank has received funds beneficially is said to be 'hopelessly confused and sits ill with legal principle and banking practice',[124] the courts have sought to distinguish between banks receiving money beneficially and when they do so in an essentially agency capacity. Even though money paid into a bank account is essentially the bank's, to use as it wishes, typical banking transactions, such as paying or receiving for customers, are considered as undertaken in an agency capacity.[125] Where, however, 'the collecting bank uses the money to reduce or discharge the customer's

---

[116] ibid 287.

[117] *Polly Peck International plc v Nadir (No 2)* [1992] 4 All ER 769, implied by Scott LJ at 777.

[118] *Agip (Africa) Ltd v Jackson* [1990] Ch 265, 291 per Millett J.

[119] *El Ajou v Dollar Land Holdings* [1994] 2 All ER 685, 700 per Hoffmann LJ.

[120] EP Ellinger and E Lomnicka, *Modern Banking Law* (2nd edn, 1994) 212.

[121] For example, C Harpum, 'The Basis of Equitable Liability' in PBH Birks (ed), *The Frontiers of Liability* (1994) Vol 1, 9, 20; S Gardner, 'Knowing Assistance and Knowing Receipt: Taking Stock' (1996) 112 LQR 56, 69, n 83; and M Bryan, 'When Does a Bank Receive Money?' [1996] JBL 165, 175.

[122] *Agip (Africa) Ltd v Jackson* [1990] Ch 265, 292 per Millett J, *Polly Peck International plc v Nadir (No 2)* [1992] 4 All ER 769, 777 per Scott LJ and *El Ajou v Dollar Land Holdings* [1994] 2 All ER 685, 700 per Hoffmann LJ. See also: *Adams v Bank of New South Wales* [1984] 1 NSWR 285, 291–292 per Moffitt P, 301 per Hutley JA, *Westpac Banking Corporation v Savin* [1985] 2 NZLR 41, 69 per Sir Clifford Richmond.

[123] *Foley v Hill* (1848) 2 HLC 28, 36–37 per Cottenham LC.

[124] R Cranston, *Principles of Banking Law* (1997) 207.

[125] *Agip (Africa) Ltd v Jackson* [1990] Ch 265, 292 per Millett J.

overdraft'[126] or a bank receives money to perform a currency exchange for a customer,[127] the bank will be considered to be taking the money beneficially.

8.47 On the necessary mental state for the claim, the authorities have been described as 'in considerable disarray'.[128] The debate has centred on whether a defendant must have knowledge of the trust and receipt in breach thereof or of facts which should have led him to be aware of the facts that form the basis of the allegation, or whether it is enough for him to have notice thereof. A sub-text to this is whether the defendant need be morally blameworthy or not,[129] although the courts have asserted that they are not looking for fraud.[130] Other conflicting policy objectives here include those of security of title and security of receipt, which may turn on the degree of enquiry to be made by a recipient. Those seeking to impose liability in the absence of knowledge in effect seek to raise the standard of enquiries to be made because liability will be imposed according to objective standards based on the facts of the situation, whether or not the defendant is aware of them.[131]

8.48 Peter Gibson J identified 'five different mental states . . . : (i) actual knowledge; (ii) wilfully shutting one's eyes to the obvious; (iii) wilfully and recklessly failing to make such enquiries as an honest and reasonable person would make; (iv) knowledge of circumstances which would indicate the facts to an honest and reasonable man; (v) knowledge of circumstances which would put an honest and reasonable man on inquiry'.[132] The first three categories may be considered to connote dishonesty, whilst the latter two are suggestive of negligence.

8.49 There is authority that the first three categories are enough for this claim, a subjective approach.[133] Another approach suggests that notice will suffice; yet, in some cases notice is considered to be based on the defendant's actual knowledge.[134] On this line of authority, the requisite mental state may be imputed if the

---

[126] ibid.

[127] *Polly Peck International plc v Nadir (No 2)* [1992] 4 All ER 769, 777 per Scott LJ. For a critique of this decision see *Nimmo v Westpac Banking Corporation* [1993] 3 NZLR 218, 225–226 per Blanchard J, New Zealand HC, and M Bryan, 'When Does a Bank Receive Money?' [1996] JBL 165, 175. It is suggested that the payment of foreign exchange is not substantively different from a client withdrawing funds from its account, a transaction that a bank is considered to undertake in an agency capacity.

[128] *Parker and Mellows, The Modern Law of Trusts* (6th edn, 1994) 266.

[129] *Westdeutsche v Islington BC* [1996] AC 669, 707 per Lord Browne-Wilkinson; *Hillsdown plc v Pensions Ombudsman* [1997] 1 All ER 862, 902–903 per Knox J.

[130] *Lipkin Gorman v Karpnale Ltd* [1987] 1 WLR 987, 1006 per Alliott J.

[131] *Barclays Bank plc v Quincecare Ltd* [1992] 4 All ER 363, 376–377 per Steyn J.

[132] *Baden v Société Générale pour Favoriser le Développement du Commerce et de l'Industrie en France SA* [1992] 4 All ER 161, 235.

[133] *Re Montagu's Settlement Trusts* [1987] Ch 264, 285 per Megarry VC, applied in *Lipkin Gorman v Karpnale Ltd* [1987] 1 WLR 987, 1005 per Alliott J. See also *Barclays Bank plc v Quincecare Ltd* (1988) [1992] 4 All ER 363, 375 per Steyn J.

[134] *Eagle Trust v SBC Securities* [1992] 4 All ER 488, 509 per Vinelott J; affirmed in *Cowan de Groot Properties Ltd v Eagle Trust plc* [1992] 4 All ER 700, 759–761 per Knox J; *Polly Peck International plc v Nadir (No 2)* [1992] 4 All ER 769, 781–782 per Scott LJ.

circumstances were such that an honest and reasonable man would have inferred that he was probably in receipt of trust assets; of course, no man can infer something on the basis of facts that he is not aware of. Another line of cases suggests that notice is based on what the defendant could have discovered if he had made the enquiries that an 'honest and reasonable man' would have made,[135] or which were in those circumstances 'the custom and practice to investigate'.[136]

The distinction between basing notice on actual knowledge and on knowledge **8.50** that the defendant should have acquired may be significant in the present context. A custodian will ordinarily have actual knowledge as to dealings with assets of which he is trustee, thus satisfying either line of authority. However, the distinction may be of greater consequence in relation to third party transferees because it may not be obvious that they are dealing with a custodian or in receipt of custody assets.

The defendant need not have had the requisite mental state at the time of receipt **8.51** of the assets. He may only have discovered or become aware of the relevant facts subsequently. 'In either case he is liable to account for the property, in the first case as from the time he received the property, and in the second as from the time he acquired' the requisite mental state.[137]

In many cases, the recipient may be a company, an abstract legal construct, pre- **8.52** senting obvious difficulties for establishing the required mental state. This is resolved by attributing the mental state of particular individuals to the company by reference to the company's own rules of attribution as contained in its constitution, company law and general principles of agency.[138] The process of attribution is best undertaken with reference to the relevant context in order to serve the rule for which it is undertaken in the most appropriate fashion.[139] The mental state of servants of a company acting in their proper capacity will generally be attributed to the company even if they do not communicate the relevant knowledge to the company, because absolving companies whose servants do not pass on the relevant information would allow the attribution of mental state to be defeated by companies encouraging their servants to act autonomously.[140]

---

[135] *El Ajou v Dollar Land Holdings plc* [1993] 3 All ER 717, 739 per Millett J.
[136] *Macmillan Inc v Bishopsgate Investment Trust plc* [1995] 1 WLR 978, 1000 per Millett J.
[137] *Agip (Africa) Ltd v Jackson* [1990] Ch 265, 291 per Millett J.
[138] *Meridien Global Funds Management Asia Ltd v Securities Commission* [1995] 2 AC 500, 506 per Lord Hoffmann. See also *Re Supply of Ready Mixed Concrete (No 2)* [1995] 1 AC 456; Law Commission, *Fiduciary Duties and Regulatory Rules* (Law Com No 236, 1995) 2.3–2.6; see also Consultation Paper No 124, sections 2.3, 18–26.
[139] *Meridien Global Funds Management Asia Ltd v Securities Commission* [1995] 2 AC 500, 507.
[140] ibid 511.

(c) Personal or Proprietary Remedy for Enrichment by Receipt?

8.53 Unjust enrichment by receipt of assets that are no longer identifiable leads to personal liability of the enriched.[141] In this respect such remedies do not confer any strategic advantage over proceeding for breach of duty upon the insolvency of the defendant, although their ability to be applied against third parties who do not owe the investor duties permits them to be applied to other solvent parties. However, the obiter dictum of Lord Templeman in *Space Investments Ltd v Canadian Imperial Bank of Commerce Trust Co (Bahamas) Ltd*[142] suggests that it may be possible to obtain a proprietary remedy by way of a general equitable charge over the assets of an enriched trustee because they have swollen the assets of the trustee.

8.54 Lord Templeman stated that the beneficiaries should enjoy a proprietary remedy because they had not accepted the risk of insolvency of the trustee whilst unsecured creditors had accepted such a risk. However, this approach may be criticised on the basis that it involves a risk analysis that may be infinitely complex. Further, this approach is inconsistent with the treatment of tort or other involuntary creditors who do not accept the risk of insolvency and would not enjoy priority in the insolvency of the trustee. In any event, the swollen assets theory has not proven attractive to English courts or academics.[143] It is likely that such a general equitable charge will not be applied if it can be demonstrated that the assets which form the basis of the claim have been dissipated or otherwise ceased to exist,[144] or if it would be inequitable to do so.[145]

Enrichment by Profiting from a Wrong

8.55 A wrongdoer may profit from the misapplication of custody assets without the assets being removed or where they are subsequently replaced. This may occur by unlawful stock-lending of custody assets or improper use of custody assets to secure another's indebtedness, for which the custodian derives fees. The investor may seek disgorgement by the custodian of what may be termed deemed agency

---

[141] *Agip (Africa) Ltd v Jackson* [1990] Ch 265, 287 per Millett J in relation to money had and received and 291 in relation to knowing receipt; *Selangor United Rubber Estates Ltd v Cradock (No 3)* [1968] 1 WLR 1555, 1582 per Ungoed-Thomas J. See also PJ Millett, 'Tracing the Proceeds of Fraud' (1991) 107 LQR 71, 85; P Birks, 'Trusts in the Recovery of Misapplied Assets: Tracing, Trusts, and Restitution' in E McKendrick (ed), *Commercial Aspects of Trusts and Fiduciary Relations* (1992) 149, 153–156.

[142] [1986] 1 WLR 1072, 1074. See also *Westdeutsche Landesbank v Islington BC* [1994] 4 All ER 890, 938 per Hobhouse J, and at the Court of Appeal [1994] 1 WLR 938.

[143] For instance, RM Goode, 'Ownership and Obligation in Commercial Transactions' (1987) 103 LQR 433, 445–447; P Birks, 'Establishing a Proprietary Base' [1995] RLR 83, 85–86.

[144] *Bishopsgate Investment Management Ltd v Homan* [1995] Ch 211, 220–221 per Dillon LJ.

[145] *Re Goldcorp Exchange Ltd* [1995] 1 AC 74, 110.

gains,[146] gains that should, if at all, have been made on behalf of the investor. Even if the gain cannot be so characterised, the investor may seek disgorgement of profits simply because they are derived from a wrong committed against him.

(a) Disgorgement for Wrong

Disgorgement may be sought by the victims of various types of wrong,[147] includ-   **8.56**
ing for fraud,[148] breach of fiduciary duties[149] and inducing breach of contract.[150] It
has been asserted that disgorgement of profits from a defendant in breach of contract where the plaintiff had suffered no loss would necessitate 'a somewhat revo-
lutionary development of the law of damages'.[151] This is doubtful, as there is both
early[152] and modern authority[153] for this. Further, if disgorgement is for wrongdoing, it seems inconsistent to permit disgorgement for inducing breach of contract and not for cynical breach of contract.[154]

Arguments that disgorgement for economically efficient breach of contract   **8.57**
inhibits economic efficiency are untenable in the face of a policy that characterises
the type of wrongdoing as unacceptable regardless of the economic arguments in
favour of it; such arguments do not prevail for torts or crimes.[155] Disgorgement

---

[146] This term is borrowed from RM Goode, 'Property and Unjust Enrichment' in A Burrows (ed), *Essays on the Law of Restitution* (1991) 219.

[147] Some of these are set out by the Law Commission, *Aggravated, Exemplary and Restitutionary Damages* (Consultation Paper No 132, 1993) 7.5.

[148] *Hill v Perrott* (1810) 3 Taunt 274, 275, 128 ER 109; *Billing v Reis* (1841) Car & M 26, 29 per Lord Denman CJ, 174 ER 392; *Refuge Assurance Company Limited v Kettlewell* [1909] KB 243; *Mahesa v Malaysia Housing Society* [1979] AC 374, 382–384.

[149] *Keech v Sandford* (1726) Sel Cas T King 61, 62 per Lord Chancellor King, 25 ER 223; *Boardman v Phipps* [1967] 2 AC 46; and *Guinness Plc v Saunders* [1990] 2 AC 663.

[150] *Lightly v Clouston* (1808) 1 Taunt 112, 114, 127 ER 774; affirmed in *Foster v Stewart* (1814) 3 M & S 191, 105 ER 582. Criticised by PH Winfield, *The Province of the Law of Tort* (1931) 174–175.

[151] *Surrey CC v Bredero Homes Ltd* [1993] 1 WLR 1361, 1364 per Dillon LJ; see also 1370 per Steyn LJ, who suggested that undue application of restitutionary damages would render the assessment of damages uncertain.

[152] *Moses v Macferlan* (1760) 2 Burr 1005, 97 ER 676. See P Birks, 'Restitutionary Damages for Breach of Contract' [1987] LMCLQ 412, 429–430.

[153] *British Motor Trade Assn v Gilbert* [1951] 2 All ER 641, 644 per Danckwerts J; *Wrotham Park v Parkside Homes* [1974] 1 WLR 798, 815 per Brightman J; *Surrey CC v Bredero Homes* [1993] 1 WLR 1361, 1369 per Steyn LJ; *Jaggard v Sawyer* [1995] 1 WLR 269, 289, 291 per Millett LJ; *A-G v Blake* [1998] 2 WLR 805, 818.
Academic support may also be cited: W Goodhart, 'Restitutionary Damages for Breach of Contract: The Remedy That Dare Not Speak its Name' [1995] RLR 3, 7–8; H McGregor, 'Restitutionary Damages' in PBH Birks (ed), *Wrongs and Remedies in the Twenty-First Century* (1996) 203, 214 and the references cited in the footnotes therein.

[154] In *A-G v Blake* [1998] 2 WLR 805, 818–819, the Court of Appeal stated, obiter, that although deliberate wrongdoing or breach of contract alone would not justify restitutionary damages, deliberate pursuit of a profit-making activity in breach of a promise not to do this may justify restitutionary damages.

[155] LD Smith, 'Disgorgement of the Profits of Breach of Contract: Property, Contract and "Efficient Breach"' (1995) 24 Canadian Business Law Journal 121, 133–135.

may also be justifiable here in that it serves a quasi-punitive purpose,[156] even though the general jurisdiction to award punitive damages is being narrowed.[157]

(b) Disgorgement upon Conversion

8.58 A custodian could be guilty of conversion of tangible custody assets,[158] as could third parties that receive such assets.[159] Upon the establishment of conversion, an account for profits may be ordered.[160] However, the need to relate a claim for conversion to tangible assets will prove an impediment in many custodial contexts.[161] For wholly dematerialised securities this type of remedy will not be available, although if there is tangible representation of the securities, such as a share certificate, and the claimant can establish a direct link thereto, the courts have been willing to reify the securities into the token in order to permit recovery by way of conversion.[162] This remedy will not be available to beneficiaries of interests under tiers of intermediary custodians.

8.59 Another difficulty in applying conversion to the modern custodial context comes from the requisite interest in relation to the converted chattel that the claimant must enjoy. It has been suggested that one needs to be the 'true owner',[163] which may be taken to mean legal title-holder. However, since there is authority that legal title will not of itself suffice in the absence of the right to immediate possession of the thing,[164] it may be the case that the right to immediate possession of the chattel may be the requisite interest of a claimant for conversion.[165] Yet, there is authority that in the absence of an immediate right to possession, a claimant who has parted with possession who enjoys a reversionary interest may bring a claim for conversion that injures this interest.[166]

8.60 The foregoing suggests that to bring a claim for conversion the claimant must enjoy an immediate right to possession or a reversionary interest in the thing

---

[156] P Jaffey, 'Restitutionary Damages and Disgorgement' [1995] RLR 30, 37.

[157] *AB v South West Water Services Ltd* [1993] QB 507.

[158] For the constituent elements, see *Lancashire & Yorkshire Railway, &c v MacNicoll* (1919) 88 LJKB 601, 605 per Lord Atkin, affirmed in *Oakley v Lyster* [1931] 1 KB 148, 153 per Scrutton LJ, and in *Caxton Publishing Co v Sutherland Publishing Co* [1939] AC 178, 201–202 per Lord Porter.

[159] *M'Combie v Davies* (1805) 6 East 538, 540 per Lord Ellenborough, 102 ER 1393.

[160] *Lamine v Dorrell* (1705) 2 Ld Raym 1216, 1217 per Holt CJ, 92 ER 303; *Re Simms* [1934] Ch 1.

[161] Torts (Interference with Goods) Act 1977, s 14.

[162] *Solloway v McLaughlin* [1938] AC 247; *BBMB Finance (Hong Kong) Ltd v Eda Holdings Ltd* [1991] 2 All ER 129; *MCC Proceeds v Lehman Brothers International, The Times*, 14 January 1998.

[163] *Lancashire & Yorkshire Railway, &c v MacNicoll* (1919) 88 LJKB 601, 605 per Lord Atkin.

[164] *Lord v Price* (1873) LR 9 Ex 54.

[165] *Bute (Marquess) v Barclays Bank Ltd* [1955] 1 QB 202, affirmed in *Lipkin Gorman v Karpnale Ltd* [1991] 2 AC 548, 587 per Lord Goff. See also WVH Rogers (ed), *Winfield and Jolowicz on Tort* (14th edn, 1994) 498; *Clerk & Lindsell on Torts* (17th edn, 1995) 13.51.

[166] *Mears v London & South Western Railway Co* (1862) 11 CB (NS) 850, 142 ER 1029; see also the General Note to Torts (Interference with Goods) Act 1977, s 1(d) in [1977] *Sweet & Maxwell's Current Law Statutes Annotated.*

converted. If this is accepted, beneficiaries of single-tier intermediary custody could claim for conversion because they could generally call for immediate possession of the underlying asset or enjoy a reversionary interest therein, as would any investor with assets in non-intermediary custody. Investors with assets in extended tiers of intermediary custody generally do not enjoy such rights and would therefore not be in a position to avail themselves of this remedy. There is authority[167] and support from academics[168] for a claimant relying on equitable title alone to claim for conversion, but this view is deprecated as 'heterodox as a matter of law, and dangerous in point of practice'.[169] It is contrary to earlier authority that either legal ownership or the right to immediate possession is necessary[170] and would lead to the anomaly of permitting one to rely on an equitable interest to bring a claim at law. This possibility has been considered and rejected by the Court of Appeal.[171]

(c) Personal or Proprietary Remedy for Enrichment from a Wrong?

Avenues of recovery that insulate the claimant from the effects of insolvency of the **8.61** defendant are important since they enable a claimant to receive more than a dividend. Does this advantage obtain where the plaintiff seeks disgorgement of profits from the use of their assets or wrongs committed against them? *AG for Hong Kong v Reid*[172] suggests that profit by a fiduciary pursuant to a breach of his fiduciary duties would, *ipso facto*, be accountable to the beneficiary of the duty by way of constructive trust from the moment the profit is received. This was said to be because in equity it is unconscionable that a wrongdoer should benefit from a wrong; and because equity considers as done that which ought to be done. There is academic support for the view that it is a proper legal policy to strip wrongdoing fiduciaries of their profits by proprietary means notwithstanding the harsh effects on third party interests.[173]

However, even if making wrongdoers disgorge is a laudable policy, this need not **8.62** be effected by proprietary remedies. By the reasoning in *AG v Reid* that equity treats as done that which ought to be done, all equitable remedies should be proprietary. No such argument is made for other equally reprehensible conduct.

---

[167] *International Factors Ltd v Rodriguez* [1979] 1 QB 351, 357; *Stroud Architectural Systems Ltd v John Laing Construction Ltd* [1994] 2 BCLC 276.

[168] NE Palmer, 'The Vindication of Commercial Security over Commodities: Equitable Pledges and Conversion' [1986] LMCLQ 218, 228; BS Markesinis and SF Deakin, *Tort Law* (3rd edn, 1994) 406.

[169] A Tettenborn, 'Trust Property and Conversion: An Equitable Confusion' [1996] CLJ 36, 38.

[170] *United Bank of Australia, Limited v McClintlock* [1922] 1 AC 240, applied in *Commercial Banking Co of Sydney Ltd v Edward Rolf Mann* [1961] AC 1, cited with approval in *Lipkin Gorman v Karpnale Ltd* [1991] 2 AC 548, 583–586 per Lord Goff.

[171] *MCC Proceeds v Lehman Brothers International, The Times*, 14 January 1998.

[172] [1994] 1 AC 324, 331.

[173] Sir P Millett, 'Bribes and Secret Commissions' [1993] RLR 7.

Profit-stripping may be equally well effected by a vigorous order to account which embraces any incidental profits of invested wealth and, if necessary, a *Mareva* injunction to prevent dissipation of such profits. The most serious objection to granting remedial proprietary interests in these circumstances is due to their effect on unsecured third party interests. Since the claimant of an account for profits for wrongs and unsecured creditors may both be innocent victims of the defendant, it is not clear why victims of wrongs should rank ahead of unsecured creditors. Indeed, given that the creditor, albeit unsecured, has added to the wealth of the insolvent, whereas the victim of a wrong may not have done so, the reverse argument may be made. Although *AG v Reid* subsists as authority for providing proprietary remedies for wrongs, indications from the Court of Appeal[174] and House of Lords[175] suggest a disinclination to applying this remedy.

8.63 *Lister v Stubbs*[176] had stood for almost a century as authority for effecting disgorgement for wrongs by a personal remedy before being disapproved in *AG v Reid*, where it was said[177] that *Lister v Stubbs* was inconsistent with the view that a wrongdoer should not benefit from his wrong. This is doubtful; the fact that only a personal remedy is provided is not inconsistent with the profit-stripping policy. If the wrongdoer is solvent, the profits are stripped by the personal remedy. If the wrongdoer is insolvent, he will not benefit from the profits because his wealth is shared amongst his creditors. Although *Lister v Stubbs* was criticised for being inconsistent with earlier authority, it has been demonstrated[178] that earlier authority was inconclusive on this point; *Lister v Stubbs* was not unprecedented.

Accessory Liability

8.64 A claimant may seek to impose accessory liability on anyone implicated in the misapplication of his custody assets. In order to establish this, however, he will have to prove breach of fiduciary obligations owed to him;[179] that the defendant assisted in that breach; and that the defendant assisted with a particular mental state. For example, a custodian could be liable in this way if implicated in misdeeds by a fund-manager, as could fund-managers, accountants, lawyers and others who are implicated in misdeeds by a custodian.

---

[174] *Halifax Building Society v Thomas* [1996] Ch 217, 229 per Peter Gibson LJ.
[175] *Re Goldcorp Exchange Ltd* [1995] 1 AC 74, 104 per Lord Mustill; *Westdeutsche Bank v Islington LBC* [1996] AC 669, 716 per Lord Browne-Wilkinson; see also *Soulos v Korkontzilas* (1997) 146 DLR (4th) 214, 229–230 per McLachlin J, SC of Canada, where although he initially stated that a proprietary remedy was available for either wrongs or unjust enrichment, he went on to qualify this by stating that this would only be available in the event of deemed agency gains.
[176] (1890) 45 ChD 1; applied in *Islamic Republic of Iran v Denby* [1987] 1 Lloyd's Rep 367.
[177] [1994] 1 AC 324, 336.
[178] D Crilley, 'A Case of Proprietary Overkill' [1994] RLR 57, 63–65.
[179] *Royal Brunei Airlines v Philip Tan Kok Ming* [1995] 2 AC 378, 382, 384, 392.

(a) Knowing Assistance

The requirement of breach of trust or fiduciary obligations is likely to be met by **8.65** the facts of typical custodial operations, but if the custodial structure results in a debtor-creditor relationship, an investor will be deprived of this remedy. Although it appears to be a requirement of *Barnes v Addy*[180] that the breach must be fraudulent, there are cases both before[181] and after[182] *Barnes v Addy* which challenge this on the basis that liability for dishonest assistance rests on the assistant's own wrongdoing, separate from any wrongdoing by the fiduciary.[183] This requirement was considered in *Royal Brunei Airlines v Philip Tan Kok Ming*[184] where the Privy Council confirmed that it is not necessary for accessory liability that the breach is fraudulent, 'what matters is the state of mind of the third party sought to be made liable, not the state of mind of the trustee'.[185]

What degree of assistance attracts liability? It is submitted that since liability for **8.66** dishonest assistance is secondary to the breach,[186] it need not be the case that the breach could not have occurred but for the assistance. Nevertheless, the assistance must be significant.[187]

Given that accessory liability is imposed as a result of wrongdoing, it is necessary **8.67** to demonstrate some degree of fault on the part of the assistant.[188] A lack of probity or 'dishonesty is a necessary ingredient of accessory liability. It is also a sufficient ingredient'.[189] This 'means simply not acting as an honest person would in the circumstances'.[190] Dishonesty involves 'a strong subjective element in that it is a description of a type of conduct assessed in the light of what a person actually knew at the time, as distinct from what a reasonable person would have known or

---

[180] *Barnes v Addy* (1874) LR 9 Ch App 244, 251–252 per Lord Selborne. See also *Belmont Finance Corporation Ltd v Williams Furniture Ltd* [1979] Ch 250, 267 per Buckley LJ; *Agip (Africa) Ltd v Jackson* [1990] Ch 265, 293 per Millett J.

[181] *Fyler v Fyler* (1841) 3 Beav 550, 49 ER 216; *Attorney-General v The Corporation of Leicester* (1844) 7 Beav 176, 179, 49 ER 1031; *Eaves v Hickson* (1861) 30 Beav 136, 54 ER at 840. See A Berg, 'Accessory Liability for Breach of Trust' (1996) 59 MLR 443, 444–445 for a differing analysis of these cases.

[182] *Midgley v Midgley* [1893] 3 Ch 282, 301 per Lindley LJ and 304 per Lopes LJ; *Soar v Ashwell* [1893] 2 QB 390, 396 per Bowen LJ. See also *Equiticorp Finance Ltd (In Liq) v Bank of New Zealand* (1993) 32 NSWLR 50, 105 per Kirby P.

[183] Many of these cases are cited by C Harpum, 'The Basis of Equitable Liability' in PBH Birks (ed), *The Frontiers of Liability* (1994) Vol 1, 9.

[184] [1995] 2 AC 378, 384–386.

[185] ibid 385.

[186] ibid 382.

[187] *Brinks Ltd v Abu-Saleh* [1996] CLC 133, 149 per Colin Rimer J.

[188] Since similar difficulties in attributing mental state to a legal construct for knowing receipt arise, reference may be made to that discussion.

[189] *Royal Brunei* (n 184 above) at 392. See also *Agip (Africa) Ltd v Jackson* [1990] Ch 265, 293 per Millett J; *Eagle Trust Plc v SBC Securities Ltd* [1993] 1 WLR 484, 496; *Polly Peck International plc v Nadir (No 2)* [1992] 4 All ER 769, 777 per Scott LJ.

[190] *Royal Brunei* (n 184 above) at 389.

appreciated . . . Thus for the most part dishonesty is to be equated with conscious impropriety'.[191] Negligence and carelessness do not amount to dishonesty but, in appropriate circumstances, recklessness might. Rimer J has stated that 'a claim based on accessory liability can only be brought against someone who knows of the existence of the trust, or at least of the facts giving rise to the trust'.[192]

8.68 Yet, in spite of the subjective element dishonesty 'is an objective standard'.[193] The 'subjective characteristics of honesty do not mean that individuals are free to set their own standards of honesty in particular circumstances',[194] 'a person . . . will not escape a finding of dishonesty simply because he sees nothing wrong in such behaviour'.[195] 'The individual is expected to attain the standard which would be observed by an honest person placed in those circumstances. It is impossible to be more specific.'[196] Pursuit of a market practice does not necessarily render the action unimpugnable. 'Actions which are basically dishonest are not rendered honest by repetition.'[197]

8.69 Millett J stated in *Agip (Africa) Ltd v Jackson*[198] that once one is suspicious of wrongdoing, even if not cognisant of the particular wrong to which one may be accessory, one may be found liable because 'such conduct is dishonest, and those who are guilty of it cannot complain if, for the purpose of civil liability, they are treated as if they had actual knowledge'. A similar argument to that adopted by Millett J was considered by Rimer J in *Brinks Ltd v Abu-Saleh*.[199] Although Rimer J's remarks on this are strictly obiter because he had already determined that the actions of the defendant did not in that case amount to assistance or constitute her an accessory to the breach,[200] he found this an unpersuasive argument[201] because by his interpretation of *Royal Brunei*, accessory liability can only be imposed on the basis of facts known to the defendant. There will be many transactions by custodians where it is not clear whether it acts in a proprietary or fiduciary capacity. Where the counter-party in such transactions is unaware of the trust, imposition of accessory liability seems impossible.

(b) Personal or Proprietary Remedy for Accessory Liability?

8.70 As with knowing receipt, although it is said that liability imposed for knowing assistance is to account as constructive trustee,[202] the liability of a dishonest assis-

---

191 *Royal Brunei* (n 184 above) at 389.
192 *Brinks Ltd v Abu-Saleh* [1996] CLC 133, 151.
193 *Royal Brunei* (n 184 above) at 389.
194 ibid.
195 ibid.
196 ibid 390.
197 *Adams v The Queen* [1995] 1 WLR 52, 63 per Lord Jauncey.
198 [1990] Ch 265, 293.
199 [1996] CLC 133.
200 ibid 149.
201 ibid 151.
202 *Agip (Africa) Ltd v Jackson* [1990] Ch 265, 292 per Millett J.

tant is personal. In this respect, this remedy does not offer any strategic advantage in the insolvency of the defendant, although if the principal malfeasors are insolvent, it permits claimants to pursue well-heeled third parties instead.[203]

F. Defences

(1) Bona Fide Purchase

8.71 This defence is effective for proprietary claims,[204] but its applicability to personal claims is doubted because the defence is primarily concerned with property rights, as an exception to *nemo dat.*[205] Nevertheless, these doubts may be countered,[206] inter alia, on the grounds that a personal claim for unjust enrichment may depend on demonstrating that the defendant received the claimant's thing. If the recipient can demonstrate that he was entitled to receive the thing, such entitlement should serve as defence to the personal claim for unjust enrichment. There is authority for this position.[207]

8.72 If the foregoing reasons for permitting the defence to personal claims are accepted, they also determine the scope of personal claims to which the defence should apply; to personal claims that depend on receipt.[208] Claims dependent on wrongs should be beyond its scope.

8.73 There is authority that it may lie on the plaintiff to show that the defendant had notice or did not provide value,[209] but there is also contrary authority suggesting that it is for the defendant to make out this defence.[210] Many academics are of the view that the preponderance of authority puts the onus of establishing this

---

[203] *Royal Brunei* (n 184 above) 381–382 per Lord Nicholls.

[204] *Eagle Trust v SBC Securities* [1992] 4 All ER 488, 500 per Vinelott J; *Agip (Africa) Ltd v Jackson* [1990] Ch 265, 290 per Millett J.

[205] P Key, 'Bona Fide Purchase as a Defence in the Law of Restitution' [1994] LMCLQ 421, 424–426, 428.

[206] E McKendrick, 'Restitution, Misdirected Funds and Change of Position' (1992) 55 MLR 377, 383–384; K Barker, 'After Change of Position: Good Faith Exchange in the Modern Law of Restitution' in PBH Birks (ed), *Laundering and Tracing* (1995) 202, 211–213. See also A Burrows, *The Law of Restitution* (1993) 472.

[207] *Lipkin Gorman v Karpnale Ltd* [1991] 2 AC 548, 574–577 per Lord Goff.

[208] PBH Birks, 'Overview: Tracing, Claiming and Defences' in PBH Birks (ed), *Laundering and Tracing* (1995) 333.

[209] *Thomson v Clydesdale Bank Limited* [1893] AC 282, 289 per Lord Herschell LC; *Union Bank of Australia v Murray-Aynsley* [1898] AC 693, 697 per Lord Watson; *Polly Peck International plc v Nadir (No 2)* [1992] 4 All ER 769, 781 per Scott LJ.

[210] *Attorney-General v Biphosphated Guano Company* (1898) 11 ChD 327, 337 per Thessiger LJ; *Re Nisbett and Potts' Contract* [1906] 1 Ch 386, 404 per Collins MR, 409 per Romer LJ; *Lipkin Gorman v Karpnale Ltd* [1991] 2 AC 548, 574–577 per Lord Goff.

defence on the defendant and that authorities that run counter to this may 'be either explained or criticised'.[211]

8.74 The exchange of any value will suffice for the defence, even if the value is release from a debt.[212] In view of the operations of modern custody, however, the difficulty will be in linking the value given to the value received. It will be necessary to go through the process of identification outlined earlier. Yet, if the law does not recognise the transaction by which the value was given, whether because contrary to policy and regarded as a void transaction,[213] or because contrary to the morality of the day,[214] the value given will not count.

8.75 If a recipient has notice of a defect in the title of the transferor, he may not resort to the defence. However, Lindley LJ has warned[215] against giving notice too expansive a meaning. He drew a distinction between situations where the recipient has enough time to conduct research into his counter-party, such as real property transactions, where it may be reasonable to readily impute notice to a recipient, and other commercial contexts where there is little time to investigate one's counter-parties and their titles. In his view, one should be slow to impute notice in the latter.

(2) Change of Position

8.76 Change of position is a defence against restitutionary claims,[216] because 'where an innocent defendant's position is so changed that he will suffer an injustice if called upon to repay or to repay in full, the injustice of requiring him so to repay outweighs the injustice of denying the plaintiff restitution'.[217] The limits of the defence were undefined so as not 'to inhibit the development of the defence on a case by case basis, in the usual way'.[218]

8.77 The defence is not available to one who changed position in bad faith or is a wrongdoer:[219] is this true of any wrongdoer? The fourth edition of Goff and Jones,

---

[211] K Barker, 'After Change of Position: Good Faith Exchange in the Modern Law of Restitution' in PBH Birks (ed), *Laundering and Tracing* (1995) 206. See also RP Meagher, WMC Gummow and JRF Lehane, *Equity: Doctrines and Remedies* (3rd edn, 1992) 257–259, PBH Birks, 'Overview: Tracing, Claiming and Defences' (n 208 above) 334.

[212] *Aiken v Short* (1856) 1 H & N 210, 144 ER 1180; *Barclays Bank v WJ Simms Ltd* [1980] 1 QB 677, 695 per Goff J.

[213] *Lipkin Gorman v Karpnale Ltd* [1991] 2 AC 548.

[214] *Banque Belge v Hambrouck* [1921] 1 KB 321, 326 per Bankes LJ, 329 per Scrutton LJ and 332 per Atkin LJ.

[215] *Manchester Trust v Furness* [1895] 2 QB 539, 545. See also *Eagle Trust plc v SBC Securities Ltd* [1992] 4 All ER 488, 507, 509 per Vinelott J; *Polly Peck International plc v Nadir (No 2)* [1992] 4 All ER 769, 781–782 per Scott LJ; *Macmillan Inc v Bishopsgate Trust (No 3)* [1995] 1 WLR 978, 1000 per Millett J.

[216] *Lipkin Gorman v Karpnale Ltd* [1991] 2 AC 548, 579–580 per Lord Goff.

[217] ibid 579.

[218] ibid 580.

[219] ibid.

of which Lord Goff was not an author, suggests that the defence should be open to wrongdoers not guilty of *mala fides*,[220] but this seems to have been rejected by the courts.[221]

The defence is valid for personal claims,[222] what about proprietary claims? If the defence relates to unjust enrichment, it should be irrelevant to a claim of pre-existing and unbroken title where the claimant does not demand his thing because of the defendant's unjust enrichment, but simply because it is his. Where, however, the claim is for traceably identifiable substitutes, the claimant does not assert a pre-existing title, the claimant is dependent on the generation of new proprietary rights in relation to a new thing in response to the unjust enrichment of the defendant.[223] There is, therefore, support for allowing the defence to proprietary claims contingent on tracing,[224] which would make it applicable to many proprietary claims in the modern custodial context. If this is accepted, the defence of change of position should also be available where the claim asserted is based on proprietary rights established by law to reverse unjust enrichment based on wrongs, as occurred in *AG v Reid*.[225] One difficulty with the application of this defence to proprietary claims is that the defence may take effect *pro tanto* in relation to a claim for a specific non-divisible thing. However, since the defence may be full or partial,[226] the suggested resolution of this difficulty is that the claimant be put 'on terms, compelling him to make good the defendant's change of position as a condition of asserting his own title'.[227]

8.78

What types of change of position may validly form a basis for the defence? Anticipatory reliance was considered in *South Tyneside BC v Svenska International*[228] where it was held that it was not the case that 'the defence of change of position can never succeed where the alleged change occurs before the receipt of the money . . . the facts of *Lipkin Gorman* itself are an example of such a case'.[229] However, permitting this type of change of position may not be 'entirely logical'.[230] It is impossible to change position based on something that has not

8.79

---

[220] G Jones, *Goff & Jones, The Law of Restitution* (4th edn, 1993) 745.

[221] *South Tyneside BC v Svenska International* [1995] 1 All ER 545.

[222] *Lipkin* (n 216 above) 580.

[223] PBH Birks, 'Overview: Tracing, Claiming and Defences' (n 209 above) 317–319.

[224] *Boscawen v Bajwa* [1996] 1 WLR 328, 341 per Millett LJ. See also P Birks, 'Tracing, Subrogation and Change of Position' (1995) 9 Trust Law International, No 4, 124, 125; R Nolan 'Change of Position' in PBH Birks (ed), *Laundering and Tracing* (1995) 176–179; PBH Birks 'Overview: Tracing, Claiming and Defences' (n 208 above) 319–322, 326–327; and Smith, *The Law of Tracing* (n 72 above) 384–385.

[225] Smith, *The Law of Tracing* (n 72 above) 384, n 26.

[226] *Lipkin* (n 216 above) 579 and 580.

[227] PBH Birks, 'Overview: Tracing, Claiming and Defences' (n 208 above) 326.

[228] [1995] 1 All ER 545, 559–568 per Clarke J.

[229] ibid 565–566. See *Lipkin Gorman v Karpnale Ltd* [1991] 2 AC 548, 582–583.

[230] *Lipkin* (n 216 above) 583.

occurred; such a change is more properly based on an expectation. The argument has been advanced[231] that all one is concerned with is to 'establish a sufficient causal link between the plus received and a minus to be set against it', followed by the assertion that 'anticipatory reliance does establish a sufficient link'. In defence of this type of change it is also suggested that the difference between change based on actual receipt and change based on expectation thereof may be fortuitous, such as if the defendant cannot know whether there has been actual receipt or not. It is stated that 'there is a valid distinction between change of position based on anticipatory action and the improper perfection or fulfilment of expectations'.[232] It is also suggested that permitting the defence does not necessarily protect mere expectancies because the defendant takes the risk that the thing expected is not actually received and that the defence merely renders 'an impugnable receipt an unimpugnable receipt'. Nevertheless, the logical inconsistency inherent in permitting change of position in relation to a receipt to be based on a change pursuant to something else, an expectation, may be difficult to overcome. Perhaps in recognition of this, one judge has stated that anticipatory reliance will be recognised only in exceptional circumstances.[233]

8.80 The defence cannot properly be invoked for changes that the defendant would ordinarily have had to effect.[234] In one sense, the change was not effected simply because of the enrichment, but because of other factors, such as regulations that make such change mandatory, such as payment of tax on receipts. However, whilst the direct cause of the change may have been an obligation, it is submitted that where the direct obligation is a logical consequence or otherwise caused by the enrichment, such obligatory payment ought to be regarded as sufficient change of position. It was because of the enrichment that the further payment, such as tax, was made.[235]

8.81 Similarly, if the actual thing received is stolen or destroyed this may count as change of position. If one did not come into receipt of that thing, then it could not have been stolen or destroyed. That is not to say that it is the receipt of the thing that caused the theft or loss. Simply, 'the receipt was a condition sine qua non of the theft or destruction and that, that connection established, the loss is, for the reason given, within the class of losses which has to count if the security of receipts is to be adequately protected'.[236]

---

[231] PBH Birks, 'Overview: Tracing, Claiming and Defences' (n 208 above) 329.
[232] R Nolan, 'Change of Position in Anticipation of Enrichment' [1995] LMCLQ 313, 315.
[233] *South Tyneside BC v Svenska International* [1995] 1 All ER 545, 566 per Clarke J.
[234] *Lipkin* (n 216 above) 580.
[235] PBH Birks, 'Overview: Tracing, Claiming and Defences' (n 208 above) 329–330.
[236] ibid 330.

(3) Equitable Allowance in Accounting for Profits

Where the defendant has been partly responsible for the generation of profits **8.82** claimed by the plaintiff, the defendant might claim allowance for his input. This is analytically distinct from a defence of change of position, although one set of facts could give rise to both types of defence. A defendant claiming change of position for sums spent in maintaining or managing something is different from one who seeks allowance for his contribution to the generation of profits thereby.

The Law Commission has observed that determining when such allowances **8.83** should be permitted is one of the most difficult problems in relation to an account for profits.[237] It has been suggested that this may be determined by reference to what was gained by the defendant and what was lost by the claimant.[238] However, if the essence of the allowance is for 'expenses, skill, expertise, effort and resources contributed'[239] by the defendant it is not clear why loss by the claimant should be relevant. A better way to determine allowance may be to focus on the basis for the liability to account.[240]

Where liability to account derives from enrichment by subtraction, to the extent **8.84** that profits derived by alienation[241] or deemed hire[242] of the plaintiff's assets did not involve the skill or material contribution of the defendant, it may be appropriate for the defendant to hand over all of the profit to the claimant. However, where the defendant has put skill, effort and money into procuring the profit, and it is accepted that the basis for account of profits is the subtractive enrichment at the plaintiff's expense, any enrichment which may be demonstrated not to have been at the claimant's expense may be allowed.

If the profit is gained by a wrong *ipso facto*, and an account is sought on that basis, **8.85** there is authority for allowance on the basis that it would be inequitable for the claimant 'to step in and take the profit without paying for the skill and labour which has produced it'.[243] However, this 'has to be reconciled with the fundamental principle that a trustee is not entitled to remuneration for services rendered by him to the trust except as expressly provided in the trust deed'.[244]

---

[237] Law Commission, *Aggravated, Exemplary and Restitutionary Damages* (Consultation Paper No 132, 1993) 7.13(c).

[238] *Warman v Dwyer* (1995) 128 ALR 201, 214, HC of Australia.

[239] ibid 216.

[240] See P Jaffey, 'Accounting for Wrongful Profits: Warman v Dwyer' [1995] LMCLQ 462 and R Nolan, 'What to Take into Account' [1996] CLJ 201.

[241] *Lamine v Dorrell* (1705) 2 Ld Raym 1216, 92 ER 303.

[242] *Strand Electric & Engineering Co Ltd v Brisford Entertainments Ltd* [1952] 2 QB 246, 254 per Denning LJ and 257 per Romer LJ; *Penarth Dock Company v Pounds* [1963] 1 QB 359, 361–362 per Lord Denning MR, sitting as an additional judge of the QBD.

[243] *Phipps v Boardman* [1964] 1 WLR 993, 1018 per Wilberforce J, affirmed *sub nom. Boardman v Phipps* [1967] 2 AC 46, 104 per Lord Cohen and 112 per Lord Hodson.

[244] *Guinness Plc v Saunders* [1990] 2 AC 663, 701 per Lord Goff.

Notwithstanding suggestions that allowance should be permitted where the equity underlying the defence is overwhelming and the circumstances of such an award does not encourage further wrongful activity,[245] where the essence of an account for profits is profit-stripping on a prophylactic or quasi-punitive basis, no allowance should be permitted.

(4) Ministerial Receipt

8.86 Ordinarily, 'an agent receiving money on account of his principal and paying it over to the principal, without notice to the contrary, is protected against any claim which the party from whom it was received would have had if the money still remained in his hands. When money so paid to an agent has once been bona fide parted with, without notice, the liability of the agent ceases, and the claim of the party paying it can be enforced only against the principal to whom the money has been handed over'.[246]

8.87 For a defendant to rely on this defence, he must be acting as agent. Trusteeship may not be conclusive of an agency,[247] though the typical facts of custody are likely to be considered an agency. There is authority that suggests that the agency must be disclosed.[248] Although there are cases to the contrary,[249] these cases are criticised on the grounds that the point was not argued and that the decisions may be explained on other grounds.[250] The requirement for disclosed agency might be a source of difficulty in the custodial context to the extent that it is not always apparent that a custodian transacts for himself or for another party.

8.88 The defence does not avail a defendant who effects transfer to his principal after notice of a plaintiff's claim, nor one involved in fraud perpetrated by his principal.[251] If the agent was not properly authorised to receive the money or acted without good faith in obtaining the payment, he may also be deprived of the defence even though he has paid the money on.[252]

8.89 What constitutes paying over? If money received for his principal remains in the agent's hands for the principal the agent may be liable for money had and

---

[245] ibid.

[246] *Holland v Russell* (1861) 1 B & S 424, 434 per Cockburn J, 121 ER 773; affirmed (1863) 4 B & S 14, 15 per Erle CJ, 122 ER 365.

[247] *Baylis v Bishop of London* [1913] 1 Ch 127.

[248] *Sadler v Evans* (1766) 4 Burr 1984, 1986 per Lord Mansfield, 98 ER 34; *Buller v Harrison* (1777) 2 Cowp 565, 566 per Lord Mansfield, 98 ER 1243; *Oates v Hudson* (1851) 6 Ex 346, 348 per Parke B, 155 ER 576; *Agip (Africa) Ltd v Jackson* [1990] 1 Ch 265, 288 per Millett J.

[249] *East India Company v Tritton* (1824) 3 B & C 280, 107 ER 738; *Transvaal Investment Co v Atkinson* [1944] 1 All ER 579.

[250] W Swadling, 'The Nature of Ministerial Receipt' in PBH Birks (ed), *Laundering and Tracing* (1995) 252–253.

[251] *Agip (Africa) Ltd v Jackson* [1990] Ch 265, 288–289 per Millett J.

[252] *Snowdon v Davis* (1808) 1 Taunt 359, 363–364 per Mansfield CJ, 127 ER 872; *Oates v Hudson* (1851) 6 Ex 346, 348 per Parke B, 155 ER 576.

received.[253] However, if the agent has allocated the sums received to any other person or purpose on behalf of the principal, although the agent has not transferred the sums received to the principal, the fact that he has done the principal's bidding with the sums will constitute payment over.[254]

---

[253] *Buller v Harrison* (1777) 2 Cowp 565, 568 per Lord Mansfield, 98 ER 1243.

[254] *Holland v Russell* (1861) 1 B & S 424, 435–436 per Cockburn CJ, 121 ER 773; affirmed (1863) 4 B & S 14, 15 per Erle CJ, 122 ER 365.

9

REGULATION OF CUSTODY BUSINESS

By the Financial Services Act 1986 (Extension of Scope of Act) Order 1996 ('the **9.01** Order')[1] the custody of investments, as defined in the Financial Services Act 1986 ('the Act'),[2] has been brought within the regulatory scope of the Act. The Order was made by HM Treasury and laid before Parliament on 25 November 1996 and came fully into force on 1 June 1997.

The Order inserted a new paragraph 13A in Schedule 1 to the Act, which sets out **9.02** the types of financial services for which a practitioner must be authorised or exempt,[3] as follows:

Custody of Investments

(1) Safeguarding and administering or arranging for the safeguarding and administration of assets belonging to another where—

(a) those assets consist of or include investments; or

(b) the arrangements for their safeguarding and administration are such that those assets may consist of or include investments and the arrangements have at any

---

[1] SI 1996/2958.
[2] 1986 c 60.
[3] Financial Services Act 1986, s 3.

time been held out as being arrangements under which investments would be safeguarded and administered.

(2) Offering or agreeing to safeguard and administer, or to arrange for the safeguarding and administration of, assets belonging to another where the circumstances fall within sub-paragraph (1)(a) or (b) above.

A. Background to, and Motives for, Regulation

9.03 Although the Order would not have substantively altered the way in which many custodians conduct their custody business, because much of their work related to investment business that was already authorisable prior to the Order, the fact that the Order was issued reflected a need for specific regulation.

9.04 It has been argued that the desire of service-providers in a free market to maintain their reputation should serve as sufficient motivation for the observance of high standards of conduct in the provision of the service.[4] However, the facts of the financial service industry would seem to suggest otherwise. There have been a number of recent scandals in England leading to the loss of reputation of the wrongdoer,[5] not all of whom were custodians. Such wrongdoers must have been aware of this risk but, driven by the overwhelming desire to generate new business or stave off impending insolvency, presumably remained undeterred by reputational considerations.

9.05 Further, the nature of politics in a democracy is such that politicians want to be seen as active in spheres of life that affect possible voters. The area of financial services is one such area.[6] The desire to do, or at least to be seen to be doing, something is recognised to be heightened following a scandal affecting large sections of the public.[7] The steps leading to the regulation of custody are in this sense unexceptional. The Securities and Investments Board (SIB) recognised that the Maxwell affair, as well as other instances where custody assets have been threatened or abused, formed the initial impetus for the review of custody business.[8]

---

[4] C Ford and J Kay, 'Why Regulate Financial Services?' in F Oditah (ed), *The Future for the Global Securities Market* (1996).

[5] Maxwell's theft of pension funds and the lack of internal controls that permitted the Barings debacle are obvious examples. Whilst custody assets in the latter were not strictly at risk, any cash held by the bank as part of the custodial function was. Further, the lack of internal control that permitted the wrongful acts by Mr Leeson could have led to wrongful acts also being perpetrated in connection with custody assets.

[6] M O'Brien, MP, 'Labour's Proposals for Regulation into the 21st Century' (1997) 5 *Journal of Financial Regulation and Compliance* No 7, 115.

[7] MJ Perry, 'Approaches to Market Regulation: The United Kingdom' in F Oditah (ed), *The Future for the Global Securities Market* (1996) 192–194.

[8] SIB, *Custody Review: Discussion Paper* (August 1993) ('*Custody Discussion Paper*') 1.3–1.7; SIB, *Custody: Consultative Paper* 90 (August 1995) ('*Custody Consultative Paper 90*') para 1.

The process of doing something commenced with a discussion paper on custody **9.06** by SIB in August 1993. At that time, although SIB recognised that regulation of custody could minimise the risk of theft or misuse of custody assets and safeguard investors' interests in the event of the insolvency of the custodian,[9] it remained unsure of the need for regulation of custody. It was felt that in the light of the costs to custodians of complying with specifically targeted regulations and the possibility of otherwise achieving investor protection, by making investment firms which use custodians insist on high standards and take responsibility for their custodians, 'it does not appear to SIB that there is a clear or sufficient case for recommending to HM Treasury that custody should be made an authorisable activity in its own right'.[10] However, based on comments received in response to the discussion paper of 1993 and further detailed consultation with market operators, including a cost-benefit analysis involving market operators,[11] a formal recommendation was made by SIB to the Treasury that custody should be an authorisable activity. This was followed by an announcement by the Economic Secretary to the Treasury on 9 May 1996 that the Treasury had decided in principle that custody should be an authorisable activity.[12]

The Treasury's motives for regulating custody are expressed in a consultation document of June 1996.[13] The motives were essentially two-fold: to achieve consistency in the regulation of all aspects of investment business and for investor protection. In relation to inconsistency in regulation, it used to be the case that dealing in and managing securities were regulated but custody thereof was not, and that custody carried out by or in connection with investment firms was regulated by virtue of the regulation of investment firms but custody by a stand-alone custodian was not regulated. This has been redressed and, in so doing, provision made for implementing the Investment Services Directive (ISD) which provides for an ISD firm's authorisation to cover non-core services such as custody, and for such services to be subject to appropriate conduct of business rules. As for investor protection, it was recognised that the sums involved with custody are large, opening investors to considerable risks if custody services were not properly controlled. It was felt that not only would regulation by the Act give investors greater confidence in custodial services, but also afford them access to the Investors Compensation Scheme in the event of loss. The view was taken that while such benefits to investors would be strong, the likely compliance burden on custodians would be light. Although the Act is broader in scope than the Order, there is a

---

[9] *Custody Discussion Paper* (n 8 above) 1.11.
[10] ibid 10.8.
[11] *Custody Consultative Paper 90* (n 8 above).
[12] SIB, *Custody of Investments under the Financial Services Act 1986: Consultative Paper 107* (March 1997) Preface, 5, para 1.
[13] HM Treasury, *Custody: A Consultation Document* (June 1996) internet address: http://www.hm-treasury.gov.uk/pub/html/reg/0696c/main.html.

fundamental compatibility between the motives that led to the establishment of the Act and the motives leading to the Order. In the White Paper setting out the Government's proposals for a new system of the regulation of financial services in the United Kingdom, which culminated in the Act, it was made clear that revision of the regulation of financial services was with a view to protecting the interests of investors.[14]

9.08 The desire for consistency in the regulatory treatment of a financial service in varying contexts is laudable. The former system of accidental[15] regulation of custody was illogical, caused uncertainty and led to inconsistent outcomes for the results of a breach of the terms of custody in differing situations. These effects of accidental regulation are unwelcome and their removal by a more principled system of regulation must be seen as beneficial.

9.09 The other principal motivation for the regulation of custody is more complex. Under the broad banner of investor protection, a number of themes are apparent. To the extent that regulation is directed to preventing the investor from suffering losses not due to market forces, and that in the event of such loss he should be afforded compensation, the motives of regulation may be rationalised on the grounds of paternalism by the State. However, it is clear that unbridled paternalism is not the only justification for investor protection because this causes the problem of moral hazard.[16] In the White Paper leading to the Act, it was made clear that *caveat emptor* remained an underlying principle of the regulation of financial services as a whole.[17] 'No regulatory system can, or should, relieve the investor of responsibility for exercising judgement and care in deciding how to invest his money. If he makes a foolish decision on the basis of adequate disclosure . . . he cannot look to any regulator to make good the losses arising from his own misjudgement.'[18]

9.10 Investor protection may also be justified on other grounds. The protection of investors from fraud seeks to ensure that the custody business market works efficiently without suffering from the distortions which would be effected by fraud. Further, it is a declared goal of the present Labour Government to encourage individuals to take care of their long-term financial needs by savings and investments.[19]

---

[14] Department of Trade and Industry, *Financial Services in the United Kingdom: A New Framework for Investor Protection* (Cmnd 9432, January 1985) ch 1, 1.2.

[15] Before 1996, regulation of custody was accidental in that custody was only regulated as an incident of regulation of the service provider's main business if such service fell within the scope of Sch 1 to the Act.

[16] Where investors do not exercise, and are absolved from exercising, due care in the manner in which they choose and monitor their investments.

[17] DTI, *Financial Services in the United Kingdom* (Cmnd 9432, 1985) ch 1, 3.3–3.4.

[18] ibid 3.3.

[19] A Darling, MP, 'Government and the Financial Services Industry' (1994) 2 *Journal of Financial Regulation and Compliance* No 2, 107, 108–109, 111.

In order to achieve this goal, confidence in the capital markets and ancillary services for investment therein must be fostered. Further, investor confidence would encourage more investors to use financial services, so allowing the benefits which accrue to the United Kingdom's GDP from the use of financial services offered in the United Kingdom to continue to grow.

Finally, although it is not obvious that systemic risk should offer justification for regulating custody business, current trends in the industry suggest that this risk may be increasing in significance. In the past, custody business has been conducted by many institutions across the range of financial services operators, with assets widely dispersed amongst the various institutions. Thus, the failure of any one, even where custody assets were jeopardised, would be unlikely to have system-wide ramifications. However, the costs of best practice, both in terms of IT[20] and skilled staff,[21] have driven some custodians out of business. Even if it is beneficial that custodians who did not conduct custody business according to best practice are driven out of business by the Order, this factor increases the trend towards consolidation in the industry.[22] If the trend develops, the result will be that a few major custodians will end up holding an increasing share of the totality of assets in custody.[23] Inevitably, this must increase systemic risk. If one of the few custodians that survive the process of consolidation faces difficulties which threaten custody assets, an unlikely event under properly constituted custodial structures, given that the custodian will be holding a sizeable proportion of the totality of custody assets in the market, there may be system-wide effects as the clients of that custodian take action to limit potential losses. An indirect systemic problem may also arise if the custodian makes good the custody losses and is thereby unable to perform its non-custody obligations in the market. **9.11**

The figures for the cost of regulating custody remain to some extent speculative. It is not until the Order has been in force for some time that definitive costs for regulating custody will be available. However, on the basis of the projections of market operators who conduct custody business already, many of whom undertake best practice and so should be in a position to comment on the costs of the **9.12**

---

[20] P Temple, 'Big Changes Afoot in a Tough Market', *Investors Chronicle*, 28 April 1995, 59; A Dack, 'Meeting the Demand for Faster Settlement', *Investors Chronicle*, 28 April 1995, 62.

[21] P Gibson, 'Getting the Right People into Custody', *Institutional Investor*, November 1995, 163.

[22] See the reported views of Roger Fishwick, treasurer of the Prudential, which decided to withdraw from the custody business, as quoted in 'Wisdom of the Prudential', *The Times*, 28 April 1995, 28.

[23] In 1993 the SIB estimated that there was £800 billion worth of UK equities held by custodians: SIB, *Custody Review, Discussion Paper* (August 1993) 5.9. Although figures for the total volume of assets in custody at the time are not available, Andrew Large, the chairman of SIB, is reported to have estimated that the top 10 UK custodians had more than £700 billion worth of assets under their care by 1995: 'SIB Seeks Safeguards for Investors' Assets', *Financial Times*, 1 September 1995, 6.

Order to their business,[24] it is anticipated that the costs of regulation should be minimal.[25]

B. Scope of Regulation

9.13 In introducing the Order to the House of Commons on 10 December 1996, the Economic Secretary emphasised that it was custody business that was sought to be regulated and not custody ancillary to a non-investment function.[26] As such, the type of custody for which authorisation would be required involves both safeguarding and administration of assets which include investments, as well as arranging or offering to arrange for such services. In principle, the regulations seek to draw the recognised distinction between safe custody of things and custody business, a similar but slightly more demanding function in relation to things as investments.[27]

9.14 Although the meaning of safeguarding, administration, assets and arranging in this context is not defined in the Order, Notes to the new paragraph 13A determine its scope and SIB has issued a Guidance Release setting out its understanding of these terms.[28]

Safeguarding

9.15 Safeguarding involves physical possession of tangible assets, physical possession of documents evidencing intangible assets, or protecting the integrity of intangible assets.[29] This interpretation of safeguarding embraces not only traditional formats of investments which are represented or evidenced by a tangible token which may be taken into possession, it also encompasses dematerialised investments which cannot be possessed but which are held in custody by being vested in the name of the custodian or its nominee.

9.16 In terms of mechanics, except in relation to intangibles, the function of safeguarding differs very little from the safe custody of things as things. The difference between the business of the custody of investments and safe custody simpliciter

---

[24] Best practice before the Order is not markedly affected by the demands of the Order.

[25] HM Treasury, *Custody: A Consultation Document* (June 1996), Annex C, internet address: http://www.hm-treasury.gov.uk/pub/html/reg/0696c/main.html.

[26] SIB, *Custody of Investments under the Financial Services Act 1986, Guidance Release 5/97* (June 1997) ('*Custody Guidance Release*') 2, para 4.

[27] This distinction is discussed in Chapter 1 on custody business.
See also Blair, Allison, Palmer and Richards-Carpenter, *Banking and the Financial Services Act* (1993) 64, para 3.45; Ellinger and Lomnicka, *Modern Banking Law*, 568–573; and M Hapgood, *Paget's Law of Banking* (11th edn, 1996) 132 in relation to safe custody simpliciter. See R Cranston, *Principles of Banking Law* (1997) 359–363 in relation to custody business.

[28] *Custody Guidance Release* (n 26 above).

[29] ibid 2–3, para 10.

becomes more apparent in relation to the types of assets kept under custody business and the additional types of action to be taken by the custodian in relation thereto.

Administration

The term is supposed to have its ordinary meaning.[30] Examples of functions which constitute administration include: maintaining accounts with clearing houses, settling transactions in investments, operating through depositories or sub-custodians, operating nominee accounts which identify each customer's assets in a ledger, cash processing in relation to customers' assets, collecting and dealing with the dividends and other income associated with safeguarded assets or carrying out corporate actions for customers in relation to assets being safeguarded. This list is not exhaustive[31] and any one of such or similar functions may constitute administration for present purposes if carried out in relation to assets being safeguarded.[32]   **9.17**

Where, however, the only functions undertaken in relation to safeguarded assets are the provision of information as to the number of units or value of assets safeguarded, the conversion of currency or the receipt of documents relating to an investment solely for the purpose of onward transmission to, from or to the order of the person to whom the investment belongs, such activity will not, for present purposes, constitute administration.[33]   **9.18**

Assets

The safeguarding and administration of any assets which actually, or may, include or consist of investments falls within the Order. It is immaterial that the assets may be wholly dematerialised.[34] However, for such assets to come within the scope of the regulations they must belong to another, which means that they are beneficially owned by another,[35] and be the subject of both safeguarding and administration.[36]   **9.19**

Given that the definition of investments[37] encompasses shares, debentures, government and public securities, instruments of entitlement to shares or securities,   **9.20**

---

[30] HM Treasury, *Custody: A Consultation Document* (June 1996), internet address: http://www.hm-treasury.gov.uk/pub/html/reg/0696c/main.html.   *Custody Guidance Release* (n 26 above) 3, para 12.

[31] *Custody Guidance Release* (n 26 above) 3, para 12.

[32] ibid 4, para 15.

[33] Art 3 of the Order, note (2) to para 13A of Sch 1 to the Act; *Custody Guidance Release* (n 26 above) 3–4, para 14.

[34] Art 3 of the Order, note (3)(a) to para 13A of Sch 1 to the Act; *Custody Guidance Release* (n 26 above) 4, para 17.

[35] *Custody Guidance Release* (n 26 above) 4, para 18.

[36] ibid 4, para 19.

[37] Sch 1 to the Act.

certificates representing securities, options, futures and rights and interests in investments, there can be little doubt that the range of activities that typically make up custody business now falls within the scope of the Act.

Arranging

9.21 The scope of new paragraph 13A extends beyond those who actually administer and safeguard assets to include those who arrange for such services. This includes where the arranger undertakes arrangements so that he performs both safeguarding and administration; he performs only one of the functions and another party performs the other function; as well as where he does not perform either of the functions but only arranges for one or others to do so.[38]

9.22 The broad scope of the regulations is based on the belief that where assets are being safeguarded and administered there will always be someone responsible for arranging all of this who should be regulated.[39] In this way, even where safeguarding and administration are being performed by separate parties, who are therefore not within the purview of the new paragraph 13A, the person responsible for the arrangements will be caught by the regulations.

9.23 Arrangements that consist of an introduction to a person permitted under paragraph 13A to provide custody services are exempt from the Order. Similarly, an introduction to a person who has neither paid for the introduction nor forms part of the same corporate group as the introducer with a view to the provision of custodial services or the making of arrangements therefor by that other person (introducee) is exempt from the Order.[40] SIB does not believe that other forms of introduction which fall outside the scope of such introductions will necessarily constitute the arranging of custody. It is only where there is a direct causal link between the introduction and the subsequent safeguarding and administration that the introduction may constitute arranging in this context.[41] Any involvement by the otherwise exempt introducer beyond the simple introduction may bring the introducer within the scope of paragraph 13A because this exemption may then become inapplicable.[42]

Exemptions Under the Order

9.24 Even if one is both safeguarding and administering assets which include investments, which would ordinarily come within paragraph 13A, the provisions will not apply to the actual custodian where another (lead or primary) custodian who

---

[38] *Custody Guidance Release* (n 26 above) 4–5, para 20.
[39] ibid 4–5, paras 20, 22.
[40] Art 3 of the Order, note (4)(a)–(b) to para 13A of Sch 1 to the Act; *Custody Guidance Release* (n 26 above) 5–6, para 24.
[41] ibid 6, para 25.
[42] ibid 5–6, para 24.

is permitted to offer custody services under the paragraph has undertaken to the beneficial owner of the assets a responsibility for the assets which is no less onerous than he would have undertaken if he (the lead custodian) were performing the functions himself.[43] This exemption is intended to exclude bare nominees, such as those operated by stockbrokers, from the need to be authorised for their custody business provided that the beneficial owner of the assets is not prejudiced by this by the undertaking of responsibility by another party, such as the stockbroker. For this exemption to take effect, the undertaking of responsibility should be a legally binding obligation in respect of the assets.[44]

Trustees are exempt from requiring authorisation under paragraph 13A, provided **9.25** they do not hold themselves out as providing custody services or do not receive additional remuneration for providing custodial services over and above remuneration for their duties as trustee.[45] The object of this is to exempt trustees who provide custody services as an incident of their trusteeship from having to seek authorisation. However, distinguishing between a trustee performing trust functions and custody business as defined in the paragraph is bound to be difficult. Trustees as a rule safeguard trust assets. They also take action, such as collecting dividends and taking corporate action on behalf of the beneficiaries, which may amount to administration. Even if not responsible for such things, they may arrange such services. As such, by sub-paragraph 22(2A)(a) of Schedule 1 to the Act, the ordinary trustee would seem to come within the terms of paragraph 13A. Nevertheless, SIB has taken the view that trustees will only be holding themselves out as providing custody services where they offer services over and above those which trustees normally provide.[46] Reaching consensus as to what services it is normal for trustees to provide is likely to prove fertile ground for disagreement. Of course, a trustee that accepts remuneration for what he takes to be trustee functions and receives additional remuneration for providing custodial services as an extra will clearly fall within paragraph 13A.[47]

Other exemptions are established by the Order. A person is exempt from para- **9.26** graph 13A where: (a) one performs custodial services for a group or joint enterprise of which one is part;[48] (b) assets in custody are held in connection with the sale of goods or supply of services and the business of the person holding the assets is to supply goods or services which do not constitute investment

---

[43] Art 3 of the Order, note (1) to para 13A of Sch 1 to the Act; *Custody Guidance Release* (n 26 above) 6, paras 27–28.
[44] ibid 7, para 29.
[45] Art 7 of the Order, inserting a new sub-para 2A into para 22 of Sch 1 to the Act.
[46] *Custody Guidance Release* (n 26 above) 7, para 30.
[47] Art 7 of the Order, inserting a new sub-para 2A into para 22 of Sch 1 to the Act, sub-sub-para 22(2A)(b).
[48] Art 4 of the Order, inserting a new sub-para (3) into para 18 of Sch 1 to the Act.

business;[49] (c) an employer company, a company in the same group or trustee holds a company's shares or debentures to facilitate an employee's share scheme;[50] (d) advice is given or arrangements made as a necessary part of a professional business which does not otherwise constitute investment business and is not separately remunerated;[51] (e) insurance companies which do not derive their authorisation to carry on investment business from section 22 of the Act, and to which sub-paragraph 2(2) of Schedule 10 to the Act applies, carry on custody business in respect of pension funds set up for the benefit of the officers or employees of the company or another company in the same group;[52] (f) an overseas person (ie a person who does not carry on investment business from a permanent place of business maintained by him in the United Kingdom) offers or agrees with a person in the United Kingdom to provide or arrange custody services if the offer or agreement is pursuant to an unsolicited or properly solicited approach by the United Kingdom person or a properly solicited approach by the overseas person.[53]

9.27 SIB has expressed the view that where a lender holds securities as collateral or takes a legal charge over them by way of security for a loan, such activity will ordinarily not constitute custody business. It has stated that even if the taking of security may in principle constitute safeguarding and administration of securities, this will not ordinarily constitute custody business because the lender looks after the assets in such circumstances to safeguard his own contingent interests, not specifically and exclusively for the beneficial owner.[54]

C. Eligibility to Perform Custody Business

9.28 Now that custody business is an authorisable activity, assuming that one's actions fall within the scope of paragraph 13A, one will need authorisation or to come within one of the exemptions properly to undertake custody business.

9.29 There are at present a number of ways by which one may be authorised under the Act, including: direct authorisation by SIB;[55] membership of a recognised self-regulating organisation (SRO);[56] holding a certificate of authorisation issued by a recognised professional body (RPB);[57] undertaking insurance business pursuant to the Insurance Companies Act 1982 which amounts to investment business;[58] a

---

[49] Art 5 of the Order, inserting a new sub-para (4) into para 19 of Sch 1 to the Act.
[50] Art 6 of the Order, amending sub-para (1) of para 20 of Sch 1 to the Act.
[51] Art 8 of the Order, inserting a new sub-para (2) into para 24 of Sch 1 to the Act.
[52] Art 9 of the Order, inserting a new para 24A into Sch 1 to the Act.
[53] Art 10 of the Order, amending sub-para (1) of para 27 of Sch 1 to the Act.
[54] *Custody Guidance Release* (n 26 above) 8, para 33.
[55] See s 25 of the Act.
[56] ibid s 7.
[57] ibid s 15. See also *Custody Guidance Release* (n 26 above) 10, para 38.
[58] ibid s 22.

friendly society operating pursuant to the Friendly Societies Act 1974;[59] as operator or trustee of a recognised collective investment scheme;[60] and as a credit institution or investment firm incorporated or established in another European Economic Area member state.[61]

In relation to custody services by a domestic firm undertaking custody in addition **9.30** to other investment business, it is likely that it will already have obtained authorisation in connection with its primary business. If not, as may be the case for a stand-alone custodian, it will be necessary to either seek authorisation by application to SIB directly or by applying to an SRO, the obvious possibilities being the Securities and Futures Authority (SFA), the Investment Management Regulatory Organisation (IMRO) or Personal Investment Authority (PIA).

However, matters are set to become simpler. The Chancellor of the Exchequer **9.31** announced to the House of Commons on 20 May 1997 that the regulation of financial services is to be reformed, the result of which would leave a single regulator responsible for the entire banking and financial services industry.[62] The current system of self-regulation will be replaced by a new and fully statutory system which is supposed to provide a single set of coherent functions and powers for the new entity, as well as a single authorisation process; a single compensation scheme; a single ombudsman scheme; a single appeals tribunal; and new powers to tackle market abuse. On 28 October 1997 the Chancellor announced at the launch of the new regulatory body that it would be called the Financial Services Authority (FSA),[63] and that it would take over responsibility for banking supervision from the Bank of England and financial services regulation from SIB and the SROs, as well as regulation of the insurance industry. In view of these developments, references in this work to SIB may be taken to read, assuming that the new regulatory body is given the appropriate powers, FSA.

In relation to custody services by firms authorised under the Second Banking Co- **9.32** ordination Directive[64] (2BCD), SIB is of the view that 2BCD only allows a relevant institution to carry on custody business for securities.[65] As 2BCD draws a distinction between securities and other types of investments[66] and only permits

---

[59] ibid s 23.

[60] ibid s 24.

[61] ibid s 31; reg 51 of the Banking Coordination (Second Council Directive) Regulations 1992, SI 1992/3218 ('2BCD Regulations') and regs 24 and 33 of the Investments Services Regulations 1995, SI 1995/3275 ('ISD Regulations'). See *SIB v Scandex A/S* [1998] 1 All ER 514.

[62] HM Treasury News Release, 'The Chancellor's Statement to the House of Commons on the Bank of England' (20 May 1997), internet address: http://www.hm-treasury.gov.uk/pub/html/press97/p49_97.html, especially at paras 12–19 of the Chancellor's statement.

[63] See generally Financial Services Authority, *Financial Services Authority: An Outline* (1997).

[64] 89/646/EEC, 1989 OJ No L386/1.

[65] *Custody Guidance Release* (n 26 above) 9–10, para 37.

[66] 2BCD Regulations (n 61 above) Sch 1, para 7.

safekeeping and administration of securities,[67] SIB's understanding would seem to be well-founded. Therefore, for custody of other types of investments, such as derivatives, it is likely that further authorisation in the United Kingdom will be necessary. The fact that 2BCD permits safe custody simpliciter[68] does not offer a loophole for general custody business, it draws a distinction between safe custody of things as things and safekeeping and administration of investments. For firms which rely for authorisation on the Investment Services Directive[69] (ISD), they may perform custody services in relation to securities, money-market instruments, futures, swaps and options.[70]

9.33 Recognised investment exchanges,[71] clearing houses,[72] including overseas investment exchanges and clearing houses,[73] the Society of Lloyd's and legitimate underwriting agents of Lloyd's,[74] listed money-market institutions[75] and appointed representatives of authorised persons[76] are or may be exempt from the need for authorisation under the Act to the extent that they are acting in the capacity for which the exemption is granted.

D. Conduct of Custody Business

9.34 If one is either authorised or exempt from authorisation, there are a number of regulations that affect one lawfully undertaking custody business. A person carrying on custody business is subject to at least the following regulations in addition to the provisions of the Act itself: SIB's Statement of Principles,[77] SIB's Core Conduct of Business Rules,[78] any rules imposed by the SRO or RPB including, indirectly, Standards for the Custody of Customers' Investments which SIB expects SROs and RPBs to ensure that its members maintain[79] and Client Money Regulations.[80] While the entirety of the regulations made under the Act may

---

[67] 2BCD Regulations (n 61 above) Sch 1, para 12.
[68] ibid Sch 1, paras 12, 14.
[69] 93/22/EEC, 1993 OJ No L141/27.
[70] ISD Regulations (n 61 above) Sch 1, ss B–C.
[71] See s 36 of the Act.
[72] ibid s 38.
[73] ibid s 40.
[74] ibid s 42.
[75] ibid s 43. See also *Custody Guidance Release* (n 26 above) 8–9, para 34.
[76] See s 44 of the Act. See also *Custody Guidance Release* (n 26 above) 9, paras 35–36.
[77] SIB, Statements of Principle: Rulebook Amendments and Additions Release 79 (1990), SIB Rules and Regulations Vol 1.
[78] SIB, The Core Conduct of Business Rules: Rulebook Amendments and Additions Release 94 (1991), SIB Rules and Regulations Vol 1.
[79] SIB, Standards for the Custody of Customers' Investments: Guidance Release 3/96 (August 1996) ('Standards Guidance Release'), SIB Rules and Regulations Vol 4.
[80] SIB, The Financial Services (Client Money) Regulations 1991; The Financial Services (Client Money) (Supplementary) Regulations 1991; The Financial Services (Investment Business Clients'

impact tangentially on custody business, it is only those of most direct application that are considered here. Many of these regulations represented best practice prior to the enactment of the Order,[81] a number of which are derived from pre-existing general law.[82]

Source of Rule-Making Powers

By section 48 of the Act, SIB is empowered to make rules for the conduct of the gamut of investment business. Although custody is not expressly dealt with in the main body of the Act, Schedule 8 to the Act, which sets out the principles according to which the conduct of business rules should be drawn up, requires in Principle 9 of that Schedule that the 'conduct of business rules . . . must make proper provision for the protection of property for which an authorised person is liable to account to another person'. **9.35**

Statement of Principles

SIB has issued principles intended to form a general statement of the standards of conduct of business and financial standing expected from all authorised persons. The Principles most relevant to custody business are considered below. **9.36**

Principle 7 states: **9.37**

'Where a firm has control of or is otherwise responsible for assets belonging to a customer which it is required to safeguard, it should arrange proper protection for them, by way of segregation and identification of those assets or otherwise, in accordance with the responsibility it has accepted.

By Principle 7, a firm is obliged to arrange proper protection for assets for which it is responsible to another. The obligation imposed by this principle varies from case to case, and is a function of the responsibilities accepted by a custodian in any particular circumstances. Thus, it appears that a contract for custodial services may determine what is proper. **9.38**

Money) (Chartered Accountants) Regulations 1988: Rulebook Amendments and Additions Release 137 (1994); The Financial Services (Client Money) (Amendment No 2) Regulations 1994; The Financial Services (Client Money) (Supplementary) (Amendment No 2) Regulations 1994: Rulebook Amendments and Additions Release 143 (1994); The Financial Services (Client Money) (Amendment) Regulations 1996: Rulebook Amendments and Additions Release 164 (1996), SIB Rules and Regulations Vol 2.

[81] For instance, the ProShare Nominee Code of August 1995 already indicated that best practice by nominees extended to providing investors with constant statements of their investments, arrangements for compensation of investors for loss or theft of their investments and greater transparency in the dealings between investor and nominee.

[82] The issue of the interplay between regulation and general law has been addressed, see Law Commission, *Fiduciary Duties and Regulatory Rules* (Consultation Paper No 124, 1992) and Law Com No 236, 1995.

9.39 The principle suggests means by which the obligation may be discharged, principally by segregation and identification of assets. By segregating customer assets from the firm's own assets, assuming proper record-keeping and no misappropriation, investor assets remain available for them to recover even in the event of the custodian's insolvency. Given that the mere pooling of investor assets does not necessarily jeopardise their ability to recover upon the insolvency of the custodian, it may be taken that the reference to the need for segregation only refers to segregating investor and custodian assets, and not necessarily segregation as between investors.

9.40 The identification of assets is a further measure by which investors' interests may be safeguarded in case of the insolvency of the custodian. Such identification may also be critical in case of a misapplication of assets, to indicate whose assets were misapplied or lost in case of any other shortfall. Since the nature of certain investments is such that they cannot be identified beyond the custodian in whose name they are vested, such as registrable shares where only legal title is recognised, identification in such circumstances will of necessity have to occur in the books of the custodian rather than in the title to the investment itself.[83]

9.41 Principle 7 permits the application of other measures which may be appropriate for protecting custody assets in any particular circumstances. In relation to derivative positions safeguarded for investors, for example, it may be necessary to ensure that funds for margin payments are always ready to meet margin calls.[84]

9.42 Principle 9 states:

> A firm should organise and control its internal affairs in a responsible manner, keeping proper records, and where the firm employs staff or is responsible for the conduct of investment business by others, should have adequate arrangements to ensure that they are suitable, adequately trained and properly supervised and that it has well-defined compliance procedures.

9.43 By Principle 9, a firm carrying on custody business is obliged to put into place a responsible system of internal organisation and control and to take steps to ensure that staff who are responsible for that business are suitable, and properly trained and supervised.

9.44 The requirement of proper records should again ensure that in the event of the insolvency of the custodian or shortfall of assets, investors would in the former scenario be able to recover their assets and in the latter scenario identify whose assets have been misapplied. This is, of course, aspirational because it is recognised

---

[83] Although it may be possible to add a pre- or suffix to the title for purposes of identification which does not alter legal ownership of the asset.

[84] On custody of derivatives see I Cullen, 'United Kingdom: Custody of Derivatives: Legal and Regulatory Issues' [1994] Futures and Derivatives Law Review, Issue 1, 43.

that in case of difficulties for a firm, proper record-keeping may be one of the first good practices to be jettisoned.[85]

9.45 The requirements in relation to staff are of a prophylactic nature. If the individuals actually responsible for the operation of the business are vetted for suitability, given proper training and are properly supervised, this should reduce the likelihood of any untoward events.

Core Conduct of Business Rules

9.46 Rule 32 states:

> A firm which has custody of a customer's investments in connection with or with a view to a regulated business must, subject to any exceptions contained in the rules of an SRO of which it is a member:
>
> a. keep safe, or arrange for the safekeeping of, any documents of title relating to them;
>
> b. ensure that any registrable investments which it buys or holds for a customer in the course of regulated business are properly registered in his name or, with the consent of the customer, in the name of an eligible nominee; and
>
> c. where title to investments is recorded electronically, ensure that customer entitlements are separately identifiable from those of the firm in the records of the person maintaining records of entitlement.

9.47 This rule applies to the custody of documents of title to investments, registrable investments and dematerialised investments. The rule does not apply to custody of money. Whilst it has been suggested that the rule also does not apply to derivatives,[86] this is doubtful. Although the term 'investment' is not defined in the Rules, it must be taken that the definition in the Act is applicable. In the Act, futures, options and contracts for differences fall within the term investments. It is unclear why any distinction should be made for the Core Conduct of Business Rules. The better view, it is suggested, is that where there is a tangible contract for derivatives, a system of registrable derivatives or where entitlement to derivatives is otherwise recorded electronically and such derivatives are entered into by a custodian on behalf of an investor, rule 32 will apply.

9.48 However, the Core Conduct of Business Rules do not apply to custodians authorised by certification by a RPB or to the extent that they act as an exempt person.[87] The implication of this is that the rule is not applicable, for instance, to firms of

---

[85] 'In the face of financial difficulties, the line between client and company funds is easily blurred': J Franks and C Mayer, *Risk, Regulation and Investor Protection: The Case of Investment Management* (1989) 77, para 2.9.

[86] Cullen (n 84 above) 54–55.

[87] See rule 40 1.c.

solicitors or accountants which undertake custody business by certification by their respective RPBs, nor for that matter to exempted overseas firms.

9.49 If the rule is applicable, the custodian will be responsible for a document of title whilst it is in the firm's safe-keeping. Whilst the argument may be made that responsibility should be passed on to the other person if the custodian arranges for another person to carry out the operations of safe-keeping, with an obligation on the custodian only to make proper arrangements, the better view is probably that the custodian will ordinarily remain liable even in such circumstances, possibly in addition to the actual operator. He should remain responsible for the assets in custody whether he chooses to perform the operation himself or he uses another party to do so.

9.50 In relation to the registration of registrable investments, the basic obligation of the custodian is to register them in the name of the investor. If, however, the investor consents, the custodian may register the investments in the name of an 'eligible nominee', that is an individual chosen by the investor who is not known by, or an associate of, the custodian, a corporate nominee with no other business or an institution authorised under the Banking Act 1987.[88]

9.51 For wholly dematerialised investments where title is electronically recorded by book (or, more accurately, computer) entry, such as under CREST, the custodian is obliged, in accordance with Principle 7, to ensure that the custodian's proprietary positions are separately identifiable from those of the investors on behalf of whom it holds assets.

Standards for Custody Business Required of SRO and RPB Members

9.52 SROs and RPBs have always had rules that affect the custody of investments. However, with the statement by SIB in August 1996 of standards it expects all SROs and RPBs to ensure that their members or certified firms meet for custody business, any former provisions will be overtaken by the new rules specifically addressed to custody business based on the new standards.[89]

9.53 Although these standards pre-date the Order that made custody business an authorisable activity, they were specifically drawn up in anticipation of, and based on, the (at the time proposed) change made by the Order.[90] The standards are set out below.

---

[88] The term is defined in SIB, The Financial Services (Updating of Glossary) Rules and Regulations 1992, Release 115 (1992), SIB Rules and Regulations Vol 1, at p 2 of 'The Financial Services Core Glossary (Third Edition)'.

[89] For example, the Council of the Law Society has made amendments to the Solicitors' Investment Business Rules 1995 by issuing Solicitors' Investment Business (Custody) Amendment Rules 1998 as set out in (1998) 95(4) *Law Society Gazette* 36–37, 41.

[90] Standards Guidance Release (n 79 above) 1, n 1.

Standard 1: Responsibilities, states: **9.54**

> The SIB looks to SROs and RPBs to require that authorised firms make custody
> arrangements with due care and clarify the responsibilities of the various parties to
> the custodial arrangements.

The underlying ethos of Standard 1 is that whatever is appropriate in any circum-   **9.55**
stances to keep the investments safe should be done.[91] A custodian may use nominees, but must ensure that the nominee acts only in accordance with proper
instructions. The custodian must accept responsibility for any of its nominees
used, to the same extent as if it held title itself, and the auditor's report on the custodian on compliance with the rules and regulations relating to client assets
should cover the nominee as well.[92] Beyond that, a custodian should be precise as
to the services it undertakes on behalf of the investor, as well as the degree of
responsibility it bears for each service,[93] but is prohibited from disclaiming losses
due to fraud, wilful default or negligence arising from it or its nominees' activities.[94]

Where overseas investments entail different settlement, legal and regulatory   **9.56**
requirements from those that obtain in the United Kingdom, the investor should
be informed of this.[95] Care should be exercised in the appointment or selection of
third party custodians and the lead custodian should inform the investor if the
third party custodian appointed or recommended is in the same group as the
lead custodian. In the event of appointment or recommendation of a third party
custodian, such a firm should be: (a) authorised under the Act to provide custody
services; (b) an EC credit institution or investment firm whose authorisation
covers custody business or an overseas custodian subject to supervision by a regulatory body; (c) a government agency; or (d) reviewed by auditors where it is
located.[96] Where a third party custodian is appointed, the agreement between custodian and investor should set out the respective responsibilities of custodian and
third party custodian in relation to loss of investments, responsibilities for the
appointment of further custodians and the responsibility of the primary custodian for loss due to fraud, wilful default or negligence of third party or further custodians appointed.[97] There should be a written agreement between the custodian
and any third party custodian appointed which obliges the latter to keep the

---

[91] ibid note 1.1.
[92] ibid note 1.2.
[93] ibid note 1.3.
[94] ibid note 1.4.
[95] ibid note 1.5.
[96] ibid note 1.6. This may be compared with revised rule 17f-5 of the Investment Companies Act
1940 of the USA that sets out criteria for the use of foreign sub-custodians. In the revision of 17f-5,
the formerly mandatory minimum capital structure for sub-custodians was dropped in favour of a
more pragmatic assessment of the appropriateness of using a particular sub-custodian.
[97] ibid note 1.8.

relevant investments safe and provides for the custodian to review the third party custodian's performance under the agreement.[98] Where an investor appoints his own third party or further custodian, the primary custodian should agree in writing any necessary consequential arrangements with the investor and the custodian appointed by the investor.[99]

9.57   Standard 2: Customers' investments held so as to be separately identifiable, states:

> The SIB looks to SROs and RPBs to require that authorised firms hold customers' investments so that they are separately identifiable from their own, and arrange for appointed third party custodians to distinguish customers' investments and hold the firm's and the firm's customers' investments so that they are separately identifiable from the custodians' own.

9.58   A custodian may not register investors' investments in its own or third party custodian's name except as agreed by the custodian's regulator. There are also a number of activities it may not undertake without the consent of the relevant investor(s) including: use client investments for its own account; pool client investments; use the investments of one client for another; use investments in pooled holdings for stock-lending (the consent of every customer with assets in the pool must be sought).[100] A custodian must also hold its own investments separately identifiable from those of its clients.[101] Where a third party custodian is appointed, the third party custodian should in turn distinguish in its own records between custodian and investor investments and hold both of such investments separately from its (the third party's) own investments.[102] If the third party custodian is overseas the foregoing safeguards as to separation should be observed where it is reasonable to insist on this, and unless the investor otherwise agrees.[103]

9.59   Standard 3: Protection against loss, states:

> The SIB looks to SROs and RPBs to require that authorised firms observe appropriate arrangements for the security and integrity of custody facilities and systems for the transfer of investments.

9.60   A custodian should provide physical custody facilities to safeguard tangible tokens of investments in proportion to the value of the underlying investments and the risk of damage, loss or misappropriation. For intangible assets, data processing facilities and records therein should also be appropriately safeguarded.[104] Where the custodian acts itself or appoints a third party custodian, it must ensure that

---

[98]   Standards Guidance Release (n 79 above) note 1.7.
[99]   ibid note 1.9.
[00]   ibid note 2.1.
[01]   ibid note 2.2.
[02]   ibid note 2.3.
[03]   ibid note 2.4.
[04]   ibid note 3.1.

tokens of investments are kept safe and that both it and the third party custodian only act on instructions given in accordance with agreed procedures.[105]

Standard 4: Identification and reconciliation, states: **9.61**

> The SIB looks to SROs and RPBs to require that the individual investments of the authorised firms' customers are clearly recorded and that, when authorised firms act as custodians or appoint third party custodians, customers' investments are frequently reconciled, authorised firms take responsibility for shortfalls, and customers receive statements on a frequent basis.

Custodians must maintain adequate records identifying at all times each cus-   **9.62** tomer's entitlements.[106] Whether acting itself or having appointed a third party custodian, the custodian should undertake frequent reconciliation of its records of client entitlements with holdings of client assets which have been independently arrived at; make good irreconcilable shortfalls for which it is responsible; separate in its records investments held as collateral and those held in custody simpliciter; and provide customers at appropriate intervals with a record of their entitlements, detailing those which are unavailable for delivery because they have been lent or used for collateral.[107]

Client Money Regulations

As custody business has become an authorisable activity, cash held or passing   **9.63** through the hands of a custodian will generally constitute client money and be subject to the client money regulations. The regulations are intended to 'protect client money from the claims of creditors in the event of a firm's insolvency' and 'to prevent firms using client funds to finance their business'.[108] This is achieved by the requirement that client money be held separately from a firm's own money,[109] in a separate bank account with an approved bank,[110] and by making provision for it to be held on trust for the clients.[111] It is doubtful whether the regulations afford more protection to investors than the general law did save, perhaps, in two respects: (a) by disapplying the rule in *Clayton's Case*;[112] and (b) by limiting contracting-out in cases of private investors.[113]

---

[105] ibid note 3.2.
[106] ibid note 4.1.
[107] ibid note 4.2.
[108] SIB, *Proposals for Amended Client Money Regulations, Consultative Paper 53* (April 1991) 7, para 17.
[109] Financial Services (Client Money) Regulations 1991 (CMR) reg 2.12.
[110] ibid reg 2.05.
[111] ibid reg 3.02.
[112] (1816) 1 Mer 572, 35 ER 781. By CMR reg 3.05 beneficiaries share pro rata, not according to the 'first in time' rule.
[113] CMR reg 2.02.

9.64 Broadly, however, the regulations do not apply to firms certified by RPBs, exempted persons in respect of the business for which they are exempt, approved banks holding money for clients with themselves as bankers to the investor[114] and authorised persons undertaking investment business that is also trustee activity, provided that the person is regulated in respect of that business by the Investment Management Regulatory Organisation (IMRO). There are also restrictions as to how the regulations will apply to insurers and friendly societies.[115]

9.65 Thus, where a custodian which is also an approved bank holds custody money with itself, possibly with a view to executing client transactions, as banker to the client it need not be concerned by the regulations. If, however, it deposits the money with another bank, assuming the custodian bank is itself an authorised entity in regard to custody business, the client money regulations will apply.[116]

9.66 European exempted investment institutions also need not be troubled by the client money regulations, but may need to consider whether and what regulations govern them in this respect in their home state.

Other Implications of Carrying On an Authorisable Activity

9.67 A firm to which the Act applies may also be subject to capital adequacy rules.[117] The need for this type of regulation has been doubted as a tool for investor protection where client assets are already required to be segregated from the intermediary's assets because the client assets should in principle be free from the claims of creditors upon the insolvency of the intermediary.[118] In an ideal world, this is correct. However, there are reasons in practice for requiring capital adequacy rules for a custodian. In the first place, contrary to the regulations, the custodian may not have properly segregated the client assets, so putting them in jeopardy upon his insolvency. Further, if it is felt desirable that the custodian should be in a position to make up for shortfalls whilst he is solvent, as may arise by negligence or fraud by its employees, capital adequacy rules are a suitable method for ensuring this. As with capital adequacy rules in any other scenario, the proper question may be to determine the required level of capital adequacy.

9.68 Whatever the arguments, as already stated, it seems that an authorised custodian is now subject to some degree of capital adequacy requirements. The precise rules to which a firm will be subject depends on which class amongst those established by the Financial Supervision Rules 1990[119] the custodian firm falls under. The

---

[114] In the event of the bank's insolvency, client money will remain at risk.

[115] CMR reg 1.02.

[116] *Custody Guidance Release* (n 26 above) 8, para 32.

[117] See s 49 of the Act.

[118] R Dale, *Risk and Regulation in Global Securities Markets* (1996) 7.

[119] SIB Release 117, as amended by the Financial Supervision (Amendment) Rules 1995, SIB Rulebook Amendments and Additions 161. See especially rules 2.01–2.04.

classification is according to the functions undertaken by the firm and covers low, medium (types A and B), high and special risk firms. It is not clear into which class custody business falls. A firm doing custody business is unlikely to be considered a low risk or type A medium risk firm, which are firms which do not hold client assets more than temporarily or, for type A medium risk firms, if they do so, only hold the assets with an eligible custodian. Given that type B medium risk firms are those that hold assets other than on a temporary basis or which conduct their investment management business without using a separate custodian, itself performing custody services for the investments it manages, it is likely that custody business may fall under this class. If not, a custody business firm would have to be considered a high risk firm. In view of the different obligations incumbent on a firm according to its classification, not only in relation to capital adequacy but encompassing a variety of other methods of financial supervision, guidance in this regard from the FSA would be welcome. The FSA may, of course, choose to add custody business to the class of special risk firms, establishing rules specifically tailored to this type of business.

Although the principal core conduct of business rule of direct application to custody business has already been discussed, there are a range of other rules which have been enacted by SIB which will ordinarily apply to a firm directly authorised by SIB and may be applicable to other legitimate custodian firms.[120] **9.69**

A firm may also be subject to cancellation rules for agreements entered into by investors, permitting the investor a 'cooling-off' period during which he may resile from the transaction.[121] Although these have been primarily aimed at the sale of life policies and unit trust products, the importance of custody business to the investment well-being of investors may lead to the introduction of rules for this as well. **9.70**

SIB is empowered to make regulations requiring authorised firms to give notice of the occurrence of specified events and to furnish it with specified information.[122] It may determine that the importance and sensitivity of the custodial function to investors is such that certain events which may impact on the ability of a custodian to discharge its functions as agreed with the investor should be reported. **9.71**

There is a general restriction on advertising for investment business unless the advertiser is an authorised person or an authorised person has approved the con- **9.72**

---

[120] See s 48 of the Act. See also the notes to the section in DA Sabalot, *Butterworths Financial Services Law Handbook* (2nd edn, 1996) 48–49.

[121] See s 51 of the Act.

[122] ibid s 52. See also SIB, Notification: Rulebook Amendments and Additions Release 158 (1995), SIB Rules and Regulations Vol 2, which incorporates The Financial Services (Notification by Recognised Bodies) Regulations 1995; The Financial Services (Notification) Regulations 1988 (Persons Regulated by the Board); and The Financial Services (Notification by Permitted Persons)

tents of the advertisement.[123] The restriction relates to advertisements inviting people to enter an investment agreement, as well as those that contain information calculated to lead directly or indirectly to persons doing so.

Stock-Lending and Sale and Repurchase (Repo)

9.73 The use of custody assets for these types of transactions is common but not generally regulated under the framework of the Act. There are, however, regulations in relation to stock-lending in specific scenarios.[124] As already indicated above on standards for the conduct of custody business, SIB has indicated in relation to pooled assets that the consent of all contributors to the pool should be obtained before any of the pooled assets may be used for stock-lending.[125]

9.74 More generally, the Stock Lending and Repo Committee (SLRC), a forum for industry participants under the chairmanship of the Bank of England, maintains a Code of Practice which covers such matters as the need for consent from beneficial owners of stock being lent; the need to take adequate collateral; and the need to monitor the respective values of the assets lent and the collateral taken. Although the use of this code is voluntary, SIB has expressed support for its general application to the practice of stock-lending.[126] SIB has also stated that serious breaches of the code by an authorised firm may 'raise questions as to its fitness and properness' and that firms should assume that SIB Principle 3, which requires firms to observe high standards of market conduct and comply with codes endorsed by SIB, would require them to comply with the code.[127]

E. Enforcement of Regulations and Remedies for Breach

9.75 No person may carry on custody business in the United Kingdom unless authorised or exempt from authorisation.[128] Anyone in breach of this provision is liable to imprisonment and/or a fine.[129] Agreements executed following such breach are unenforceable against the client, who may seek recovery of any money paid or

---

Regulations 1988. This was amended by SIB, The Financial Services (Notification by Permitted Persons) Regulations 1996: Rulebook Amendments and Additions Release 166 (1996), SIB Rules and Regulations Vol 2.

[123] See s 57 of the Act, and also s 58 for exceptions to the general rule.

[124] In relation to stock-lending of the assets of unit trusts, SIB has made The Financial Services (Regulated Schemes) Regulations 1991, see Section L, and issued *Stocklending by Unit Trusts*, Guidance Release 4/91 (June 1991).

[125] Standards Guidance Release (n 79 above) 5, Note 2.1.e.

[126] SIB, *Stock Borrowing and Short Selling: Implications for the UK Equity Markets*, Consultative Paper 100 (November 1996) 11, para 33.

[127] *Custody Review, Discussion Paper* (n 23 above) 49, para 7.12.

[128] See s 3 of the Act.

[129] ibid s 4.

transferred following such agreement.[130] SIB may also seek restitution orders against the person in breach, as well as any other person that the court determines was 'knowingly concerned' in the contravention, to restore the status quo ante.[131] Since the object of this remedy is to restore the status quo ante, the order against those in breach must be accompanied by orders for the investor concerned to make restitution of benefits received.[132] In anticipation of breach, SIB or the Secretary of State may seek an injunction restraining such a contravention.[133]

A person to whom the Act applies who makes a misleading statement or performs acts which give a misleading impression as to the value of investments, to persuade another to enter into an investment agreement or in relation to the exercise of rights conferred by an investment agreement, may be guilty of an offence.[134] **9.76**

As a rule, an investment agreement entered into following an unsolicited call may be unenforceable against the person to whom the call was made.[135] However, there are exceptions to this, including where the person called understood the nature of the agreement and the risks involved, and entered into it following discussions which effectively superseded the initial call. **9.77**

SIB enjoys powers of intervention where it perceives that intervention is desirable for the protection of investors; that a firm is not fit to carry on investment of a particular kind which it currently does or proposes to undertake; where a firm is in breach of any provision of the Act or the rules and regulations made thereunder; or where a firm has furnished SIB with false, misleading or inaccurate information.[136] This may also occur in case of breach of the SIB Principles.[137] These powers are generally only exercisable against firms directly authorised by SIB. Whilst it is a condition of the recognition of an SRO that it also makes similar provisions in relation to its members,[138] there is no such obligation in relation to RPBs. These powers of intervention enable SIB to: restrict the business of a firm,[139] prohibit a firm or its appointed representative from disposing of or otherwise dealing with **9.78**

---

[130] ibid s 5.

[131] ibid s 6(2); for the meaning of the expression 'knowingly concerned', see *Burton v Bevan* [1908] 2 Ch 240; *A-G's Reference (No 1 of 1995)* [1996] 1 WLR 970; *SIB v Pantell (No 2)* [1993] Ch 256; *SIB v Scandex A/S* [1998] 1 All ER 514. The right of restitution is not, however, that of SIB or the Secretary of State but of the affected investor, see *Scandex* per Hobhouse J at 525. The statutory restitution is not a class remedy, it is directed at specific and identified investors.

[132] See s 6(2) of the Act. Such an order may be better termed an order to disgorge since some of those who are ordered to perform 'restitution' will not have received anything from the investor. See *SIB v Pantell (No 2)* [1993] Ch 256; *SIB v Scandex A/S* [1998] 1 All ER 514.

[133] See s 6(1) of the Act.

[134] ibid s 47.

[135] ibid s 56. See also SIB, Common Unsolicited Calls Regulations, Release 101, SIB Rules and Regulations Vol 2.

[136] See s 64 of the Act.

[137] ibid s 47A(3).

[138] ibid Sch 2, para 3(3).

[139] ibid s 65.

any of its assets,[140] require assets which belong to the firm or investors to be transferred to a trustee appointed by the regulator,[141] and/or require the firm to maintain assets in the United Kingdom.[142] In the event of breach of the obligations
imposed by SIB in this way, the firm leaves itself open to public censure by SIB or
for SIB to seek an injunction against the firm or an order for the firm to make disgorgement.[143]

9.79   Where an authorised firm is a company or partnership, SIB may apply to court for
it to be wound up. The court may grant such an order if the firm is unable to pay
its debts or the court is of the opinion that it is just and equitable that the firm be
wound up.[144] The various regulatory bodies may petition the court for the
appointment of an administrator under the insolvency legislation for a company
that is an authorised person or an appointed representative.

9.80   In case of a breach of the SIB Principles[145] or rules and regulations established
within the context of the Act, a number of sanctions may be brought to bear. SIB
may withdraw or suspend the domestically obtained authorisation of a firm where
the holder is not considered to be a fit and proper person to carry on the investment business it actually does, or proposes to, carry on or has breached any of the
regulations established under the Act.[146] For those authorised to conduct investment business in the United Kingdom by virtue of authorisation in another
member state of the EU, such authorisation may be suspended or terminated for
breach of regulations under the Act or for providing false, inaccurate or misleading information.[147] A disqualification direction may also be issued by SIB in relation to any individual who is not fit and proper to be employed in investment
business,[148] as may a public statement be made as to a person's actual miscon-
duct.[149] Where it is anticipated that a breach of the rules and regulations made
under the Act will occur, SIB may apply to court for an injunction to prevent this.
In the event of actual breach, SIB may seek a court order requiring the party in
breach as well as any other person knowingly concerned in the breach to take such
steps as the court may direct to remedy the breach.[150]

---

[140] ibid s 66.
[141] ibid s 67.
[142] ibid s 68.
[143] ibid s 71.
[144] ibid s 72.
[145] ibid s 47A(3).
[146] ibid s 28.
[147] ibid s 33.
[148] ibid s 59.
[149] ibid s 60.
[150] ibid s 61. Such an order may include an order to disgorge, see *SIB v Pantell (No 2)* [1993] Ch
256; *SIB v Scandex A/S* [1998] 1 All ER 514.

Although criminal sanctions are in the main restricted to undertaking investment **9.81**
business unlawfully, and not for breach of standards, there are severe sanctions for
breach of certain rules of conduct. A person who makes a misleading statement or
performs acts which give a misleading impression as to the value of investments,
to persuade another to enter into an investment agreement or in relation to the
exercise of rights conferred by an investment agreement, may be guilty of an
offence for which the sanction is prison and/or a fine.[151] SIB may also seek a court
order for those in default of this provision to take steps to remedy the breach.[152]
The question has arisen whether money paid following an investment agreement
entered into because of such a breach, misleading statement or acts may be
ordered to be repaid. Doubts have been expressed as to whether this may be
achieved under section 61(1) of the Act because this sub-section provides a remedy for breach and such a payment would not have been made directly pursuant
to the breach (the misleading), but pursuant to the agreement entered into as a
consequence of the breach.[153] Nevertheless, other provisions of section 61, especially sub-section (4), may afford SIB the opportunity to seek a court order to
effect such a repayment.[154]

As a general rule, in relation to breach of the rules and regulations made under **9.82**
Chapter V of the Act by which an investor suffers loss, the investor has a right of
action against the party in default for breach of statutory duty.[155] Breach of SRO or
RPB regulations by members thereof and those certified thereby are equally action-
able. However, this remedy is not available for breach of the SIB Principles.[156]

Unless otherwise provided for, this right of action is generally only open to private **9.83**
investors.[157] A private investor for these purposes is an individual acting other than
in the course of carrying on investment business or a firm acting other than in the
course of carrying on business of any kind.[158] One situation in which a non-
private person may bring this type of action is where the non-private person acts
in a fiduciary or representative capacity and the cause of action arises as a result of
anything done when the beneficiary of the fiduciary or representative was a private
person and any recovery would be exclusively for the benefit of such a person and
could not be effected through action brought otherwise than at the suit of the

---

[151] See s 47(6) of the Act.
[152] ibid s 61.
[153] *SIB v Pantell (No 2)* [1993] Ch 256, 279 per Scott LJ.
[154] See PL Davies, *Gower's Principles of Modern Company Law* (6th edn, 1997) 434–435.
[155] See s 62 of the Act. Unlike with the statutory power for SIB to force a defaulting party and
others implicated in the default to disgorge under ibid ss 6 and 61, the statutory right of action for
compensation under ibid s 62 is only effective as against the party in default.
[156] ibid s 47A(3).
[157] ibid s 62A.
[158] Financial Services Act 1986 (Restriction of Right of Action) Regulations 1991, SI 1991/489.

representative.[159] This provision will in some circumstances be capable of being utilised by a custodian for the benefit of his investors.

9.84 By section 54 of the Act, SIB has established a funded central compensation scheme for investors where an authorised firm is unable or unlikely to be able to meet its civil liability in connection with its investment business. The compensation scheme for firms authorised by SIB directly or those authorised by SRO is run by a separate management company, the Investors Compensation Scheme Ltd (ICSL).[160] Under ICSL when a firm goes into default, leaving a shortfall in customers' assets for their investment business, compensation of up to £48,000 may be available. Each RPB has its own compensation arrangements.

9.85 The defaulting custodian may be an authorised firm under the Act, as well as an institution recognised under the Banking Act 1987, thereby permitting it to hold the cash deposits for customers by itself. It may be possible, therefore, that the investor applies for compensation under the bank's Deposit Protection Scheme on the basis that he is identified by the bank as depositor of the funds in question or that he, the investor, is the beneficiary of a bare trust in respect of such funds.[161]

---

[159] ibid reg 3(d).

[160] See generally *R v Investors Comp. Scheme, ex p. Bowden* [1996] 1 AC 261; *ICS v West Eromwich BS* [1998] 1 All ER 98.

[161] Banking Act 1987, s 61(3). See generally *Deposit Protection Board v Dalia* [1994] 2 AC 367.

10

CROSS-BORDER CUSTODY

10.01 The assumption in the foregoing chapters that the parties and assets under consideration are based in England makes for a clearer exposition of the principles underpinning the custody of investments, but such a scenario will often not obtain in practice. Modern investment is increasingly cross-border.[1] A single transaction or investment structure may bring together an investor in one country, tiers of intermediary custodians in other countries and an underlying asset in yet another country. On these facts, the laws of a number of different countries may be relevant to the nature of rights of the ultimate beneficiary and to transactions involving custody assets.

10.02 If it is not possible to determine in advance which law applies to rights enjoyed at any tier, it becomes difficult to assess precisely what the investor is entitled to and the effectiveness of action taken in relation to custody assets. The investor's concerns are likely to be that the custodial structure is not so characterised by any

---

[1] It was estimated by Mr Jurgen Marziniak, global head of custody services for Deutsche Bank, that as of 1997 there was US$40,000 billion worth of assets in custody world-wide, including cross-border assets of US$7,000 billion. He suggested that of the US$50,000 billion worth of assets that is anticipated to be in custody by the year 2000, US$12,000 billion worth of the assets would be cross-border. See 'The Big Get Bigger as the Sector Grows', Survey on Global Custody, *Financial Times*, 11 July 1997, I.

relevant law as to leave him with the credit risk of any of the intermediaries and that transactions undertaken, such as creating security,[2] will not be re-characterised leading to undesired and/or unanticipated legal consequences. Given the volume and value of investments in custody and the fact that risk management is a critical element in any investment strategy, any uncertainty as to the law applicable to transactions in relation to cross-border custody assets is unwelcome.[3] The object of this chapter is to identify to what degree one can predict the law applicable to ownership rights and the validity of transactions in the context of cross-border custody.

10.03 The complexity of an inquiry into a conflict of laws in this area is limited only by the imagination of participants in international investment transactions and the willingness of far-flung members of the increasingly global marketplace to undertake commercial activity with one another. Given the myriad possible custodial scenarios, the present analysis does not attempt to provide answers to every conceivable dispute that may arise. Rather, an attempt is made to identify principles by which disputes that involve an element of a conflict of laws may be resolved. It is assumed that the inquiry is undertaken by an English court.

10.04 Figure 10.1 illustrates the possible nature of conflicts of law in a custodial structure.

10.05 The structure represented by Figure 10.1 may be described as follows:

(1) Utopian securities are issued in favour of Utopian nominee.

(2) Utopian nominee holds the benefit of these securities for Utopian Central Securities Depository (CSD).

(3) Utopian Central Securities Depository holds for the International Central Securities Depository (ICSD) based in Nirvana.

(4) The Nirvana ICSD's entitlement is also not beneficial; it holds as intermediary custodian for the UK lead custodian.

(5) Again, the lead custodian's entitlement is non-beneficial. Whatever benefit is derived by this entitlement from the ICSD (in relation to the ICSD's entitlement to assets held by the local depository) must be passed on to the UK investor.

(6) The investor is beneficially entitled to benefits that accrue to the lead custodian from the intermediary custodian.

---

[2] For instance, what is intended to be an outright transfer may be re-characterised as an attempt to create real security that is invalid or of inferior priority due to the non-observance of formalities for the creation of security interests. The issue of re-characterisation is more fully developed by Joanna Benjamin, 'Recharacterisation Risk and Conflict of Laws' (1997) 12 BJIBFL 513.

[3] R Guynn and M Tahyar, 'The Importance of Choice of Law and Finality to PvP, Netting and Collateral Arrangements' (1996) 4 *Journal of Financial Regulation and Compliance* No 2, 170.

Figure 10.1: Conflict of laws

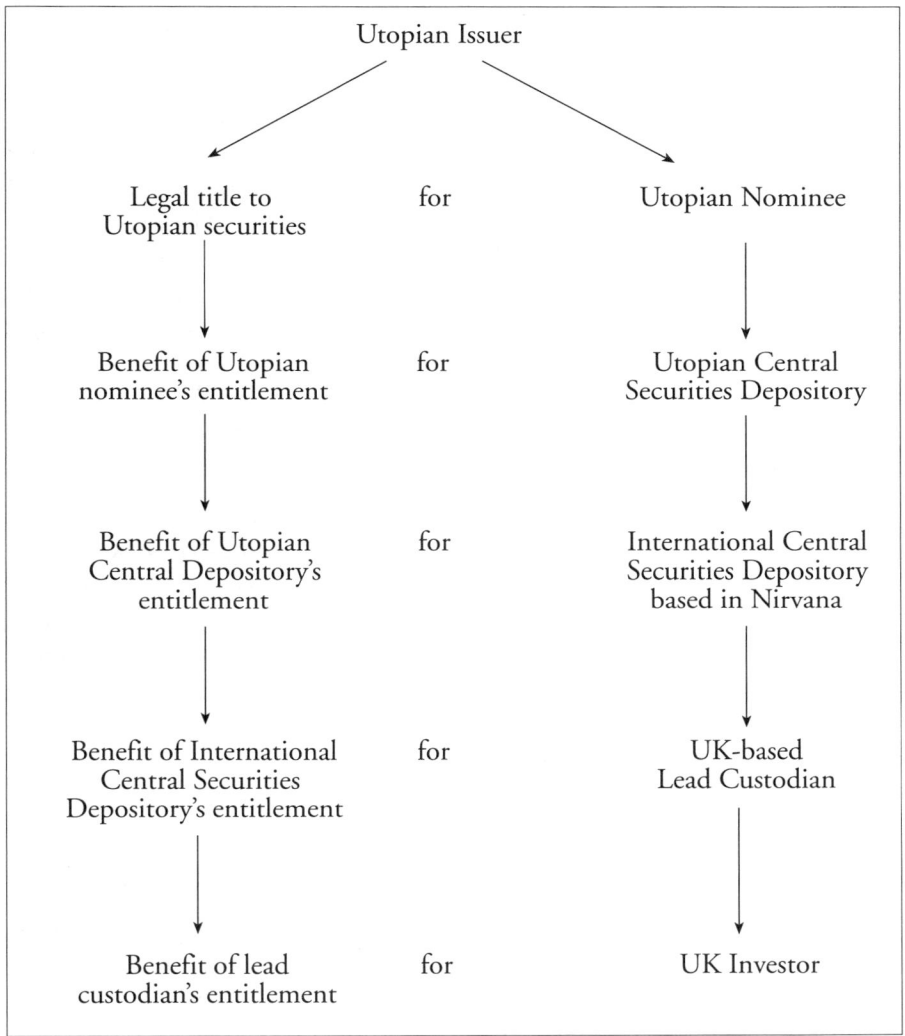

A. Applicable Law

Where there is a conflict of laws, an English court determining the substantive law **10.06** applicable to the dispute should undertake a three-stage process, ie characterise the issue before the court; select the conflict of laws rule that lays down a connecting factor for the issue in question; and identify the system of law which links the connecting factor to the issue characterised.[4] This process is essentially

---

[4] *Macmillan v Bishopsgate Investment Trust plc (No 3)* [1996] 1 WLR 387, 391–392 per Staughton LJ; applied in *Re Harvard Securities Ltd* [1997] 2 BCLC 369, 373–375 per Neuberger J.

governed by the *lex fori*, albeit with due regard to the general circumstances of the case.[5] This application of *lex fori* may be justified on the basis that the law with which the matter to be determined is most closely connected cannot be known at the outset.

10.07 The first two stages of this process are closely bound together and, on this basis, the argument has been made that it is rules of law that are characterised and not issues.[6] It is suggested that even where there is an apparent characterisation of issues, this in fact involves the characterisation of rules of law.[7] There is some force in this argument. Yet, a process of enquiry which conflates the first two stages of the above process into one of characterising a rule of conflict of laws alone may be misleading because it conceals the precise manner in which the relevant rule of law being characterised is arrived at. It is submitted that it is because of the nature of the dispute that a particular rule of conflict of laws is employed. For this reason, the three-stage process of enquiry may be preferable to the two-stage process that has been suggested.

10.08 The identification of the nature of the dispute before a court is essential to a court deciding which rule of conflict of laws to apply in determining the applicable substantive law to the dispute.[8] It is only by knowing precisely what is at issue that one can most sensitively approach the question of which rule of conflict of laws should be invoked to identify the relevant system of law.[9] One important implication of this approach is that it permits the application of the correct system of law to each issue in dispute, notwithstanding that several issues governed by separate systems of law fall to be resolved in a particular case.[10]

B. Characterisation

10.09 The two issues that are likely to concern investors most are how they enjoy rights to investments in custody and how such assets may be effectively alienated, whether outright or by way of security. Where this involves a conflict of laws, it is essential first of all to characterise the nature of the issues in order to be able to determine the applicable substantive law. In view of uncertainty as to how these issues should be characterised, this question requires detailed consideration.

---

[5] *Macmillan (No 3)* (n 4 above) 407 per Auld LJ, accepted per Aldous LJ at 417.
[6] C Forsyth, 'Characterisation Revisited: An Essay in the Theory and Practice of the English Conflict of Laws' (1998) 114 LQR 141.
[7] ibid 148–150.
[8] *Macmillan (No 3)* (n 4 above) 417, CA per Aldous LJ.
[9] *Macmillan v Bishopsgate Investment Trust plc (No 3)* [1995] 1 WLR 978, 988 per Millett J; [1996] 1 WLR 387, 399, CA per Staughton LJ, 407 per Auld LJ, 418 per Aldous LJ.
[10] *Macmillan (No 3)* (n 4 above) 418, CA per Aldous LJ.

Investor's Rights to Custody Assets

In relation to how investors enjoy rights to investments held by their custodians **10.10** there are two aspects to the question of characterisation. The first is the effectiveness of the transfer of assets to the custodian. The second is the nature of rights in relation to the asset or otherwise that the investor enjoys post-transfer, in particular whether the investor enjoys such rights in relation to the custody assets that would survive the insolvency of the custodian.

The question of the effectiveness of the transfer to the custodian is simply a pro- **10.11** prietary issue and the applicable rule of conflict of laws will be applied to this. The characterisation of whether the investor enjoys beneficial rights in relation to the custody assets is more complex and may be approached in at least two ways. One may approach the issue directly as a proprietary issue, an enquiry as to whether the investor has acquired rights in relation to the custody assets.[11] However, this approach does not address how such a proprietary right comes into existence or is retained after transfer of the assets. In the present context, such beneficial rights may arise from a transfer to the custodian on terms that it holds for the investor. From the perspective of an English investor, the issue may be characterised as one of trusts or bailment. Where the transfer to the custodian does not demand that he holds for the investor, but may simply effect delivery of equivalent assets to the investor on demand, the issue may be characterised as the establishment of personal contractual rights. The establishment of proprietary rights does not necessarily exclude the co-existence of personal rights; an investor may enjoy personal rights in addition to any proprietary rights he enjoys.[12]

One implication of the separation of the various strands that constitute an **10.12** investor's rights in relation to custody assets is that each strand may fall to be characterised differently. What is in substance the single question of whether an investor enjoys rights in relation to custody assets may involve separate rules of conflicts of laws, with the consequence that the question is determined by different substantive laws depending on how the question is framed.

Custody Assets as Collateral for Security

The use of custody assets as collateral for security may also be better addressed in **10.13** its separate components for the purposes of characterisation rather than the adoption of a blanket approach for all issues.[13] In the first place, there may be a contract

---

[11] This is implied in *Re Harvard Securities Ltd* [1997] 2 BCLC 369, 373–375 per Neuberger J.

[12] The distinction between personal and proprietary rights which may make up the parcel of rights of a person with assets in custody, as well as the fact that such rights may co-exist, seems to be recognised by L Collins (ed), *Dicey and Morris on The Conflict of Laws* (12th edn, 1993). See, for example, the discussion on bailment at 1336–1337.

[13] M Moshinsky, 'The Assignment of Debts in the Conflict of Laws' (1992) 109 LQR 591.

for security and it may be necessary to identify the proper law of such contract. Beyond the contract, depending on the nature of security created, there may be some element of transfer of property or creation of security interests in favour of the creditor that will be characterised as a proprietary issue. Since questions relating to a contract for security differ from proprietary issues which give the security effect,[14] as will be observed shortly, the applicable rules for resolving conflicts of laws are different and may lead to different aspects of a single security transaction being subjected to different systems of law.

Priority Disputes

10.14 Priority disputes may arise if one asset is purportedly assigned more than once where both assignments have complied with the formalities for transfer. A priority dispute may also arise if one party claims title to an asset by tracing whilst another person claims the same asset by assignment from the person in control thereof, or where an assigned asset is attached by a judgment creditor. The simple question is who between two or more innocents should take the benefit of the thing apparently transferred.

10.15 In resolving priority disputes it is necessary to draw a distinction between the effect of an assignment between assignee and obligor, on the one hand, and the priority of competing claims to the assigned asset on the other.[15] This view suggests a distinction between who is owed the obligations of a chose in action and who owns the obligations, with the possibility that these two questions may be resolved by different systems of law.[16] Some implications of this are that it is possible to enjoy priority to something without directly affecting the obligor of the assigned thing.[17]

10.16 Although the argument could be made that there is an inherent contradiction in the proposition that one may enjoy priority to a chose in action and not affect the obligor, such a criticism would be misguided. The question at issue is who enjoys property in an obligation, not who may enforce it. It may be that it is the person who enjoys the property therein who may enforce it directly against the obligor, but it may be that the obligation can only be directly enforced by another person.

---

[14] *Macmillan v Bishopsgate Investment Trust plc (No 3)* [1995] 1 WLR 978, 994 per Millett J, [1996] 1 WLR 387, 419 per Aldous LJ.

[15] This distinction is adopted, for instance, by Goode, *Commercial Law* (2nd edn, 1995) 1128–1130 and Moshinsky (n 13 above) 591.

[16] See, for example, *Macmillan Inc v Bishopsgate Investment Trust plc (No 3)* [1995] 1 WLR 978, 997, 1006 per Millett J, who suggested that although legal entitlement to registrable shares is determined by the law of the issuer, priorities to the shares in dispute were to be determined according to the *lex loci actus*.

[17] 'The assignment of an intangible is a transaction between the assignor and the assignee and does not necessarily concern the debtor at all.' See JG Collier, *Conflict of Laws* (2nd edn, 1994) 253.

If the question of priorities is understood in the foregoing light, it is apparent that **10.17**
the issue should be characterised as a proprietary one.

Perfection

The grant of real security may entail perfection, the twin goals of which, as set out **10.18**
below, may influence the law applicable to the issue. In the first place, perfection
involves acts intended to protect the security interest of a secured party against
third parties by 'the taking of any additional steps prescribed by law for giving
public notice of the security interest so as to bind third parties'.[18] This question
relates to the entitlement of the secured creditor; it may therefore be appropriate
to characterise it as a proprietary issue.

Beyond this, perfection also addresses the problem of false wealth whereby, in the **10.19**
absence of public notice of security interests, secured debtors may appear to be
more solvent than they actually are.[19] This issue, in particular, raises questions as
to where perfection should be undertaken in order to achieve this additional goal.

C. Rule of Conflict of Laws

The foregoing section identified the types of issues which may fall to be deter- **10.20**
mined in relation to custody assets. In this section, the appropriate rule of conflict
of laws for resolving each of such issues is identified.[20]

Bailment, Trusts and Contracts

The law applicable to bailment, trusts and contracts is generally that chosen by the **10.21**
relevant parties. In the absence of choice, the applicable law is that with which
the trust or contract is most closely connected.[21] There are rules for determining
the law with which the contract or trust is most closely connected.[22]

---

[18] Goode, *Commercial Law* (n 15 above) 674. This issue is developed in more detail in Chapter 5.

[19] PR Wood, *Comparative Law of Security and Guarantees* (1995) 181–183.

[20] This issue has recently been extensively debated by academics and practitioners. See, for example, J Benjamin, 'Determining the Situs of Interests in Immobilised Securities' (1998) 47 ICLQ 923; and the collection of articles in 'The Oxford Colloquium on Collateral and Conflict of Laws—Held at St John's College, Oxford University' (1 May 1998), a BJIBFL Special Supplement, September 1998.

[21] On bailment see *Dicey and Morris* (12th edn, 1993) Rule 185. On trusts see Arts 6 and 7 of the Hague Convention on the Law Applicable to Trusts (1986) which was enacted into English law by the Recognition of Trusts Act 1987. On contracts see Arts 3 and 4 of the Rome Convention on the Law Applicable to Contractual Obligations (1980) which was enacted into English law by the Contracts (Applicable Law) Act 1990.

[22] See *Dicey and Morris* (12th edn, 1993) Rule 153, 1091–1092 in relation to trusts; Rule 176, 1230–1239 in relation to contracts; and Rule 185, 1336–1337 in relation to bailment.

General Rule for Proprietary Matters

10.22 The general rule of conflict of laws for the resolution of proprietary issues, including the proprietary aspects of contracts, is that of *lex situs*,[23] the system of law where the relevant property is situate. One of the supposed advantages of the *lex situs* rule is that it should provide for certainty.[24] Whilst this rule does provide certainty in relation to tangible assets, problems in the use of *situs* for determining the applicable law to intangibles are manifest. The location of a tangible asset is beyond doubt, but there are inherent difficulties in the metaphysical exercise of localising in a physical sense something devoid of corporeal form. Any ascription of *situs* to an intangible asset is necessarily fictitious since it cannot have an actual locality,[25] therefore making the process of determining *situs* unpredictable.[26]

Rule for Securities

10.23 The unpredictability of the use of *situs* to determine the law governing transactions with respect to intangibles is demonstrated by the divergent views that have been expressed in relation to the application of *situs* to securities. For example, in the Court of Appeal in *Macmillan Inc v Bishopsgate Trust (No 3)*, although there was general agreement that it was the location of the certificate that determined the *situs* of negotiable securities,[27] Staughton LJ and Aldous LJ considered that the place of incorporation of the issuer was critical for registrable securities,[28] whilst Auld LJ was of the view that it was the place where the register was kept which normally determined *situs*.[29] In practice, of course, this divergence is likely to be of little importance because the register is often located at the same place as the incorporation of the company took place.

Situs of Registrable Securities

10.24 It has been suggested that securities are located at the place at which they 'can be effectually dealt with'.[30] In the case of registrable shares this may be interpreted as the place where the register is. There is authority that if such shares may be dealt

---

[23] *Macmillan (No 3)* (n 4 above) 399–402 per Staughton LJ, 410 per Auld LJ, 424 per Aldous LJ.

[24] ibid 412 per Auld LJ.

[25] *Lee v Abdy* (1886) 17 QBD 309, 312 per Day J.

[26] For a critical appraisal of *lex situs* as a rule of conflict of laws for resolving proprietary disputes, see PJ Rogerson, 'The Situs of Debts in the Conflict of Laws: Illogical, Unnecessary and Misleading' [1990] CLJ 441; RM Goode, 'The Nature and Transfer of Rights in Dematerialised and Immobilised Securities' [1996] BJIBFL 167, 172; and R Stevens, 'The Law Applicable to Priority in Shares' (1996) 112 LQR 198, 201.

[27] [1996] 1 WLR 387, 405 per Staughton LJ, 411 per Auld LJ.

[28] [1996] 1 WLR 387, 405 per Staughton LJ, 423 per Aldous LJ.

[29] [1996] 1 WLR 387, 411 per Auld LJ.

[30] *Erie Beach Co v Attorney-General for Ontario* [1930] AC 161, 168. See generally, *Dicey and Morris* (12th edn, 1993) Rule 114, 931–932.

with at more than one location, then *situs* may be ascribed to the particular place at which the share would be dealt with in the ordinary course of events;[31] or that if the company has more than one register, the share may be situated at the place at which the certificate is located.[32] There is also Canadian authority that the *situs* of a registrable share is the place of incorporation of the issuer thereof.[33]

Of the above options in relation to registrable shares, it is the location of the shares **10.25** at the place of incorporation of the issuer which can best be supported on grounds of principle and commercial reality.[34] Since a share is simply a set of rights, a chose in action, it is consistent with the intangible nature of the asset that the location ascribed to it is the place of the system of law by which the rights are given existence. Further, where *situs* is defined otherwise than by the place of incorporation of the issuer, it is accepted that 'the law of the place of incorporation may always override the *lex situs* of the register or document: it may refuse to recognise the effects of what happens under that law and it may itself provide for a transfer of title, by expropriation or otherwise'.[35] In view of this, and in an effort to avoid unnecessary disputes, it may be a useful development for the use of *situs* in determining the applicable law for registrable securities to be abandoned and regard simply to be had to the law of the place of incorporation of the issuer of the securities.

Situs of Negotiable Securities

Is the foregoing altered by virtue of the existence of a negotiable documentary **10.26** token representing the securities?[36] Even if the certificate is negotiable, it is not the essential object of ownership by the holder. What the holder desires are the rights represented by the certificate. In this sense, a negotiable certificate may be approximated to the register for registrable shares and the argument made that the negotiable certificate is merely evidence of entitlement to the rights represented by the certificate[37] and that if the register is not the same as the rights represented by the registrable shares recorded therein, the distinction between the certificate of negotiable securities and the securities represented thereby should remain. This line of reasoning finds support from at least one North American case.[38] It has also been accepted in some old cases[39] that the underlying rights that constitute the

---

[31] *Standard Chartered Bank v IRC* [1978] 1 WLR 1160.
[32] *Re Clark* [1904] 1 Ch 294, 299 per Farwell J.
[33] *Braun v The Custodian* [1944] 4 DLR 209, 213–214 per Kerwin J, SC of Canada; *Brown v Beleggings-Societeit NV* (1961) 29 DLR(2d) 673, Ontario High Court.
[34] J Bird, 'Choice of Law for Priority Disputes in Relation to Shares' [1996] LMCLQ 57, 62–63.
[35] *Dicey and Morris* (12th edn, 1993) Rule 114, 932.
[36] See generally, *Dicey and Morris* (12th edn, 1993) Rule 114, 930–931.
[37] *Attorney-General v Bouwens* (1838) 4 M & W 171, 192–193 per Lord Abinger CB, 150 ER 1390. Of course, there remains a distinction in the manner of transfer of such securities.
[38] *Brown v Beleggings-Societeit NV* (1961) 29 DLR(2d) 673, Ontario High Court.
[39] *Attorney-General v Dimond* (1831) 1 C & J 356, 371 per Lord Lyndhurst, 148 ER 1458; *Attorney-General v Hope* (1834) 1 CM & R 530, 149 ER 1191.

securities represented by a certificate are located where the securities may be enforced, which is not necessarily where the certificate is.

10.27 Conversely, the argument may be made that the underlying rights represented by a bearer or negotiable security are where the relevant certificate happens to be. Cases such as *AG v Bouwens*[40] and *Winans v AG (No 2)*[41] may be cited in support of this proposition. However, the authority of these cases is weak because both cases consider the issue from the narrow perspective of revenue law. Indeed, doubts as to their relevance for the general determination of the *situs* of securities have been expressed by academics[42] and the courts.[43] In both cases there was property in England for fiscal purposes because the foreign instrument had a local market value which, although obviously related to the underlying rights, could be traded as a chattel in its own right. The certificate could be sold for a certain amount; it therefore had a value and constituted an asset in England that could be taxed as such. This does not necessarily impinge upon the location of the rights represented by the instrument; the instrument is not the security/underlying rights which it represents.[44]

10.28 Nevertheless, there are significant practical reasons for ascribing the *situs* of negotiable securities to the location of the certificate. The basis for this position is the manner of transfer of such securities. Negotiable securities are transferred by delivery of the certificate. What constitutes delivery at any place can only be determined by the law governing the place where the certificate is. Of course it is by the law of incorporation of the issuer that the securities come into existence at all and it is by this law, or by whatever other system of law the issue of securities is made, that the securities are constituted as negotiable securities. However, it is only by the law of the place where the certificate is that the effectiveness of the delivery can be judged.[45]

Rule Governing Entitlements Via the Custodian

10.29 The analysis in Chapters 2 to 4 indicates that it is not only in relation to underlying securities that transactions will take place. Investors will often instead enjoy proprietary rights in the entitlements of their custodian. The question arises as to the rule of conflict of laws for resolving disputes in relation to the assignment or creation of interests in relation to such investors' rights.

---

[40] (1838) 4 M & W 171, 150 ER 1390.

[41] [1910] AC 27. *Attorney-General v Bouwens* was affirmed by Lord Gorell at 39.

[42] *Dicey and Morris* (12th edn, 1993) 930.

[43] *Re Clark* [1904] 1 Ch 294, 298 per Farwell J.

[44] *Attorney-General v Bouwens* (1838) 4 M & W 171, 192–193 per Lord Abinger CB, 150 ER 1390.

[45] *Alcock v Smith* [1892] 1 Ch 238, 255–256 per Romer J, affirmed on appeal; *Re Maudslay, Sons & Field, Maudslay v Maudslay, Sons & Field* [1900] 1 Ch 602, 609–610 per Cozens-Hardy J; *Embiricos v Anglo-Austrian Bank* [1904] 2 KB 870, 874–875 per Walton J; [1905] 1 KB 677 affirming the first instance decision.

Where the investor's interest is via an intermediary-trustee, by virtue of Article 10.30
1(2)(g) of the Rome Convention,[46] it is clear that that Convention is inapplicable.
Therefore, one resorts to the default rule of *lex situs*. However, the uncertainty that
exists in relation to *situs* of securities is also present in relation to the location of the
beneficial interest under a trust. Citing a number of cases, *Dicey & Morris*[47] suggests that there is a distinction for the *situs* of a beneficial interest under a trust
according to whether the beneficiary enjoys a beneficial right in the trust property[48] (*situs* is where trust assets are) or can only resort to court to get his rights
under the trust enforced[49] (*situs* is at place of intermediary). Yet, the purported distinction between whether beneficiaries enjoy rights in the trust assets or the right
to get the trust executed is fraught with difficulty. Indeed, it is difficult to discern
the precise basis of distinction in the facts of some of the cases relied upon by *Dicey
& Morris*.

The cases relied upon for fixing the beneficial interest directly to the trust assets do 10.31
not indicate that the beneficiaries enjoyed more of a direct link to the trust assets
than the beneficiaries in the cases relied upon for fixing the interest at the place
where the trust may be enforced. In neither set of cases is the beneficiary supposed
to enjoy the very assets held on trust, but usually only the sums to be realised from
sale or other forms of income. Doubts as to the application of the distinction are
evident in the text of *Dicey & Morris* itself.[50]

Assuming the distinction suggested in *Dicey & Morris* were tenable, it would lead 10.32
to uncertainty in the governing law of dealings in the beneficial interests of trusts.
Anyone dealing with the investor would, if he wanted to be sure of the correct governing law, be required to know the internal workings of the investor's custodian
even though there are no guarantees that the investor himself would know this.
Specifically, the counter-party would have to know whether the assets were held in
such a way as to give the investor a direct interest and not just a right to get the
trust executed. Reliance on an investor who got his facts as to the method of holding wrong would lead to the situation that the wrong law was applied with potentially disastrous consequences for the counter-party.

The approach of *Dicey & Morris* also leads to the unwelcome consequence, for 10.33
investors who are adjudged to enjoy direct links with the trust assets, that any
transaction in relation to their interest in an investment portfolio will be governed

---

[46] See the Contracts (Applicable Law) Act 1990, the Convention is set out in the Schedule.
[47] See *Dicey and Morris* (12th edn, 1993) Rule 114, 933. *Archer-Shee v Garland* [1931] AC 212
is cited as an illustration of the distinction.
[48] *Re Berchtold* [1923] 1 Ch 192; *Philipson-Stow v Inland Revenue Commissioners* [1961] AC 727.
[49] *Re Cigala's Settlement Trusts* (1878) 7 ChD 351; *Lord Sudeley v Attorney-General* [1897] AC
11; *Re Smyth* [1898] 1 Ch 89; *Attorney-General v Johnson* [1907] 2 KB 885; *Favorke v Steinkopff*
[1922] 1 Ch 174; *Com'r of Stamp Duties (Q'd) v Livingston* [1965] AC 694.
[50] See the query in relation to the categorisation of *Attorney-General v Johnson* [1907] 2 KB 885,
in the text of *Dicey and Morris* (12th edn, 1993) 933, n 22.

by the laws of all of the shares which make up the portfolio. This would add to the cost of transactions and permit greater scope for mistakes to be made during the more extensive process of due diligence that would have to be undertaken. This approach would also slow the pace at which transactions could be effected.

10.34 For those who are taken only to enjoy rights to be enforced against the trustee, there are difficulties in deciding where the trust can be enforced. It is taken as given in *Dicey & Morris* that the place of enforcement of the trust is the place of residence of the trustee. However, doubts are cast on this by the fact that judges in a number of cases seemed to be equally swayed by the law under which the trust arose,[51] locating *situs* of the beneficial interest in the trust in the country of the law which gave the trust force, which will not always be where the trustees are located.

10.35 If one were to abandon *situs* as the criterion for choosing the applicable law for dealings in beneficial interests under a trust, because this approach can be practically unworkable, there are some obvious principles by which the governing law may otherwise be determined. One could look to the place of the underlying assets on which the rights are based; or look to the place of the intermediary through whom the rights are claimed. Although these may point to the same system of law, with modern investment practices they may differ.

10.36 The place of the underlying assets should be rejected because the investor's rights are not directly linked to those assets, but are linked to the intermediary through whom they must be exercised. It would also be unworkable because each transaction with respect to the investor's interest would have to comply with the laws of all the securities that make up the portfolio. The better approach may be to situate the interest where the trustee is located. This may be supported on grounds of predictability; it is to this system of law that parties to a dispute may instinctively look. By this approach, the relevant system of law is also made unchanging and readily discernible. There are indications in some cases that such a method of determining the applicable system of law is consistent with the *lex situs* of beneficial interests under a trust.[52]

Summary of Law Applicable to Transactions in Relation to Custody Assets

10.37 Transactions with respect to custody assets are generally characterised as involving two elements, contractual and proprietary. The contractual aspects, ie the personal relationship between the two parties to the transaction, are governed by the governing law of the contract. The proprietary element is governed by the law of

---

[51] For example, see *Kelly v Selwyn* [1905] 2 Ch 117 as interpreted in *Macmillan (No 3)* (n 4 above) 401 per Staughton LJ, 424 per Aldous LJ; *Re Cigala's Settlement Trusts* (1878) 7 ChD 351, 357 per Jessel MR; and *Favorke v Steinkopff* [1922] 1 Ch 174, 177–178 per Russell J.

[52] *Re Cigala's Settlement Trusts* (1878) 7 ChD 351, 357 per Jessel MR; and *Favorke v Steinkopff* [1922] 1 Ch 174, 177–178 per Russell J.

the *situs* of the asset. Particular care, however, must be paid to the precise asset concerned by the transaction. The *situs* and governing law for the transaction may differ according to whether it is the underlying asset or the rights of the investor that are involved in the transaction.

Where it is the underlying securities that are being dealt with, *situs* is taken to be **10.38** where they can be effectively dealt with. For registrable securities, this is generally the place of incorporation of the issuer, although *situs* may also be taken to be the place where the register is located. For negotiable securities, *situs* is where the certificate is.

If it is the investor's rights (which would generally be beneficial rights under a trust **10.39** with custodian as trustee) that are the relevant asset, the *situs* of these rights would generally be located where the investor's direct custodian is. Although there is authority that *situs* may be where the underlying assets are, the nature of custodial relationships are such that the interests of investors would generally be located at the place of their particular intermediary. There is increasing statutory support, both domestic and offshore, for the view that the proprietary aspects of transactions with respect to such rights are governed by the law of the place of the intermediary through whom the rights are dealt with.

Regulation 23 of the Financial Markets and Insolvency (Settlement Finality) **10.40** Regulations 1999[53] states that the governing law for the holder of security where the collateral consists of rights with respect to securities or rights claimable via a securities intermediary is the law of the place where the register, account or settlement system is located. This Regulation is applicable to all registers, accounts and settlement systems located in the European Economic Area.

There is pre-existing legislation in some European countries to similar effect, **10.41** including Article 10 of Belgian Royal Decree No 62 of 10 November 1967 Facilitating the Circulation of Securities, which is applicable to Euroclear; and Article 8(3) of Grand-Ducal Decree of Luxembourg dated 17 February 1971 on the Circulation of Securities, which is applicable to Cedel, as amended by the Grand-Ducal Amending Decree of 8 June 1994.

Under the Uniform Commercial Code of the USA, it is the system of law under **10.42** which the issuer is organised that will determine questions of title to securities such as shares issued by it, and where this is permitted, eg in relation to some debt instruments, it is the law chosen by the issuer that will govern securities issued by it.[54] Where securities are held with an intermediary, the law governing the interest claimed via the intermediary is that which the parties agree should govern, or

---

[53] SI 1999/2979. Based on Article 9(2) of EU Directive (98/28/EC) on Settlement Finality in Payment and Securities Systems adopted on 19 May 1998.
[54] Uniform Commercial Code, s 8-110(a) and (d).

whatever jurisdiction the parties agree that the entitlement is held within. In the absence of such choice, the applicable law will be imputed by reference to the particular branch of an entity at which one's entitlement appears to be held or, failing the identification of a particular branch, the jurisdiction in which the chief executive office of the intermediary is located.[55] The location of a certificate representing underlying investments, the law of incorporation of the issuer of the underlying investment and the location of the facilities for recording the entitlement are not relevant to the law applicable to the interest claimed via the intermediary.[56]

Priorities

10.43 If it is accepted, as suggested in the section on characterisation, that the question of priorities is a proprietary issue, this would suggest that priorities be determined by the *lex situs* of the relevant interest. In relation to securities, this may be taken to mean the law of incorporation of the issuer;[57] proprietary rights under a trust would be determined by the law of the place of the trustee/intermediary.[58] The application of the law of *situs* to questions of priority for securities[59] and other choses in action[60] may be justified on the grounds that it is the law to which the parties would naturally look. It may ultimately be to that system of law that the winner must have recourse in order to enforce his rights.[61]

Perfection

10.44 If the object of perfection is to protect the creditor's security interest, a proprietary right, then, as with other proprietary rights, perfection should be undertaken where the assets are situate. This may take the form of filing or some other system of public notice. This is where third parties would in all likelihood make enquiries in relation to the asset.[62] This approach seems to be accepted by *Dicey*

---

[55] ibid s 8-110(b) and (e). This is also applicable to the determination of governing law for questions of priority.

[56] ibid s 8-110(f).

[57] *Macmillan (No 3)* (n 4 above) 411–412 per Auld LJ, 424 per Aldous LJ.

[58] *Kelly v Selwyn* [1905] 2 Ch 117, 122 per Warrington J; see also *Macmillan (No 3)* (n 4 above) 401 per Staughton LJ, 424 per Aldous LJ.

[59] A Briggs, 'Restitution Meets the Conflict of Laws' (1995) 3 Restitution Law Review (Autumn) 94, 95, n 10; and J Bird, 'Choice of Law Rule for Priority Disputes in Relation to Shares' [1996] LMCLQ 57, 62.

[60] Wood, *Comparative Law of Security and Guarantees* (n 19 above) 191, 13–24.

[61] *Macmillan (No 3)* (n 4 above) 424 per Aldous LJ; Bird, 'Choice of Law Rule for Priority Disputes in Relation to Shares' [1996] LMCLQ 57, 62; G Moss and F Toube, 'Cross-Border Enforcement of Security—Parts 1 and 2' (1997) 16 IBFL 1, 9, 11.

[62] *Macmillan (No 3)* (n 4 above) 405 implied per Staughton LJ; and Bird (n 61 above) 62.

& Morris,[63] as well as the courts[64] and legislature[65] of England and other countries.[66]

It is important that perfection is also undertaken where the debtor is, even if the **10.45** charged assets are situated in another jurisdiction, because whether perfection has been carried out or not may have consequences for the validity of the security or ability of the secured creditor to enforce the security at the debtor's domicile. The scope of anti-false wealth provisions is often extra-territorial, extending to all assets of the debtor regardless of their locality.[67]

Given that security may need to be enforced by legal action, it would also seem **10.46** prudent to perfect wherever the creditor anticipates that a third party may challenge his interest or where the creditor may seek to enforce his security. If this statement appears imprecise, this is a direct consequence of the myriad permutations of parties and locations of assets that may arise. Different jurisdictions use different connecting factors to assume insolvency jurisdiction, and may apply their avoidance provisions thereto. Until international comity leads to some rationalisation of the perfection requirements of all countries,[68] the simple fact of the matter is that the creditor will need to perfect his security in every jurisdiction where he anticipates that his interest may be challenged or in which he may wish to enforce his security.[69] If the debtor does not have a presence in such jurisdictions, such perfection may take place by way of any forms of notice acceptable in such jurisdiction. Given the costs that this would entail, this will involve a cost-benefit analysis of the likelihood of the challenge or the need to enforce on the one hand versus the cost and bother of perfection on the other.

---

[63] *Dicey and Morris* (12th edn, 1993) 1150.

[64] *Liverpool Marine Credit Company v Hunter* (1867) LR 4 Eq 62; (1868) 3 Ch App 479; *Re Maudslay, Sons & Field* [1900] 1 Ch 602; *Macmillan (No 3)* (n 4 above) 405 per Staughton LJ, 412 per Auld LJ.

[65] Companies Act 1985, s 398(3).

[66] In the USA, questions of perfection are determined in the same fashion as are questions of title, see Uniform Commercial Code, s 9-103(6)(b)–(d), as well as point 9, para 1 of the Official Commentary thereto.

[67] Companies Act 1985, s 395, imposes mandatory perfection requirements on UK companies in relation to assets used as collateral, regardless of the location of the asset. See Wood, *Comparative Law of Security and Guarantees* (n 19 above) 115–116, 9–11.

[68] As advocated by R Guynn, *Modernizing Securities Ownership, Transfer and Pledging Laws* (Capital Markets Forum of the International Bar Association, 1996); see also R Guynn and M Tahyar, 'The Importance of Choice of Law and Finality to PvP, Netting and Collateral Arrangements' (1996) 4 *Journal of Financial Regulation and Compliance* No 2, 170.

[69] JD Falconbridge, *Essays on the Conflict of Laws* (2nd edn, 1954) 481; and I Jameson and X Louveaux, 'Cross-Border Securities Collateralisation: Lenders Beware' [1996] BJIBFL 466, 469.

D. Identifying the System of Law

10.47   Based on the issue characterised and the relevant rule of conflict of laws one arrives at a system of law by which the issue is governed. Using the structure of offshore holdings in Figure 10.1 as an example, we shall demonstrate how the issue of characterisation and the rule of conflict of laws may take effect in practice.

Benefits

10.48   The custodial structure depends on the underlying Utopian securities being properly transferred according to Utopian law (as *lex situs* of the securities) to the nominee to be held for the Utopian CSD.

10.49   The passing of benefits by the Utopian CSD will also have to conform to Utopian law (as *lex situs* of the interest of CSD). If Utopia is a common law jurisdiction that recognises the institution of trusts, this would be the obvious method of passing the benefits on. By virtue of the Utopian CSD holding on trust for the ICSD, the ICSD is equitably entitled (under the Utopian trust) to the benefit of entitlements enjoyed by CSD.

10.50   However, ICSD's entitlement is not beneficial. It also seeks to pass on the benefit of its entitlement to the UK lead/global custodian employed by the investor. For example, the ICSD may be Euroclear or Cedel,[70] which are located in Belgium and Luxembourg respectively, civilian countries which do not recognise the institution of the trust, with the result that this method of transferring benefit would not be available. Entitlements held by Euroclear/Cedel for their clients would ordinarily run the risk of being characterised as giving their clients only contractual rights. Lead or global custodians holding assets via an ICSD in such circumstances would by this scenario be unsecured creditors of the ICSDs in competition with other general creditors upon the insolvency of the ICSDs. This highlights the risk of re-characterisation of entitlements that can occur at any tier of intermediary custody involving foreign laws. Of course, they could establish trusts under English law in favour of the global custodian, which could be enforced by an English court with jurisdiction over the ICSD,[71] but there would remain the risk that the trust would not be enforceable in their country of domicile and benefits accruing from their entitlement could be seized upon their insolvency.

10.51   Fortunately, however, both Belgium and Luxembourg have enacted specific legislation to address this risk. By article 10 of the Belgian Royal Decree No 62 of 10 November 1967 Facilitating the Circulation of Securities, the clients of Euroclear

---

[70] See generally F Christie and H Dosanjh, 'The Practical Elements of Settlement and Custody' in F Oditah (ed), *The Future for the Global Securities Market* (1996).

[71] *Chellaram v Chellaram* [1985] Ch 409; *Dicey and Morris* (12th edn, 1993) 1097.

are entitled to a co-ownership right in the entitlements held by Euroclear with *revendication* rights which rank ahead of the rights of its general creditors. Similarly, article 9 of the Grand-Ducal Decree of Luxembourg dated 17 February 1971 on the Circulation of Securities, as amended by the Grand-Ducal Amending Decree of 8 June 1994, provides that clients of Cedel enjoy *revendication* rights in relation to the entitlements held by Cedel which rank ahead of those of its general creditors. By these provisions, although there is no trust in the English sense of the word, the global custodian and other clients of Euroclear and Cedel enjoy entitlements via the ICSDs that are insulated from the insolvency risk of the institutions.

Again, the entitlement of the UK-based global custodian is not beneficial. He **10.52** holds for the investor who instructs him. As discussed in Chapters 2 and 3, it is likely that this would be effected by virtue of a trust governed by English law, which if not chosen expressly would in all likelihood be the system of law with which the trust has its closest connection.

Security

In view of the tiered nature of custody, a secured creditor could take as collateral **10.53** or enjoy a security interest in relation to different things in a custodial structure. He may enjoy rights in relation to the underlying securities, or take security in relation to an investor's rights exercisable via the custodian. From any party in the tier, the secured creditor may enjoy rights in relation to the rights of the debtor from its own intermediary or the issuer, or in relation to subsidiary rights carved therefrom. Given that the tiers, and therefore the things offered as security, may be located in different jurisdictions, the question that arises is what system of law governs the security offered.

Where the nominee or CSD seeks to use the legal or equitable title to the under- **10.54** lying securities for security, as a proprietary issue this would be governed by the *lex situs* of the securities or beneficial interest under the trust in favour of the CSD, which is the law of Utopia.

Where the security is granted by ICSD, the governing law will be Utopian law. **10.55** The rights used for security by ICSD are located with the CSD in Utopia, the law of which must therefore determine the validity of dealings in relation thereto.

If the UK global custodian sought to offer security, since the *res* is the entitlement **10.56** due from ICSD the applicable law would be that of Nirvana, on the basis that it is in Nirvana that the obligation subject to the security is located.

Where the investor offers his entitlement from the global custodian as security, **10.57** the security offered will be governed by English law. The entitlement from the custodian is located in England.

10.58 As indicated above, perfection should be undertaken according to the *situs* of securities or interests to which the security interest created attaches, as well as in the jurisdiction of the debtor.

E. Effect of Tiers of Custody on the Conflict of Laws

10.59 As recognised by Staughton LJ in *Macmillan Inc v Bishopsgate Trust (No 3)*,[72] dealings in relation to portfolios of securities spread over numerous jurisdictions would ordinarily necessitate complying with the formalities of each jurisdiction where the securities are located. Such an obligation would be tedious, time-wasting, expensive and beyond the capabilities of many investors. This process would also permit greater scope for mistakes to be made in the extensive process of due diligence that would have to be undertaken. Such mistakes could be disastrous for the economic value of an investor's rights, such as if the custodial structure he sets up leaves him with the credit risk of an uncreditworthy intermediary. The same could be true for a purported secured creditor who fails to establish real security by the law applicable to the transaction.

10.60 However, an investor, and secured creditors claiming through him, can reduce these difficulties. In the establishment of the custodial structure the investor could employ a global custodian who would be better able to ensure, at more efficient cost, that a structure is established that gives the investor the benefits desired from the assets in circumstances that insulate him from the insolvency of the custodian or sub-custodian. The most significant consequence of this is that the portfolio of securities will, in effect, have been re-packaged into a single new asset (rights to be claimed via the intermediary) in relation to which due diligence obligations will be less onerous. Transactions will be undertaken in relation to the new rights localised in the one jurisdiction under which the custody trust is established.

10.61 Characterisation of the beneficiary interest in this way is desirable from the point of view of consistency, in that it gives the interest a single applicable law, as opposed to changing applicable law as underlying assets are bought and sold. A beneficial interest governed by the *lex situs* of the underlying assets would be highly inconvenient. Ascertaining what is necessary to deal with an interest located at one place is preferable to having to master the necessities of dealing with interests scattered in various jurisdictions. This re-packaging does not substantively prejudice the investor or those claiming through him. A properly constituted relationship confers rights on the investor and those claiming through him by which they get to enjoy, albeit indirectly, the economic and other benefits of

---

[72] [1996] 1 WLR 387, 405.

the underlying securities in a manner which insulates them from the insolvency of the holder and other intermediaries.

However, the creation of intermediary structures is not wholly without risk. **10.62** There may be the risk of re-characterisation at every tier and any global custodian responsible for custody assets will need to have undertaken due diligence at every tier to ensure that benefits will pass along the tiers smoothly. In particular, it will be necessary to verify that, notwithstanding properly constituted trusts, the underlying assets are not situate in jurisdictions with mandatory laws which over-reach the trust(s) jeopardising the interests of those claiming thereby.

Where security is given via a lower tier intermediary or beneficiary claiming via a **10.63** global custodian, this reduces any necessary perfection obligations. Due diligence would only need to be performed in one place, at the deemed *situs* of the securities taken as collateral. However, this does not obviate the need for due diligence in other jurisdictions in which one may seek to enforce. Indeed, until all nations achieve harmonisation as to conflict of laws it will remain necessary to perform due diligence in as many jurisdictions as one may reasonably anticipate enforcing in, not only because of the possibility of mandatory rules there, but also because even if they adopt the *lex situs* theory in relation to perfection requirements, their conception of *situs* may be different.

The tiered nature of custody reduces or localises much of the difficulty involved **10.64** in cross-border custodial activity. The only relationship of direct concern to the investor is that with his custodian. It is then up to the custodian to make sure that the features of the custodial structure desired are present in his own operations. If the custodian is overseas, the investor will need to ascertain by the opinion of local counsel whether the features desired out of the custodial structure are permissible. The custodian would in turn need to do the same with whomsoever he sub-delegates the task of holding the underlying assets in other countries, so that nothing impedes the stream of benefits that should ultimately reach the investor. This will have saved the investor much due diligence; it will instead be the job of the custodian.

ANNEX

CHECKLIST OF THE MAIN LEGAL ISSUES IN ASSESSING CUSTODIAL ARRANGEMENTS

TRANSFER INTO CUSTODY

1. What are the terms of transfer of assets to the custodian? What is the common intention of the investor and the custodian?

2. The point may be made explicit, if that is indeed the case, that the customer does not enjoy direct relations with the issuer of the security he holds in custody with his intermediary custodian.

3. Are there particular instructions for the handling of bearer securities? Are there restrictions as to whose name registrable securities may be registered in?

TERMS OF HOLDING

4. From whom is the custodian supposed to take instructions?

5. Are the assets with the custodian held on loan or are they held in a fiduciary capacity, such as on trust or bailment, by which the assets should not be threatened in the event of insolvency of the custodian?

6. How are the assets to be held: in a segregated client account, pooled with identical assets belonging to other clients or in omnibus holdings containing the assets of both clients and the custodian?

7. Is the investor entitled to make its own sub-custodial or other arrangements where third parties may be necessary for some element of the custodial operations?

(RE-)DELIVERY OBLIGATION OF CUSTODIAN

8. Is the (re-)delivery obligation of the custodian specific, tied to a particular pool or simply generic?

SETTLEMENT

9. Is the custodian entitled to alienate the assets in custody free of the investor/depositor's interest?

10. Are there any restrictions as to which settlement systems the custodian may effect the investor's instructions on?

Liability

11. At whose risk is the failure to deliver or non-payment by any counter-party to a transaction entered by the custodian following the client's instructions?

12. Who is liable for losses to the investor arising from the fraud or negligence of the custodian? What is the degree of any exculpation or limitation of liability provisions in favour of the custodian?

13. Who is liable for losses to the investor arising from the fraud or negligence of a sub-custodian or other third party to whom some elements of the custodial operations are delegated? Is this influenced by whether the investor chose, or was consulted on the appointment of, the third party? What is the degree of any exculpation or limitation of liability provisions in favour of the custodian or third party?

Conflicts of Interest

14. How are potential conflicts of interest, such as the custodian executing transactions for the investor with a counter-party to which it (the custodian) is related, to be treated? Does the fact of any potential conflict impose any restrictions on activities that may be undertaken by the custodian?

Use of Custody Assets

15. Who may use the assets in custody, what for and on what terms?

16. Is stock-lending permissible? If so, on what terms?

Reporting and Monitoring Obligations

17. What are the reporting or other monitoring and administrative obligations of the custodian? What details are supposed to be contained in the reports and how frequently should they be issued?

18. Is the custodian expected to oversee, verify and question instructions issued to him? Is there a 'whistle-blowing' obligation on the custodian where there is a third party, such as a fund-manager appointed by the investor, who may lawfully issue instructions to the custodian?

Security Interest in Favour of Custodian

19. Does the custodian enjoy a lien or other form of security interest with respect to assets in his care for fees, out-of-pocket and other expenses that he may incur on behalf of customers?

Exercise of Rights Attached to Securities in Custody

20. How are the voting rights with respect to securities in custody to be exercised? Does the custodian undertake to refrain from exercising such rights, to exercise the rights as directed by the investor or simply to act in the best interests, as the custodian sees them, of the investor?

21. How will corporate action by issuers, such as the payment of dividends or offer of bonus securities, be dealt with by the custodian? Is the custodian obliged to ensure that any benefits that arise by virtue of the securities are credited to the investor's account or otherwise vested in the custodian or its nominee on behalf of the investor?

LAW GOVERNING RELATIONSHIP BETWEEN CUSTODIAN AND INVESTOR

22. What is the governing law of the relationship between the investor and custodian?

BIBLIOGRAPHY

ALLCOCK, B, 'Restrictions on the Assignment of Contractual Rights' [1983] CLJ 328

AMERICAN LAW INSTITUTE AND THE NATIONAL CONFERENCE OF COMMISSIONERS ON UNIFORM STATE LAWS, *Uniform Commercial Code, Official Text with Comments* (14th edn, 1995)

ANDREWS, NH and BEATSON, J, 'Common Law Tracing: Springboard or Swan-Song' (1997) 113 LQR 21

ANON, 'Super-Priority of Securities Intermediaries under the New Section 9-115(5)(c) of the Uniform Commercial Code' (1995) 108 Harvard Law Review 1937

AUSTIN, RP, 'Moulding the Content of Fiduciary Duties' in Oakley, AJ (ed), *Trends in Contemporary Trust Law* (1996), ch 7

BAKER, PV and LANGAN, PStJ (eds), *Snell's Equity* (29th edn, 1990)

BARKER, K, 'After Change of Position: Good Faith Exchange in the Modern Law of Restitution' in Birks, PBH (ed), *Laundering and Tracing* (1995), ch 7

BEAVES, AW, 'Global Custody: A Tentative Analysis of Property and Contract' in Palmer, N and McKendrick, E (eds), *Interests in Goods* (1993), ch 10

BELL, AP, *Modern Law of Personal Property in England and Ireland* (1989)

BENJAMIN, J, 'Custody: An English Law Analysis' [1994] BJIBFL 121, 187

BENJAMIN, J, 'Determining the Situs of Interests in Immobilised Securities' (1998) 47 ICLQ 923

BENJAMIN, J, 'Recharacterisation Risk and Conflict of Laws' [1997] BJIBFL 513

BENJAMIN, J, *The Law of Global Custody* (1996)

BERG, A, 'Accessory Liability for Breach of Trust' (1996) 59 MLR 443

BIRD, J, 'Choice of Law for Priority Disputes in Relation to Shares' [1996] LMCLQ 57

BIRKS, PBH, 'Restitutionary Damages for Breach of Contract' [1987] LMCLQ 412

BIRKS, PBH, 'Trusts in the Recovery of Misapplied Assets: Tracing, Trusts, and Restitution' in McKendrick, E (ed), *Commercial Aspects of Trusts and Fiduciary Relations* (1992), ch 8

BIRKS, PBH, 'Mixtures' in Palmer, N and McKendrick, E (eds), *Interests in Goods* (1993), ch 16

BIRKS, PBH, 'Establishing a Proprietary Base' [1995] RLR 83

BIRKS, PBH, 'Overview: Tracing, Claiming and Defences' in Birks, PBH (ed), *Laundering and Tracing* (1995), ch 11

BIRKS, PBH, 'Tracing, Subrogation and Change of Position' (1995) 9 Trust Law International, No 4, 124

BISHOP, W and PRENTICE, DD, 'Some Legal and Economic Aspects of Fiduciary Remuneration' (1983) 46 MLR 289

BLACKSTONE, W, *Commentaries on the Laws of England, Volume II*, with an introduction by AWB Simpson (The University of Chicago Press, 1979)

BLAIR, W, ALLISON, A, PALMER, K and RICHARDS-CARPENTER, P, *Banking and the Financial Services Act* (1993)

BRADGATE, R and WHITE, F, 'Sale of Goods Forming Part of a Bulk: Proposals for Reform' [1994] LMCLQ 315

BRAZIER, MR (ed), *Clerk & Lindsell on Torts* (17th edn, 1995)

BRIGGS, A, 'Restitution Meets the Conflict of Laws' [1995] RLR 94

BROWN, I, 'Admixture of Goods in English Law' [1988] LMCLQ 286

BROWN, I, 'Divided Loyalties in the Law of Agency' (1993) 109 LQR 206

BRYAN, M, 'When Does a Bank Receive Money?' [1996] JBL 165

BURNS, T, 'Better Late than Never: The Reform of the Law on the Sale of Goods Forming Part of a Bulk' (1996) 59 MLR 260

BURROWS, AS, *The Law of Restitution* (1993)

CAPPER, D, 'Compensation for Breach of Trust' [1997] Conveyancer 14

CENTRAL GILTS OFFICE, *Central Gilts Office Reference Manual*, version No 1 (October 1997)

CENTRAL MONEYMARKETS OFFICE, *Central Moneymarkets Office Reference Manual*, version No 2 (May 1997)

CHRISTIE, F and DOSANJH, H, 'The Practical Elements of Settlement and Custody' in Oditah, F (ed), *The Future for the Global Securities Market: Legal and Regulatory Aspects* (1996), ch 8

COLLIER, JG, *Conflict of Laws* (2nd edn, 1994)

COLLINS, L (ed), *Dicey and Morris on The Conflict of Laws* (12th edn, 1993)

CRANSTON, R, *Principles of Banking Law* (1997)

CREST, *CREST Reference Manual* (May 1996)

CREST PROJECT TEAM AT THE BANK OF ENGLAND, *CREST: The Business Description* (December 1994)

CRESTCo LIMITED, *CREST: Cross-Border Settlement* (December 1997)

CRILLEY, D, 'A Case of Proprietary Overkill' [1994] RLR 57

CROWTHER COMMITTEE, *Report on Consumer Credit* (Cmnd 4596, 1971)

CULLEN, I, 'United Kingdom: Custody of Derivatives: Legal and Regulatory Issues' (1994) Futures and Derivatives Law Review, Issue 1, 43

DACK, A, 'Meeting the Demand for Faster Settlement', *Investors Chronicle*, 28 April 1995, 62

DALE, R, *Risk and Regulation in Global Securities Markets* (1996)

DARLING, A, 'Government and the Financial Services Industry' (1994) 2 *Journal of Financial Regulation and Compliance*, No 2, 107

DAVENPORT, B and Ross, A, 'Market Overt' in Palmer, N and McKendrick, E (eds), *Interests in Goods* (1993), ch 17

DAVIES, PL, *Gower's Principles of Modern Company Law* (6th edn, 1997)

DEPARTMENT OF TRADE AND INDUSTRY, *Financial Services in the United Kingdom: A New Framework for Investor Protection* (Cmnd 9432, 1985)

DIAMOND, AL, *A Review of Security Interests in Property* (HMSO for the Department of Trade and Industry, 1989)

DONOHUE, J and ATKINS, C, 'Settling Trades in the UK Moneymarkets' (1993) 12(3) IFLR 35

ELLINGER, EP and LOMNICKA, E, *Modern Banking Law* (2nd edn, 1994)

FALCONBRIDGE, JD, *Essays on the Conflict of Laws* (2nd edn, 1954)

FARRAR, JH, 'Floating Charges and Priorities' (1974) 38 Conveyancer 315

Financial Times, 'A More Cautious View of Risk Prevails', Survey on Pension Fund Investment, 27 April 1995, I

Financial Times, 'SIB Seeks Safeguards for Investors' Assets', 1 September 1995, 6

Financial Times, 'The Big Get Bigger as the Sector Grows', Survey on Global Custody, 1 July 1997, I

FINN, P, 'The Fiduciary Principle' in Youdan, TG (ed), *Equity, Fiduciaries and Trusts* (1989), ch 1

FINN, P, 'Fiduciary Law and the Modern Commercial World' in McKendrick, E (ed), *Commercial Aspects of Trusts and Fiduciary Relations* (1992), ch 1

FORD, C and KAY, J, 'Why Regulate Financial Services?' in Oditah, F (ed), *The Future for the Global Securities Market: Legal and Regulatory Aspects* (1996), ch 9

FORSYTH, C, 'Characterisation Revisited: An Essay in the Theory and Practice of the English Conflict of Laws' (1998) 114 LQR 141

FOX, DM, 'Property Rights and Electronic Funds Transfers' [1996] LMCLQ 456

FRANKS, J and MAYER, C, *Risk, Regulation and Investor Protection: The Case of Investment Management* (1989)

GABRIEL, P, *Legal Aspects of Syndicated Loans* (1996)

GARDNER, S, 'Knowing Assistance and Knowing Receipt: Taking Stock' (1996) 112 LQR 56

GETZLER, J, 'Gentlemen do not Collect Rents: Fiduciary Obligations and Principal/ Agency Problems', paper delivered at WG Hart Legal Workshop on 'Liability, Regulation and Risk Management: Reorienting the Legal Debate' at the Institute of Advanced Legal Studies, University of London, 5 July 1995

GIBSON, P, 'Getting the Right People into Custody', *Institutional Investor*, November 1995, 163

GLOVER, J, *Commercial Equity: Fiduciary Relationships* (1995)

GOODE, RM, 'Inalienable Rights?' (1979) 42 MLR 553

GOODE, RM, 'Ownership and Obligations in Commercial Transactions' (1987) 103 LQR 433

GOODE, RM, *Legal Problems of Credit and Security* (2nd edn, 1988)

GOODE, RM, 'Property and Unjust Enrichment' in Burrows, A (ed), *Essays on the Law of Restitution* (1991), ch 9

GOODE, RM, *Commercial Law* (2nd edn, 1995)

GOODE, RM, 'The Nature and Transfer of Rights in Dematerialised and Immobilised Securities' [1996] BJIBFL 167; Oditah, F (ed), *The Future for the Global Securities Market: Legal and Regulatory Aspects* (1996), ch 7

GOODHART, W, 'Trustee Exemption Clauses and the Unfair Contract Terms Act 1977' [1980] Conveyancer 333

GOODHART, W, 'Restitutionary Damages for Breach of Contract: The Remedy That Dare Not Speak its Name' [1995] RLR 3

GOODHART, W, 'Trust Law for the Twenty-First Century' in Oakley, AJ, *Trends in Contemporary Trust Law* (1996), ch 11

GOUGH, WJ, *Company Charges* (2nd edn, 1996)

GREEN, B, 'Grey, Oughtred and Vandervell: A Contextual Reappraisal' (1984) 47 MLR 384

GUMMOW, THE HON MR JUSTICE, 'Compensation for Breach of Fiduciary Duty' in Youdan, TG (ed), *Equity, Fiduciaries and Trusts* (1989), ch 2

GUYNN, R, *Modernizing Securities Ownership, Transfer and Pledging Laws* (Capital Markets Forum of the International Bar Association, 1996)

GUYNN, R and TAHYAR, M, 'The Importance of Choice of Law and Finality to PvP, Netting and Collateral Arrangements' (1996) 4 *Journal of Financial Regulation and Compliance*, No 2, 170

HAM, R, 'Trustees' Liability' (1994) 61 BPL (November) 1

HANBURY, HG, 'The Field of Modern Equity' (1929) 45 LQR 196

HANDLEY, KR, 'Reduction of Damages Awards' in Finn, PD (ed), *Essays on Damages* (1992), ch 6

HAPGOOD, M, *Paget's Law of Banking* (11th edn, 1996)

HARPUM, C, 'The Basis of Equitable Liability' in Birks, PBH (ed), *The Frontiers of Liability*, vol 1 (1994)

HARPUM, C, 'Fiduciary Obligations and Fiduciary Powers: Where Are We Going?', a paper delivered at SPTL Seminars for 1996 on Pressing Problems in the Law XI

HART, WG, 'What is a Trust?' (1899) 15 LQR 294

HAYTON, DJ, *Hayton and Marshall, Cases and Commentary on the Law of Trusts* (9th edn, 1991)

HAYTON, DJ, 'Uncertainty of Subject-Matter of Trusts' (1994) 110 LQR 335

HAYTON, DJ, 'Equity's Identification Rules' in Birks, PBH (ed), *Laundering and Tracing* (1995), ch 1

HAYTON, DJ, *Underhill and Hayton, Law Relating to Trusts and Trustees* (15th edn, 1995)

HAYTON, DJ, 'The Irreducible Core Content of Trusteeship' in Oakley, AJ, *Trends in Contemporary Trust Law* (1996), ch 3

HOHFELD, WN, *Fundamental Legal Conceptions: As Applied in Judicial Reasoning* (Cook, WW (ed), 3rd printing, 1964)

HOLMES, OW, 'Grain Elevators', an unsigned article in (1872) 6 Am LR 450 at 457–459, attributed to Holmes by Samuel Williston, *The Law Governing Sales of Goods* (rev edn, 1948), vol 1, 412, n 16

HONORÉ, AM, 'Ownership' in Guest, AG (ed), *Oxford Essays in Jurisprudence* (First Series, 1961), ch V

JACKSON and POWELL, *Jackson & Powell on Professional Negligence* (4th edn, 1997)

JAFFEY, P, 'Accounting for Wrongful Profits: Warman v Dwyer' [1995] LMCLQ 462

JAFFEY, P, 'Restitutionary Damages and Disgorgement' [1995] RLR 30

JAMESON, I and LOUVEAUX, X, 'Cross-Border Securities Collateralisation: Lenders Beware' [1996] BJIBFL 466

JONES, G, 'Delegation by Trustees: A Reappraisal' (1959) 22 MLR 381

JONES, G, *Goff & Jones, The Law of Restitution* (4th edn, 1993)

KEY, P, 'Bona Fide Purchase as a Defence in the Law of Restitution' [1994] LMCLQ 421

KHURSHID, S and MATTHEWS, P, 'Tracing Confusion' (1979) 95 LQR 78

KINDLEBERGER, CP, *Manias, Panics and Crashes* (2nd edn, 1989)

KLOSS, DM, 'Assignments Without the Consent of the Debtor' (1979) 43 Conveyancer 133

LANGBEIN, JH, 'The Contractarian Basis of the Law of Trusts' (1995) 105(2) Yale LJ 625

LAW COMMISSION, *Fiduciary Duties and Regulatory Rules* (CP No 124, 1992; and Law Com No 236, 1995)

LAW COMMISSION, *Aggravated, Exemplary and Restitutionary Damages* (CP No 132, 1993)

LAW COMMISSION, *Sale of Goods Forming Part of a Bulk* (Law Com No 215, 1993)

LAW COMMISSION, *The Law of Trustees: Delegation by Individual Trustees* (Law Com No 220, 1994)

LAW COMMISSION, *Offences of Dishonesty: Money Transfers* (Law Com No 243, 1996)

LAW REFORM COMMITTEE, *Twelfth Report, Transfer of Title to Chattels* (1966, Cmnd 2958)

LAW SOCIETY'S STANDING COMMITTEE ON COMPANY LAW, *Custody Review: Comments on the Discussion Paper issued by the Securities and Investments Board* (No 291, October 1993)

LIGHTMAN, G and Moss, G, *The Law of Receivers of Companies* (2nd edn, 1994)

MAITLAND, FW, *Equity: A Course of Lectures* (Chaytor, AH and Whittaker, WJ (eds), rev by Brunyate, J, 1936)

MARKESINIS, BS and DEAKIN, SF, *Tort Law* (3rd edn, 1994)

MATTHEWS, P, 'The Efficacy of Trustee Exemption Clauses in English Law' [1989] Conveyancer 42

McCORMACK, G, 'Mixture of Goods' (1990) 10 Legal Studies 293

McCORMACK, G, 'The Eye of Equity: Identification Principles and Equitable Tracing' [1996] JBL 225

McGREGOR, H, 'Restitutionary Damages' in Birks, PBH, *Wrongs and Remedies in the Twenty-First Century* (1996), ch 9

McKENDRICK, E, 'Restitution, Misdirected Funds and Change of Position' (1992) 55 MLR 377

MEAGHER, RP, GUMMOW, WMC and LEHANE, JRF, *Equity: Doctrines and Remedies* (3rd edn, 1992)

MERCER, C and SANDY, D, 'Security over Unascertained Shares' (1997) 12(8) BJIBFL 399 and (1997) 11(9) *Corporate Briefing* 3

MILLER, D, 'Transfer of Title: A New Legal Regime in Only Three Paragraphs' [1994] LMCLQ 322

MILLETT, PJ, 'Tracing the Proceeds of Fraud' (1991) 107 LQR 71

MILLETT, SIR P, 'Bribes and Secret Commissions' [1993] RLR 7

MOIR, C, 'Sub-Custodians: Quest for Clear Rules', *Financial Times*, Survey on Global Custody, 11 July 1997, III

MOONEY, JR, C, 'Beyond Negotiability: A New Model for Transfer and Pledge of Interests in Securities Controlled by Intermediaries' (1990) 12 Cardozo Law R 307

MOONEY, JR, C, ROCKS, SM and SCHWARTZ, RS, 'An Introduction to the Revised UCC Article 8 and Review of Other Recent Developments with Investment Securities' (1994) 49 The Business Lawyer 1891

MOSHINSKY, M, 'The Assignment of Debts in the Conflict of Laws' (1992) 109 LQR 591

Moss, G and TOUBE, F, 'Cross-Border Enforcement of Security' (1997) 16 IBFL 1, 9

MOWBRAY, WJ, *Lewin on Trusts* (16th edn, 1964)

Nobles, R, 'Trustees' Exclusion Clauses in Jersey and England' (1996) 10(3) TLI 66

Nolan, R, 'Change of Position' in Birks, PBH (ed), *Laundering and Tracing* (1995), ch 6

Nolan, R, 'What to Take into Account' [1996] CLJ 201

Norris, W, 'Uncertainty and Informality: Hunter v Moss' [1995] Private Client Business 43

North, P, *Essays in Private International Law* (1993)

O'Brien, M, 'Labour's Proposals for Regulation into the 21st Century' (1997) 5 *Journal of Financial Regulation and Compliance*, No 7, 115

Oakley, AJ, *Parker and Mellows, The Modern Law of Trusts* (6th edn, 1994)

Oakley, AJ, 'Proprietary Claims and their Priority in Insolvency' [1995] CLJ 377

Ockelton, M, 'Share and Share Alike?' (1994) 53 Camb LJ 448

Oditah, F, *Legal Aspects of Receivables Financing* (1991)

Oditah, F, 'Financing Trade Credit: Welsh Development Agency v Exfinco' [1992] JBL 541

Ogus, AI, *Regulation: Legal Form and Economic Theory* (1994)

Oliver, P, 'The Extent of Equitable Tracing' (1995) 9 Trust Law International, No 3, 78

Page, AC and Ferguson, RB, *Investor Protection* (1992)

Palmer, NE, 'The Vindication of Commercial Security over Commodities: Equitable Pledges and Conversion' [1986] LMCLQ 218

Palmer, NE, 'Quasi-Bailment' [1988] 1 LMCLQ 34

Palmer, NE, *Bailment* (2nd edn, 1991)

Papaspyrou, N, 'Immobilisation of Securities' [1996] JIBL 430, 459

Percy, RA and Walton, CT (eds), *Charlesworth & Percy on Negligence* (9th edn, 1997)

Perry, MJ, 'Approaches to Market Regulation: The United Kingdom' in Oditah, F (ed), *The Future for the Global Securities Market* (1996), ch 11

Phillips, M and Oditah, F, 'Securities over Moveables: An Understanding of the English Position', *Insolvency Lawyer*, 1995 Conference Special Issue (1996), 11

Pollock, F and Wright, RS, *An Essay on Possession in the Common Law* (1888)

Porat, A, 'The Contributory Negligence Defence and the Ability to Rely on the Contract' (1995) 111 LQR 228

Reynolds, FMB, 'Annotating Bowstead on Agency (15th edn)' [1994] JBL 144

Rogers, JS, 'Negotiability, Property and Identity' (1990) 12 Cardozo Law R 471

Rogers, JS, 'An Essay on Horseless Carriages and Paperless Negotiable Instruments: Some Lessons from the Article 8 Revision' (1995) 31 Idaho L Rev 689

Rogers, WVH, *Winfield and Jolowicz on Tort* (14th edn, 1994)

Rogerson, PJ, 'The Situs of Debts in the Conflict of Laws: Illogical, Unnecessary and Misleading' [1990] CLJ 441

Rudden, B, 'Things as Things and Things as Wealth' (1994) 14 Oxford Journal of Legal Studies 81

Rudnick, D, 'Finding a Way Through the Emerging Minefield', *Investors Chronicle*, 28 April 1995, 65

Ryan, R, 'Taking Security over Investment Portfolios Held in Global Custody' (1990) 10 JIBL 404

Schroeder, JL, 'Is Article 8 Finally Ready This Time? The Radical Reform of Secured Lending on Wall Street' [1994] Colum Bus L Rev 291

Scott, AW, 'The Nature of the Rights of the Cestui Que Trust' (1917) 17 Col LR 269

Sealy, L, 'Fiduciary Obligations, Forty Years On' (1995) 9 Journal of Contract Law 37

Securities and Investments Board, *Custody Review: Discussion Paper* (August 1993)

Securities and Investments Board, *Custody* (Consultative Paper 90, August 1995)

Securities and Investments Board, *Standards for the Custody of Customers' Investments* (Guidance Release 3/96, August 1996)

Securities and Investments Board, *Custody of Investments under the Financial Services Act 1986* (Consultative Paper 107, March 1997)

Securities and Investments Board, *Custody of Investments under the Financial Services Act 1986* (Guidance Release 5/97, June 1997)

Sharp, B, 'Insolvent Banks as Custodians' in Oditah, F (ed), *Insolvency of Banks: Managing the Risks* (1996), ch 8

Sheridan, LA, *Keeton and Sheridan's The Law of Trusts* (12th edn, 1993)

Shipwright, A, 'Shares, Claret, Grain and Bricks: Certain Uncertainty?', *Tax Journal*, 19 May 1994, Issue No 260, 9

Smith, LD, 'Tracing, "Swollen Assets" and the Lowest Intermediate Balance: Bishopsgate Investment Management Ltd. v Homan' (1994) 8 Trust Law International, No 4, 102

Smith, LD, 'Disgorgement of the Profits of Breach of Contract: Property, Contract and "Efficient Breach"' (1995) 24 Can Bus Law J 121

Smith, LD, 'Tracing in Taylor v Plummer: Equity in the Court of King's Bench' [1995] LMCLQ 240

Smith, LD, 'Tracing into the Payment of a Debt' [1995] CLJ 290

Smith, LD, 'Constructive Fiduciaries?', a paper delivered at SPTL Seminars for 1996: Pressing Problems in the Law XI

Smith, LD, *The Law of Tracing* (1997)

Stevens, R, 'The Law Applicable to Priority in Shares' (1996) 112 LQR 198

Stone, HF, 'The Nature of the Rights of the Cestui Que Trust' (1917) 17 Col LR 467

Swadling, W, 'The Nature of Ministerial Receipt' in Birks, PBH (ed), *Laundering and Tracing* (1995), ch 9

Sykes, E and Walker, S, *The Law of Securities* (5th edn, 1993)

Temple, P, 'Big Changes Afoot in a Tough Market', *Investors Chronicle*, 28 April 1995, 59

Tettenborn, A, 'Trust Property and Conversion: An Equitable Confusion' [1996] CLJ 36

Thomas, R and Sabalot, D, 'Unfair Terms in Consumer Contracts Regulations: The Impact on the Financial Services Industry' (1995) 10 BJIBFL 214

The Oxford Colloquium on Collateral and Conflict of Laws—Held at St John's College, Oxford University (1 May 1998), a BJIBFL Special Supplement/September 1998

The Times, 'A Game for Big Players', Focus on Global Custody, 28 April 1995, 28

The Times, 'New Worlds to Conquer', Focus on Global Custody, 28 April 1995, 28

The Times, 'Wisdom of the Prudential', Focus on Global Custody, 28 April 1995, 28

Treasury, HM, *Custody: A Consultation Document* (June 1996)

Treitel, GH, *The Law of Contract* (9th edn, 1995)

Weinrib, EJ, 'The Fiduciary Obligation' (1975) 25 Univ of Toronto LJ 1

WEIR, T, *A Casebook on Tort* (8th edn, 1996)

WILLIAMS, G, *Joint Torts and Contributory Negligence: A Study of Concurrent Faults in Great Britain, Ireland and the Common Law Dominions* (1951)

WILLIAMS, GL, 'The Doctrine of Repugnancy' (1943) 59 LQR 343; (1944) 60 LQR 69, 190

WINFIELD, PH, *The Province of the Law of Tort* (1931)

WOOD, PR, *Comparative Law of Security and Guarantees* (1995)

WOOD, PR, *Title Finance, Derivatives, Securitisations, Set-off and Netting* (1995)

INDEX